TO RUTH
WITH LOVE

JOHN
XXX.

TO RUTH
WITH LOVE

JOHN
XXX.

WINE
AND
DINE

WINE
AND
DINE

Introduced by Robin Young

HAMLYN

Editor: Susie Ward
Designer: Glynis Edwards
Production: Richard Churchill

Published 1986 by Hamlyn Publishing
a division of The Hamlyn Publishing Group Limited,
Bridge House, London Road,
Twickenham, Middlesex, England

ISBN 0 600 32664 0

Printed and bound in Hong Kong

Weight and measures
Both metric and imperial measurements are given. As these are not exact equivalents, please work from one set of figures or the other. Use standard measuring spoons.

Time symbols
The time needed to prepare the dish is given on each recipe. The time symbols are as follows:

quick to prepare

takes up to 1 hour to prepare

time-consuming to prepare

start at least a day ahead

Contents

Introduction
by Robin Young

For the first time in history there are now more Britons regularly drinking wine than beer, though even now our consumption of wine is modest when compared with the annual intake of our wine-producing Continental neighbours. We are still taking our first tentative and timid steps in wine appreciation, and as yet we are mostly missing out on much of the marvellous fun that wine affords. That is because, for many of us, the vinous repertoire is still restricted to just a few tried and tested popular brands which we know we like.

By playing it safe with just a handful of commercial blends we deny the whole point about wine, which is its diversity and infinite variety. If we wanted to be absolutely safe we should no doubt stick to water, an innocuous drink which goes pretty unobjectionably with anything and everything. Wine has a bit more to say for itself. It can, accordingly, argue or be difficult to accommodate. But it can make a powerful positive contribution. Water we drink to survive.

Wine is for pleasure, excitement, delight.
There is no shortage of books about wine, or about cooking. What is exceptional, though, is a book which concerns itself with both. Such a book you have in your hands right now. *Wine and Dine* is a complete wine primer, easy to understand and full of useful information for those who are introducing themselves to the wonderful world of wine. But it is also a collection of thoroughly tested and mouthwatering recipes. Every dish is paired with a carefully considered wine suggestion, so that you can use your choice of food to guide your exploration of the huge choice of wines available.

Used properly, wine is the most exciting and stimulating condiment of all – a spur to the appetite, a relish to the meal, an aid to the digestion and a health-giving food in its own right. Plenty of wines are delicious alone and served at any time, but most are at their best when properly partnered in a perfect marriage with food. Wines not only taste different from each other; the same wine will taste different according to what it accompanies. *Wine and Dine* shows you the way.

In addition, for every wine you choose, you will find a page in this book devoted to the area from which it comes, with pictures that capture the atmosphere and spirit of the place. It makes every mealtime a mini-holiday!

Wine know-how

Learning to fully appreciate wine demands some attention to detail. Of course, reading about the varieties of grape and national or regional characteristics of wines is important. But there are more practical points to take into account. Whether a particular wine should be served chilled or at room temperature, and the best corkscrew to use, are very basic. But even these considerations, together with partnering the right wine with the right glass, come just before you raise the wine to your lips for that moment of pure enjoyment. The more you know about how wine is actually made, so that you can make an informed choice from the styles of wine on offer, and the more you know about storage requirements – position, temperature and putting down – the more you will enjoy that moment of truth.

Finally, learning how to savour a glass of good wine – to roll it around your tongue and inhale its bouquet – is not the mark of a *poseur*. Done unostentatiously, it need never be noticed, and will give you much more pleasure than simply gulping it down. Good wine deserves to be treated with respect – from the moment you buy it to the moment you proudly serve it with food you know will complement it.

Serving wine

Just as important as understanding vintages and wine regions is the correct way to prepare wine for the table. Is it best brought to room temperature or served chilled? How long should it be allowed to breathe? Here are a few guidelines to make your enjoyment as perfect as possible.

Whatever wine you are serving, whether it is red, rosé or white, cheap or expensive, it is worth making sure that it is at its best when it arrives in the glass. This need not be a complicated ritual, just a matter of ensuring that the bottle is opened at the right time and the contents poured at the right temperature into an appropriate glass.

Temperature
The rules about the temperature for serving wine are basic and easy to remember. It is common knowledge that white wines and rosés should be served chilled and the red wines at room temperature, but over-enthusiasm can lead to white wines that are frozen into tastelessness and red wines that are almost as warm as the soup! This is a waste of wine however low the price.

As a general rule, the cheaper or sweeter the white wine, the cooler it should be, but about 7°C /45°F should be cold enough for any wine. Better quality white wines, cham-

pagne and other sparkling wines, as well as rosés, need only be as cool as the ideal cellar – 10° /50°F or, more realistically for most of us, the temperature of the bottle after an hour in the refrigerator.

A quicker way to chill white wine is to plunge it into a bucket filled with water and a handful of ice-cubes. A few minutes in the freezer or a couple of ice-cubes in the glass are acceptable emergency measures for ordinary wines.

The chemicals that give red wine its bouquet and flavour come alive at higher temperatures than those in white wine, so it makes sense to serve red wine rather warmer. Think of 'room temperature' as a term coined in the days before central heating – 15°C /60°F is quite warm enough for red wine, if not for living rooms. Allow the bottle to warm up gradually, perhaps in the

The bubbles in champagne look best in tulip-shaped glasses.

kitchen as you cook, but not next to the cooker or on a radiator. If you are buying a bottle of red wine and do not have time to bring it to the right temperature, look for a beaujolais or a red Loire wine, or perhaps an Italian Valpolicella, all of which can be served cool.

Most red wines improve with being allowed to 'breathe' for an hour or two before they are drunk, whether you simply draw the cork to let the air in or pour the wine into another glass container (a process known as decanting, even if you are using an old jug rather than an antique decanter). Before wine-making techniques improved, decanting was essential to get rid of all the sediment; nowadays most wines are crystal clear in their bottles and only fine claret, old burgundies and vintage port are likely to need decanting. For most purposes, therefore, decanting is just a useful way of getting air to the wine and an equally useful way of disguising its possibly humble supermarket origins. All in all it is a matter of personal choice. Similarly the wicker baskets that are designed to stop the sediment being shaken up as the wine is poured, are, in the vast majority of cases, an unnecessary affectation.

Opening a wine bottle
Opening the bottle is often the most difficult part of serving wine, particularly if you are confronted with a plastic covering which has to be sliced with a knife. A conventional lead covering (the capsule) should be scored with the point of a knife and then peeled off. Any mould should be wiped away from the rim of the bottle with a clean cloth.

The best corkscrew is a simple, sturdy spiral with a good sharp point. Avoid gimmicky contraptions, particularly those that operate by pumping gas into the bottle. If a cork refuses to budge, run hot water over the neck of the bottle until the glass expands and allows the cork to be eased out with a corkscrew.

The best way to open sparkling wine is to take off the wires, hold the cork wrapped in a clean cloth in one hand and twist the bottle in the other until the cork eases out. There is no need for dramatic explosions.

Pouring the wine into a glass is, of course, the final stage of serving wine. The colour and clarity of the wine is (or should be) something to be appreciated, and coloured or ornate glass make this difficult. Fine, thin wine glasses are an enjoyable luxury but uncut, plain bowl or tulip-shaped glasses with a stem are cheap, easily obtainable and quite adequate for all table wines including champagne. The traditional saucer-shaped champagne glasses are not the best glasses for serving champagne, as they allow the bubbles to escape too quickly. Fortified wines are usually served in small glasses. The one point that all glasses should have in common, is that they are sparkling clean and free of cupboard smells and any trace of dust.

Last of all, the glass should not be overfilled. A third to half full is generous enough. The vapours from the wine will collect in the upper half of the glass and will increase the pleasure of drinking the wine.

Glasses

Just as you use a different sort of knife for meat or for cheese, so there are different glasses available to suit the particular drink you intend to serve. A whole array of gleaming glasses in the drinks cupboard may look inviting but unless you know how to select and use glasses to best advantage, they will add little to the pleasures of drinking.

Traditional shapes: the Paris goblet, Alsace hock glass and champagne flute.

General points

The three remarkable qualities of any drink are its colour, bouquet and taste. Consequently, the best glasses are always clear, to show the real colour without any distortion. This is especially valuable in the case of wines and fortified wines, which reveal a lot about their age, style and freshness through their colour.

With the exception of tumblers, the best glasses are bowl shaped, tapering towards the rim to contain and concentrate the bouquet for you to inhale. Bowl-shaped glasses should also be large enough to hold a good measure without being more than a third to half full. This is because, before you take the first sip, you should swirl the wine around in the glass to fill the glass with the bouquet.

All wine and fortified wine glasses also have stems, so that you can hold the glass by the stem, not the bowl. This is so that your hand does not affect the temperature of the wine. Holding the glass by its stem will also prevent you from smearing the glass. There are three primary sizes and shapes of glasses which, between them, are quite adequate on their own. The three types are: a small stemmed glass which narrows towards the rim for sherry, port, Madeira or liqueurs; a bowl or tulip-shaped stemmed glass for white or red wine; and a tumbler for spirits and long drinks. This, however, is really the bare minimum, and over the years it can be rewarding to collect a much wider range. Some people say that wine actually tastes – as well as looks – better in a thin glass. This is just psychological – but then psychology does play its part in the enjoyment of wine. Certainly it is true that delicate glass rests more lightly on the lips and guides the bouquet artfully to the nose, because its shape too is usually more carefully designed. But do not let lack of fine glassware mar your pleasure. Vineyard owners in France drink their wine from mustard glasses, washed and kept for everyday drinking. No one enjoys their wine more than they!

There are many designs of glasses associated with wines from different regions and individual shapes have developed for mixed drinks and cocktails. Here we describe some of the more common types.

Table wine glasses

Champagne: the best glass to use for champagne or sparkling wine is the tall, slim flute which preserves the 'mousse' or bubbles for as long as possible. The common wide-brimmed saucer became popular in Victorian times, but it is a very poor substitute for the classical flute design; it encourages the bubbles to die quickly in the glass besides being easy to spill.

Paris goblet: This round bowl-shaped glass is the commonest wine glass available. It is best suited to red wines, although if you have a limited choice of glasses it will do for white wine too.

Alsace: the glass traditionally used for the delicate young white wines made near the eastern border of France has an extra long stem of green glass, supporting a wide bowl. The wines of the area are very fresh and are complemented by the greenish reflection.

Anjou: a long stem is also a feature of the typical straight-sided glass used for the white wines of Anjou and the Loire. The extra long stem is not merely for elegance, but also keeps the wine well clear of any warmth transmitted by your hand.

Moselle: cut glass is frowned upon by purists and wine buffs as distorting the appearance of wine. However, in the Moselle area, cut glass is entirely typical and gives an added glint to white wines.

Hock or Rhine: hock was a Victorian name for the German wines of the Rhine. In their homeland, these aristocratic white wines are served in an unwieldy glass with a thick bobbly stem. However, it is unlikely that you will come across these unusual, old-fashioned glasses outside Germany.

9

Drinking wine

In order to get the utmost pleasure out of drinking wine, it is worth knowing a bit about the way the wine should look, smell and taste. The best method of assessing these points is to follow the procedure used by professional wine tasters. Here is a simple guide on how to judge wine.

Before drinking any wine, it is vital that the wine is at the right temperature and that it is served in clean wine glasses. If you are really seriously trying to assess the wine, the room should not have an off-putting smoky or scented atmosphere and you should not have recently eaten strongly-flavoured food, such as peppermint.

The routine for tasting a wine is to start by pouring two or three mouthfuls of wine into a glass. The clarity of the wine is the first thing to examine. Raise the glass to eye-level and look straight through it to see how clear the wine is. You should hold the glass by its stem, not by its bowl or your fingers will smear the glass and affect your judgement of the wine's clarity. All wine, whether red or white, should be clear. 'Star-bright', 'brilliant' and 'clear' are the terms usually used for good wine, but if you find that 'murky' or 'muddy' is a closer description of the wine you are looking at, it will not be at its best.

Looking at the colour

A wine's colour can tell you a great deal, and its importance should not be underestimated. It is claimed that daylight from a north-facing window is the ideal source of light by which to judge colour, but obviously this is not always available. Normal artificial lighting can be used but you should make allowances for its slight distortions. Fluorescent lighting is the worst light by which to judge wine, since it is often very blue – it tends to make red wines look strangely browny-purple and sometimes almost blue! Candles give off a yellowish light. Electric lightbulbs are probably the next best pure source of light, after natural daylight, although even they can add some blue or yellow to the wine's colour.

Hold the glass over a white surface, tilt it slightly and look at the colour of the wine. You will see that in a red wine the colour is most intense at its deepest part and palest at its shallowest. Young red wine is purple but changes to red as it ages, and later becomes almost brown. It is easiest to judge a wine's age by looking at the paler edge where any browning will be more evident.

Generally, wine of a good vintage will have more colour, and will turn brown more slowly than the same type of wine from a bad year. For instance, clarets of 1970 are deeper and redder than the clarets of 1972, a bad year. Quite often Beaujolais has a purple hue to it. Burgundies are noted for having a velvety-red colour, while red Rhône wines, especially Châteauneuf du Pape, are often so intensely red that they seem almost black.

White wines are judged in the same way but because they are naturally pale, the gradation of colour is much harder to detect. However, you will see that sweet white wines, such as Sauternes, are yellow-gold when young, becoming gold or even burnt gold with age. They also have a thicker texture than dry white wines.

Of the dry white wines, Chablis is known for having a very faint greenish tinge, as do German wines from the Mosel. The dry white wines of the Loire have a touch of yellow to them, while Alsatian wines are definitely yellow.

Smelling the wine

Having examined the colour, you then have to assess the smell or 'nose'. Just as the wine should look good, so it should smell good. Your first sniff will tell you most about the wine – take a good deep sniff and concentrate on it.

Surprisingly, grapes do not figure very highly in people's descriptions of the smell of wine. Clarets often smell of blackcurrants or even cedar wood, pencils and antique shops. Beaujolais and Côtes du Rhônes are often said to smell of freshly dug earth or raspberry sorbet.

White wines come closest to smelling like grapes, especially those from Germany, although 'melon' often crops up in descriptions of white wines. Sweet white wines from Germany, Sauternes and the Loire valley will usually have a honey-like nose. Meursault, a white from Burgundy, is famous for smelling of asparagus and wines made from the Riesling grape have a curiously petrol-like bouquet. Probably the most distinctive white wine, easily identified by its aroma, is the Alsatian Gewürztraminer. This has a very spicy smell. Champagne is said to smell of fresh bread, or even toast!

Tasting the wine

Once you have examined the sight and smell of the wine, you are ready to actually taste it! Take enough into your mouth to allow you to swirl it about and chew it, so that it reaches every part of your mouth. Keep it there for at least 5 seconds before swallowing.

Your taste buds register sweetness (at the tip of the tongue), acidity (at the sides of the tongue), saltiness (towards the back) and bitterness (at the back). As a result of the positioning of these taste buds, wines usually begin by tasting sweet or rich and end with an impression of acidity. All other sensations are those of touch. These include the density or weight of the liquid – sweet wines are usually 'thicker'. With red wine the tannin, which gives the sensation that your gums and cheeks are puckered, is most evident in young clarets – this effect lessens with age.

In a good wine the sensation of sweetness or richness should be equally proportioned with acidity, so that neither appears to be in excess. An equally proportioned wine is known as a balanced wine.

Having swallowed the wine, you should still be able to smell and taste it – the length of time that these sensations remain with you is the best guide to the quality of the wine. A minor wine will be forgotten in 2–3 seconds, but a great wine will last for 10 seconds or more. Don't confuse this with the length of time your tongue registers the presence of acid in your mouth, as this will probably last for longer than 10 seconds.

Gently swirl the wine in the bowl of the glass. Breathe in to assess the 'nose'.

Storing wine

Cheap, everyday wine is nowadays ready to drink as soon as it it bottled, so there is not much to be gained from filling up a wine cellar with it. Buy it and drink it as and when you need it. However, better quality wines, even quite modest ones, do benefit from 'laying down'.

How and where

The first question for most wine drinkers is how and where to store even a limited number of bottles. The ideal, of course, is a cool dark cellar with a steady temperature of about 10°C /50°F. But very few modern houses have cellars, so the alternative is to look around for a dark place where the bottles can lie undisturbed.

The storage place must be dark – because light can affect the colour of the wine – and free from strong smells (paint or detergent), that could penetrate the cork. There should also be no local vibrations that might shake up the bottles and stir up the sediment.

The temperature of the 'cellar' is crucial too, although it is more important that it should be constant rather than particularly cool. Anywhere free from draughts that is not near a radiator, central heating boiler or hot water tank should be adequate – in practice this means the back of a broom cupboard or a recess under the stairs. A shed or garage may be suitable, but it is vital that it is well enough insulated for there to be no risk of the bottles freezing in winter. It should, of course, also be kept securely locked.

Wine bottles should be stored lying horizontally. This is to ensure that the corks are kept in contact with the wine, so that they do not dry out and let in too much air. Wine merchants' cardboard boxes lying on their sides will just about do for a limited number of bottles, but for a more serious cellar, wine racks are essential. Do-it-yourself enthusiasts can make their own built-in racks, and most good department stores sell quite cheap and perfectly adequate racks that will hold 12, 24 or 48 bottles. Some types are collapsible, which is useful for itinerant flat dwellers.

As your cellar fills up, keep it well organized. Store whites below reds because they like to be cooler and heat rises. Keep all necks pointing outwards, labels uppermost so that you can see what is where without too much rooting about. You may even find it fun to keep a 'cellar book', with the dates of purchases and comments on the wines as you drink them. Wine accessory shops often sell smart, leather-bound ones, but an exercise book does just as well.

What to store

Fine clarets and red Burgundies, classy white Burgundies, Sauternes and vintage port used to be the staples of the traditional cellar, laid down to mature for a decade or so, much longer in the case of very great wines. During these years, tiny amounts of air seep in through the cork and combine with the wine. Gradually the raw elements knit together and the marvellous bouquet builds up, to be savoured when the bottle is eventually opened and drunk.

For those who can afford to buy fine wines when they first come on the market and are able to lay them down until they are ready to drink, it is a major and highly important financial investment. However, right at the other end of the scale, for those of us who can only afford to buy a few modest bottles at a time, it still makes economic sense to bulk buy and lay down.

The most important reason for storing wine is that certain wines improve dramatically with keeping. Some cheap young reds will taste much better after six months or a year. Big red wines like those from the northern Rhône, Italian Barolos, Chiantis and Barbarescos, Spanish red and white Riojas, and meaty Californian and Australian reds (made from Shiraz, Pinot Noir and Cabernet Sauvignon grapes) will benefit from keeping considerably longer. Better quality heavyweight Chilean, Argentinian and South African reds, too, deserve to be stored for a couple of years. Look out for any wines from these areas that you particularly like, with a view to laying down. Of course, if you are going to invest money in a large volume of wine, make sure you taste it carefully before you buy it.

Lighter reds, anything that says 'fresh and fruity' to you when you taste it, may well benefit from just a few months 'rest' in their bottles, but need not be kept any longer. Southern Rhône wines, vins de pays, Valpolicella and Beaujolais fall in this category. As a general guide, the 'bigger' and 'heavier' a wine tastes, the longer it needs to mature.

Generally speaking, most of the more ordinary white wines will not benefit from more than a very few months 'rest'. Drink light, dry whites such as Muscadet, Mâcon, any Sauvignon and the Italian whites as soon as you like. Sweet dessert white wines, however, do improve with keeping. Non-vintage champagne does not need laying down – just buy it when you need it. Vintage champagne does benefit from laying down, however.

Apart from the definite improvement in taste, there are two or three other good reasons for buying wine in bulk and keeping it in your cellar. Wine prices are rising all the time, and what is cheap now will not be any cheaper in a year's time. Wine merchants will often give a discount of a few per cent on 'bulk' purchases too – generally a case or more, sometimes a mixed case of several different wines. Finally, if you have a comfortably stocked cellar, there is no chance of running out of wine in the middle of a particularly thirsty dinner party!

Wine should be stored on its side, necks pointing outwards, label uppermost.

Wine as an aperitif

The most important function of an aperitif is to stimulate the appetite gently, and wine fulfils this purpose admirably. Spirits and strong cocktails may be fashionable and more popular, but they tend to deaden the tastes of the food and wine to come. Many people also find spirits too much to cope with on an empty stomach, particularly at the end of a long day.

Wine is not only cheaper and gentler as an aperitif than spirits, but it can also have the advantage of being a much more original choice, especially if it is chosen with care, bearing in mind the subsequent meal.

Whatever wine you choose to offer your guests as an aperitif, remember everyone will be hungry, or at least empty, so it is considerate and sensible to offer them something to nibble at the same time. A bowl of olives, some nuts or cocktail biscuits are all that is really necessary; avoid over-salty tit-bits, however, because these simply increase the thirst.

Champagne is definitely the king of aperitifs. The festive sparkle is guaranteed to break the ice and lift everyone's spirits – invaluable if your guests do not know each other well. As only a glass each (two at the most) is necessary at the aperitif stage, it need not be too expensive a choice either, particularly as a non-vintage or the house champagne of one of the big merchants is perfectly good for this sort of drinking.

A cheaper alternative with the same effect might be a non-champagne sparkler such as sparkling Moselle or hock from Germany (also known as Sekt), or Asti Spumante from Italy. Astis are usually sweet, but there are dry ones too and these make particularly good aperitifs. Other possibilities would be a dryish sparkling Vouvray or Saumur from the Loire, or one of the Spanish sparklers that are made by the *méthode champenoise*.

For a popular and economical aperitif, still white wine is the most obvious choice. It is refreshing, and if you are not offering any alternatives it is the most widely acceptable drink. Bear in mind that very dry whites that are high in acidity are rather hard to drink without food – light wines with fragrance and plenty of fruit are the ones to go for. In Europe the wines of Alsace fit this bill perfectly. Look out for those made from the Riesling or – cheaper – Sylvaner grapes. A Muscat from Alsace would be a more unusual choice – elsewhere the Muscat grape makes sweet wines but these are dry, distinctively perfumed, and mouth-wateringly spicy.

Other white wines that would make suitable aperitifs are Sancerre or Pouilly from the Loire (these can be expensive though), a fresh and fruity Saumur from the Anjou district, a good white Mâcon from Burgundy or a dry white Graves from Bordeaux. Outside France you might choose an Italian Soave or a Frascati, a German Kabinett or a Qualitätswein, a Yugoslavian Riesling or – to be slightly unusual – a Portuguese *vinho verde* with its slight tingly 'prickle'. All these white aperitif wines should be served cool.

Do not feel, however, that aperitif wine must be white. One of the drier rosés can be an excellent choice. Look out for the pale pink wines of Saumur.

It is more difficult to start off an evening's drinking with red wine, just because the majority of them tend to be heavier than whites, and full-bodied enough to demand food. However, if you think that red wine would suit your guests or your menu there is no reason why you should not serve it. Try a Bourgeuil, a delicate, fruity wine from Touraine, or perhaps a light young Beaujolais. With a little careful planning, any of the above wines can go on from the aperitif stage to be drunk with the first course.

More unusual choices

If you are looking for an idea that is a little more special than serving plain wine, the answer might be one of the wine cups or cocktails. Buck's Fizz (champagne mixed half-and-half with fresh orange juice) is wonderful at lunchtime, and some people swear by it as a morning-after hangover cure. Vin blanc cassis is popular for summer drinking – make it from any dry white wine mixed with the blackcurrant syrup in the proportions five of wine to one of syrup. More exotic is a similar drink made with raspberry syrup instead of blackcurrant.

Hock and seltzer is refreshing and can be made with any sweeter white wine (not necessarily hock) with an equal splash of soda. Many books of cocktails also give recipes for more elaborate concoctions, often mixing wine with brandy or other spirits. These can look very innocent with their decorations of fresh fruit, and they can taste exciting, but they are deceptively potent, so pour them sparingly.

If you are aiming at real originality you could serve either a white port or a Muscat de Beaumes de Venise. White port is a succulent golden colour, although it is now more often dry than sweet. As such it is a stimulating aperitif although, because it is a little heavy, most people will probably not want more than one glass.

Muscat de Beaumes de Venise is most unusual. A sweet wine, made from the Muscat grape in the southern Côtes-du-Rhône, with a beguiling tang of herbs, it is best known as a *digestif*, but if it is served lightly chilled it is delicious as an aperitif.

Serve sparkling wine to start your party with a swing.

Wine and food

Although it is perfectly possible to drink any wine with any food, it is worth at least considering general guidelines accumulated from the experience of others, over the years, of eating and drinking. These may help to avoid real disasters and increase the combined enjoyment of food and wine.

When trying to match wine to food there are a few sensible points that are worth remembering. One is that it is best to balance the type of wine to the type of food, so that neither overpowers the other – a light meal requires a light wine, whilst richer, heavier fare calls for a more robust wine. The way in which the food has been prepared may influence the balance. For instance, a white or light red wine will happily complement a plain roast chicken, but if the bird has a rich stuffing, a fuller-bodied red wine would taste better.

Food from a particular region will often match a type of wine from the same region. Bear in mind that if you use a particular wine in the making of a dish, it is likely to be the best one to drink with the dish.

The order in which wines are generally served is also based on practical experience and common sense. If you are serving two wines in succession, or even an aperitif and then a wine at dinner, take care that the first one does not spoil the effect of the second. Make sure that you serve dry before sweet, light-weight before full-bodied, delicate before spicy, fruity or intensely flavoured white before red, young before old and a cheaper wine before a better quality one. Like all rules, there are some exceptions, such as serving sweet white wines with a slightly tart dessert.

Difficult combinations

Although, in general, food and wine are natural partners, there is some food which clashes or is difficult to combine with wine. Try to avoid drinking good wine with food that contains vinegar. Acidic fruit, like oranges, lemons and pineapples, react badly with wine, as does chocolate.

If you do serve a dressed salad as a side dish, try to keep the dressing light (preferably made with lemon juice rather than vinegar) and serve something bland, such as bread, to act as a barrier between the salad and the wine. Salad as a main course can be partnered by one of the dry, stronger rosés such as Tavel, a light Provençal red wine or a light Italian red wine such as Valpolicella.

Eggs and egg dishes mask wines so there is no point serving them with one which is fine or delicate. Keep the wine simple and on the robust side, for example a Côtes du Rhône or a dry sherry. Highly spiced food, and curries which are not too hot, may be served with fuller-flavoured white wines such as Gewürztraminers, while Chinese food only requires a light, sweetish rosé (Mateus or Rosé d'Anjou) or a Riesling.

Although cheese and wine are the classic companions, really strong cheese can overpower all but the most robust of wines (such as a Rhône) or dessert or fortified wines.

If possible, avoid serving full tannic red wines with fish – not only do these wines 'swamp' delicate fish, but they tend to make the fish taste metallic. However, very light red wines, which have acidity rather than tannin, like red vinhos verdes, can be drunk with fish such as salmon, especially when it is served hot. Red wines do not combine well with rich puddings either. Although combinations of red wine with some fruit (such as strawberries, peaches and pears) can work well, the dryness and tannin of a red wine will clash with a rich pudding.

Good Combinations

There are certain combinations of food and wine that are particularly good, when the food and wine can improve each other.

White meat, such as chicken or veal, should be served with fairly 'full', not too dry, white wines – for instance, southern burgundies, white Rhône, Frascati and Riesling. Stronger rosés like Tavel, or light reds, such as Bordeaux, Chianti or Italian Merlot also go well with white meat.

Red meat cooked plainly, and white meat cooked in a rich sauce or with a stuffing, call for the classic accompaniment of claret or medium-bodied reds like Chianti classico, Bardolino, Barbaresco and Dão.

Game and rich beef dishes are best served with Burgundy or Rhône wines – especially Châteauneuf du Pape – or with full-bodied red wines, such as Argentinian, Chilean, Barolo, Riojas, South African Pinotage or Australian Shiraz.

Light fish, simply prepared, goes well with any dry white wine – try a white burgundy, Australian Chardonnay, South African Chenin Blanc or Steen. Pouilly Fuissé or Fumé, Sancerre, Soave or a Mosel wine. Richer fish dishes need a fuller flavoured white wine such as Graves, Orvieto or white Penedes, while shellfish calls for light, crisp white wine (a Muscadet or Mâcon would be an excellent choice).

Light red wines combine pleasantly with dishes made with rice, pasta, pizzas, pastries and bread. Where these are 'national' dishes, as quite a few are, the natural thing to drink is the wine of the area. For example, drink chianti with a pizza.

With gateaux and not too creamy desserts, it would be appropriate to serve a sweet white wine. Sauternes, Muscat de Beaumes de Venise, Monbazillac, Bonnezeaux and sweet sparkling wines are suggestions.

A wedding reception, Portuguese style: local wine to accompany local dishes.

The geography of wine

The grape vine is a plant which is traditionally associated with the Mediterranean – the mild damp winters and hot dry summers of that region provide ideal conditions for it to flourish. However, the climate described as 'Mediterranean' is also found outside Europe, most notably in California, South Africa, southern Australia and parts of Chile and Argentina. Vines are cultivated in all these areas and their wines, previously drunk locally, are now gaining wider recognition in other parts of the world.

Climate

Of the three main geographical factors in the production of wine – climate, soil and site – climate is the most important. There must be sufficient rain at the right time of year to sustain growth and a period of at least a hundred warm sunny days after flowering to enable the fruit to ripen. In Europe these conditions are normally only found below latitude 50°N.

Producing wine can never be a straightforward business, in that even a 'reliable' climate is subject to occasional extremes. It is also a strange fact that the greatest European wines come not from the areas around the Mediterranean itself where conditions would appear to be most suitable, but from the northern fringe areas of Bordeaux, Champagne and Burgundy in France and the Rhine and Mosel valleys in Germany. The vine may be a sensitive plant but it seems that it also needs an element of challenge to bring out the best in it.

Of all the extremes of weather which affect these growing areas, drought is the least likely to do damage. The roots of the wine go very deep, and even the prolonged dry heat of 1976 did little harm – on the contrary, most regions produced an outstanding vintage.

Frost is another matter; sharp springtime frosts which attack the budding plants can severely limit the year's output, as happened in Bordeaux in 1977. Deep penetrating winter frosts are even worse, for they can kill the entire plant, as occurred widely in France in 1956 and 1963. Hail is another great hazard, though usually a local one, which can ruin an unfortunate grower's entire crop.

Even rain can be harmful if it comes at the wrong time. A cool damp flowering period will mean a small crop, though if the weather later improves, the quality is not necessarily affected. The year 1961 followed this pattern in Bordeaux, and the resulting vintage was very fine.

A wet harvest period is more serious, as many grapes may become mildewed and rot on the vines. This is a particular problem in Germany where a portion of the crop is traditionally harvested late, when the grapes have the maximum possible sugar content, to produce the rich 'Spätlese' and 'Auslese' wines. If the weather breaks too soon, the grower may not be able to produce any of these wines at all.

Even when there are no major disasters, persistent cool, cloudy weather can result in an inferior crop of unripe grapes. These give an unbalanced wine with too much acidity and too little alcohol.

As a result of all these possible variations in climate, vintage charts can be a useful guide as to when the best growths occurred. However, it would be a mistake to regard the charts as gospel, for a number of reasons. In the first place, weather can vary significantly from place to place within a small area – one slope may be exposed to rain or cold winds from a certain quarter while another is sheltered. One village may be more susceptible to summer storms than another a few miles away. These local variations, or 'microclimates', can mean that even in a bad year one estate or chateau may be able to produce a much better wine that its neighbours.

Soil and site

Not only do vines produce their finest results in areas where the climate is least predictable, they can also flourish on soils and sites which appear very unpromising. Appearances can be deceptive – a stony topsoil, which anyway has the advantage of efficient drainage, may conceal rich subsoils beneath. However, it seems that vines struggling to extract the maximum benefit from the soil, producing vigorous root growth, achieve the best results in quality of fruit – provided, of course, that the plants themselves are skilfully pruned and tended.

The steep-sided hill slopes of the Mosel valley, for example, with their thin slaty soil, produce some of the finest results from the Riesling grape. Farther south in the Rhine district of the Palatinate, better wines are made on the hills of the Haardt Mountains than on the rich alluvial plains of the valley floor.

Soil conditions vary from area to area as with microclimates. In Burgundy, for example, some of the most spectacular – and expensive – wines in the world, with names like Romanée-Conti and Le Montrachet, come from very small and unspectacular-looking patches of ground only a few acres in extent.

Of course, for every bottle of Romanée-Conti there will be millions of bottles from more humble and probably more easily cultivated vineyards whose uncomplicated table wines provide the staple of wine-drinking the world over. Greatness, however, is less easily achieved, depending as it does on several factors still imperfectly understood, and containing always an element of mystery.

A vineyard in Germany

Grape types

It is an obvious enough fact that grapes do not all look or taste the same: aside from the basic division into black and white, there are all sorts of subtle differences in appearance and flavour. These differences will naturally also appear in the fermented juice of the grape (the wine) and are largely responsible for the many varied styles of wine available today.

Colour

Many people think that black grapes produce red wine, and generally speaking this is so; it is the broken grape skins present in the vats during fermentation that give colour to a wine. However, the juice of any grape, even a black grape, is pale yellow – and if the black skins are carefully removed before the juice ferments, a white wine will result. Champagne, for example, is made mainly from a black grape which, by a different process of fermentation, also produces the great red wines of Burgundy.

Grape varieties

There are over 5000 varieties of the one species of vine, *Vitis vinifera*, from which wine is made. Sometimes several names are given to one variety. For instance, the variety Syrah, the best red grape of the Rhône and the one which produces Hermitage, is known in Australia and South Africa as Shiraz.

Some closely related grape varieties come under a family name. One family which is encountered again and again in the making of wine is the Pinot family – Pinot Noir (the

Pinot Noir – the burgundy grape

red burgundies); Pinot Chardonnay (Chablis and the great white burgundies); Pinot Gris (full-bodied whites); Pinot de la Loire (the name often used for the classic white grape of the Loire); Pinotage (a South African grape crossed with the Pinot Noir) and so on.

Grape regions

Most of the good European wines are named after the château or estate, or at least the region, from which they come, so you do not really need to know the grape from which they are made.

However, certain grape types are best suited to certain areas, and in order to maintain the quality and reputation of a wine, the independent governing bodies which control wine-making will usually specify which varieties are to be used. For example, in the area of Bordeaux there are only six grape types authorized for red wines, and of these Merlot, Cabernet Franc and above all Cabernet Sauvignon make up the bulk of the crop. Unless these varieties are used, the wine will not qualify for the *Appellation Contrôlée* which is the mark of the finest French wines.

In Germany and Italy similar controls are applied: an approved wine will be labelled *Qualitätswein* or *Denominazione di Origine Controllata* (D.O.C.).

Varietal wines

Some wines are, however, known by the grape rather than the place of origin. These are called varietal wines. The French district of Alsace, for example, traditionally names its white wines in this way as Riesling, or Sylvaner, or Gewürztraminer.

Riesling is a particularly familiar grape name to be found on labels. True Riesling is regarded as the king of grapes in Germany and Alsace, where it produces magnificent, fragrant and fruity wines. This true Riesling is also grown successfully in Austria, Australia, South Africa, California and parts of Europe, when it is usually called Rhine, White or Johannisberg Riesling depending on the country of origin.

The true Riesling grape has a doubtfully related cousin that is grown in northern Italy and all over Eastern Europe. It produces a lighter, cheaper wine and will often be labelled as Laski Riesling, Olasz Riesling, Welschriesling or Italian Riesling.

The Muscat wines are another good example of varietal wines. Muscat wine is easily recognizable as it has a distinctively fragrant, grapy smell. The naturally high sugar content of the grape results in the dessert wines of southern France, such as Muscat de Beaumes de Venise, as well as the sweet sparkling Italian wine, Asti Spumante. However, in Alsace, it produces a wine that is surprisingly dry.

Quite different from Muscat is Muscadet, which many people probably do not think of as a grape because it is always associated with the small area around the mouth of the Loire where it is grown. The white wine Muscadet produces is refreshingly dry.

The Gewürztraminer grape is by far the easiest grape to identify as it has a very strong and spicy flavour. It is at its best in the fruity, dry wines of Alsace but it also makes good wine in Germany, Australia, California and Eastern Europe.

The Cabernet Sauvignon grape, aside from its reputation in the making of claret, is a name increasingly seen on labels from many countries such as Australia, Argentina, Chile, South Africa and California. In fact the Cabernet Sauvignon grape is the pride of California and while in Bordeaux this grape is almost always blended with others, some of the best Californian wines are pure Cabernet Sauvignon. There is also America's own variety, Zinfandel, which produces a fruity red wine.

Shopping around among varietal wines is a good way of discovering just how many different flavours there are to be enjoyed. It can also be interesting to compare wines of the same grape type, but from different areas – a Chardonnay from California is obviously going to share certain basic characteristics with a Chardonnay from Burgundy, but soil, climate and the wine-making method differ from place to place and year to year, affecting the finished product. This is a discouraging thought for those who want their wine always to taste the same, but not for those who enjoy variety.

How wine is made

The natural process of fermentation, which transforms crushed grapes into wine, is as old as time. In very simple terms, fermentation means that the sugar in the sun-ripened grapes is converted by substances in the wine called yeast enzymes, into alcohol and carbon dioxide. Modern wine makers prefer to leave nothing to chance and so their techniques are very sophisticated, but at the heart of all their high-powered technology lies the same ancient equation that has been used since wine was first made.

An old-fashioned manual wine press from the Beaujolais region

Fermentation

Once the grapes are ripe (which in the northern hemisphere happens sometime between August and November, depending on the weather and the latitude), they are picked by hand or by machines and brought into the winery in lorry-loads. The grapes are then crushed, and the stalks removed – in a modern mechanized winery this is done at the same time in a stemmer-crusher. The ancient method of crushing the grapes with the feet is rarely seen today, except perhaps on a few small farms in some parts of France, Spain, Portugal and Italy.

The traditional method of making wine was to press the grapes in a manual press and then leave the juice to ferment. Nowadays, however, red wine is made by pumping the crushed grapes, with their skins and pips, into huge fermentation vats. It is the skins that give red wine its colour so the grapy mixture may be left on the skins for as long as three weeks. The newly-fermented alcohol sucks up colour, and also the tannin that will make the wine powerful and long-lasting.

White wines may be made from red or white grapes, or a mixture. The juice is usually pressed out of the grapy mixture and the skins and pips are left behind when the juice is put into vats to ferment. Rosé wines always include some red grapes. The juice is removed ('racked off') from the skins after only a day or so, when it is delicate pale pink. The pale pink grape juice is then left to ferment.

Before fermentation is allowed to begin the wine maker often removes the yeasts that are naturally present on the grape skins and substitutes a more effective strain of his own. The amount of sugar in the grapes is critical too. If there has been too little sun during the summer it may well be in short supply, so the wine maker is allowed to add a specified amount to raise the future alcoholic strength (this is known as 'chaptalization'). Another crucial factor is temperature. Fermentation will not happen at all if the vats are too cool. On the other hand, if there is too much heat, the fermentation will be over-vigorous and the resultant wine will be short on subtlety.

Once under way, fermentation of red wine is allowed to go on happily until all the sugar has been converted into alcohol. The new wine (known as *vin de goutte*) is then run off the used-up skins and pips and left in vats so that it can settle. The remaining used-up skins and pips are sometimes then pressed, resulting in a rough wine (known as *vin de presse*) which is extremely harsh and very dark.

Ageing

The next stage is to transfer the new wine to the casks to acquire some 'age'. These casks are traditionally wooden, but nowadays they are often made of something less picturesque, such as stainless steel. The time that red wines are left in barrel varies widely, depending on the quality of the wine – it can be anything from several years to just long enough for the lingering deposits to settle.

For white wines the procedure is slightly different because fermentation may be stopped artificially so that some sugar remains, resulting in a sweeter wine. White wines are not usually aged in barrels, being left instead in stainless steel tanks for up to a year until the deposits settle.

Final stages

Before bottling, the wine is filtered and 'fined' – treated with chemicals to make it completely clear. In some cases there is yet another piece to be fitted into the puzzle – blending. This is a highly skilled operation by the wine maker, who may take wine from different grapes and different vineyards and even different years and vinify them together to produce his individual end product – the cuvée. Blending can improve the quality of even the greatest wines, or it can simply produce an acceptable table wine. It all depends on the type of wine the wine maker is aiming for. It is not, as some people think, a shady procedure to be frowned on by purists, but one of the most important operations in the winery.

Bottling, corking, capsuling and labelling are the last stages in the process, nowadays done almost exclusively by huge machines. Finally, the wine may be left for years to acquire 'bottle age', or it may be shipped straight off to appear on the supermarket shelf within days.

Wine Regions

Wine is now grown the world over, on every continent. In some areas, like South Africa, South America and Australia, it is a relatively new industry, with young vines and the benefit of expertise brought over from older European viniculture. In other areas – like Greece, Turkey and the Balkan States – wine has been produced for hundreds, even thousands, of years for a mainly local market, and is only recently beginning to compete with more established exporters for world attention. North America – particularly California – is a case apart. There vines have been grown since the time of the Spanish missions, but the last twenty-five years have seen enormous growth, both in the number and acreage of wineries, and in the interest of wine connoisseurs everywhere. The new processing techniques being pioneered in California's Napa Valley are being brought back for incorporation into the Continent's long-established industry. Here, in Europe, France is the undisputed king, producing the best-known and most respected red, white and rosé wines – and, of course, champagne. But Germany, Italy, Spain, Portugal, Austria and Hungary all have venerable traditions of wine-making, and England too has recently revived a history of white wine-making begun with the Romans and carried on by the monks until the supression of the monasteries by not-always-good King Henry. The styles of wine – from sweet to dry, from sparkling to still, in red, white or rosé – may vary from region to region within a country, but all growers and winemakers share a proud common heritage that ensures they learn from one another and exchange new ideas – for wine-making is more than an industry. It is a way of life.

FRANCE

France's reputation as a wine producer rests firmly on her greatest wines, which continue to set standards for all other countries. Her two best-known regions, Bordeaux and Burgundy, have become by-words, but the variety and richness of her wine heritage extends far beyond these two.

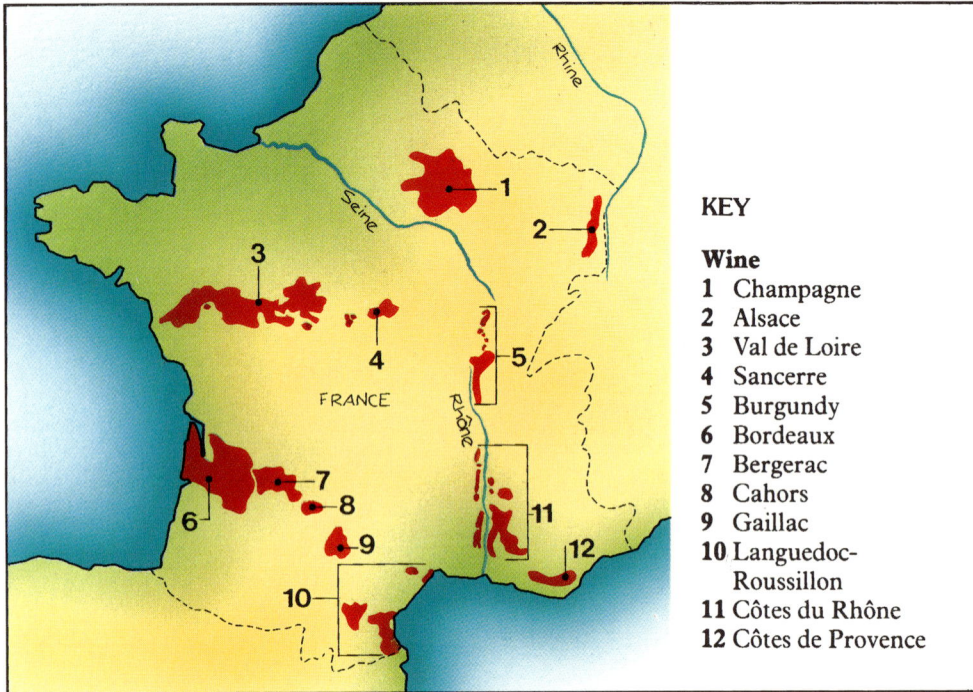

KEY

Wine
1 Champagne
2 Alsace
3 Val de Loire
4 Sancerre
5 Burgundy
6 Bordeaux
7 Bergerac
8 Cahors
9 Gaillac
10 Languedoc-Roussillon
11 Côtes du Rhône
12 Côtes de Provence

Despite her large land area, France is not the most productive of wine-growers, but she produces more quality wines than any other country. A quarter of the 75 million hectolitres which flow annually from French wineries are *Vins de Qualité produits dans les régions determinées* – the official EEC designation for fine wines. This proportion is likely to increase, as many growers in the lesser-known areas are ambitious to achieve a higher status for their wines, and land is being set aside for the cultivation of classic grape varieties.

The demand for these fine wines exceeds even France's capacity to supply them, so that many have become expensive and some prohibitively so. The greatest red wines from Bordeaux and Burgundy are now more often bought as an investment than for drinking; over the past twenty years, they have proved good inflation-beaters. But it seems a pity that after all the hard work, patience and skill which goes into making such a wine, it should end up not in a glass but on a balance-sheet. Fortunately, most of the wines even from these classic regions do not have to be considered in this light and are, if not everyday drinking, at least an affordable luxury.

Why are the best French wines so good? There is no complete answer to that question. In the first place, there is a tradition of wine-making extending back for hundreds of years, even to the Roman occupation; given enough time and practice, skills will develop and be handed on. There has also been an enthusiastic and sophisticated market for the product, not only in France but abroad; the English court developed a taste for Bordeaux wines after the region fell under control of the Crown in the Middle Ages, and at the end of the eighteenth century Thomas Jefferson was there, arranging for cases of his own favourites to make the trans-Atlantic crossing. Georgraphy too is significant; the right combination of soil and site for particular vines, and a climate which is equable but with just enough variation of temperature and rainfall to test their toughness and flexibility. Then in recent years there has been a stringent set of government regulations, controlling the types of grape grown in each region, the maximum yield allowed, and permitted alcoholic strength.

French wines are outstanding not only for their quality but also for their variety. Somewhere in France there should be a wine for every palate. If you like dry wines, then there is a Muscadet from the Loire, Entre deux Mers from Bordeaux, or one of the White Burgundies. Something with a little more fruit? Try a Riesling from Alsace. For red wine, Bordeaux and Burgundy are unrivalled, or if you prefer a lightweight, Beaujolais. Pink perhaps? Then there is a choice between the light rosés of Anjou and the fuller-flavoured ones from Provence. As for sparkling, what could be better then Champagne? We shall be looking at all these – and many others – in the following pages.

The Pinot Noir vendage in Cahors.

French wine labels

In order to get the best value for money, it is essential that you understand the labels on bottles of wine. Once you are familiar with the technical details and sometimes flowery language, you can gather a surprising amount of information from them as to the quality of the wine inside.

Table wine
In the case of French wines, just under three-quarters of the two billion gallons produced every year is ordinary table wine (*vin de table*). The 'Chasse Royale' pictured here is a typical example and, as always, it is the small print on the label that counts. 'Produce of France' means that the wine is made from a blend of French-grown grapes, and 'vin de table' indicates that it is the most basic quality. *'Mise en bouteille par . . . négociant à F. 21700'* indicates which shipper blended and bottled the wine, and where – in this case the French département 21700. The wine's commercial or brand name, and the flowery descriptions like 'La Bonne Bouteille du Patron', are colourful and eye-catching but, in fact, do not tell you anything about the wine.

Ordinary graded wine
Moving further up the scale, the remaining quarter or so of French wine is governed by a complex system of laws designed to stop ordinary wine being passed off as something more special. There are three grades to watch out for. The lowest is *'vins de pays'*. These are really table wines, mostly from the south, made with a little more care by producers conscious of their reputation. Next comes VDQS wines, *Vins Delimité de Qualité Supérieure*. The rules applying to these are less stringent than those governing the next class up, but they do set certain standards and wines in this category can be good value for money.

AC wines
At the top of the pyramid, making up about 20% of the total, are AC or *Appellation Contrôlée wines*. When you look at the label of an AC wine, remember that the more specific the appellation (in geographical terms) the better the quality of the wine. An AC Bordeaux or an AC burgundy will be a decently made wine, but could come from anywhere in a big area. If the wine all comes from a particular area within the region (Médoc, say, in Bordeaux or Côte de Beaune in Burgundy) the label will say so, and likewise if it comes from an even more specific source, whether it is a particular commune, group of villages, area of hillside or even individual château or vineyard, the label will proudly declare it.

So, when you are checking the pedigree of your wine, one of the things to watch out for is brand-name wines with smart labels that are trying to look like, say, château-bottled claret. Look for the give-away words 'AC Bordeaux' (the lowest possible claret appelation). These may be perfectly acceptable wines – Mouton-Cadet is the best-known example – but they are nothing like as good as the producers would like you to think. Remember too that more specific descriptions like *'Côtes de X' 'Coteaux de X'* (hillside(s) of) and *'X Villages'* indicate a slightly better quality wine than one entitled to give itself only the basic place name.

The label can tell you many important things about the wine you are buying.

Thus AC Beaujolais-Villages is superior to plain AC Beaujolais. The Mâcon-Villages illustrated below comes from certain designated villages within the Mâcon area, and is also bottled by the established négociant Loron et Fils. One qualifying word to be wary of is *'supérieur'*. It is not necessarily superior – this designation simply means over 10.5% alcohol and most wines in a good year reach this anyway.

At the top end of the AC system, wines from certain of the best vineyards (in the Médoc, Côte d'Or and Chablis, for example) may be described as *cru classé* or classed growth. These classes range from *grand cru* down through *premier cru* to *cinquième cru* (first to fifth growth, in the case of the Médoc) with *cru bourgeois* below that: the latter is often good value. The claret shown here, from the property Lamothe Bergeron, is a château-bottled cru bourgeois, entitled to the appelation Haut-Médoc – the most prestigious region of Bordeaux.

Bottling
Where the wine was bottled and who shipped it are important clues to quality. The best wines are *'mise en bouteille à la propriété'*, *'. . . au château'* or *'. . . à la domaine'*, which means that the grower bottled them himself at the individual property with due care and attention. *'Mise en bouteilles dans nos caves'* or *'. . . nos chais'* is gently misleading. It means *not* bottled at the property. *'Nos caves'* (our cellars), after all, could be almost anywhere. *'Mise par le négociant'* or *'mise par Monsieur X'* means that a shipper bought the wines from the grower(s), blended them and arranged the bottling. 'Shipped and bottled *by*' is more encouraging than 'shipped and bottled *for*', whether the words are in French or English. If you have any choice go for a shipper whose reputation you know and trust.

Vintage
The vintage date may also be important. Few people can carry around in their heads all the information about every vintage of wine, and there are plenty of books that set it all down. On the other hand, it is worth having a rough idea of what years are best.

Varietal wines
From time to time you may come across a wine that is labelled according to the grape variety rather than where it was grown – the so-called 'varietal' wines. These are most likely to come from California or Australia and will be labelled accordingly, but French examples might be 'Gamay' or 'Sauvignon de . . .'. Read the rest of the label, and choose a trustworthy négociant or shipper.

Degree of sweetness and sparkle
Brut: bone dry
Sec: dry
Demi sec: medium sweet
Doux: sweet
Champagne: made by the méthode champenoise in the Champagne area of France
Mousseux: sparkling
Crémant: less sparkling than Mousseux
Pétillant: with a tingly fizz
Perlant: just a touch of fizz

Introducing Burgundy

Most wine experts are agreed that the best of Burgundy's wines are among the greatest in the world. Almost all burgundy is very expensive nowadays and the famous single-vineyard or even top commune wines are way beyond the reach of the ordinary wine-buyer. But it is still possible, armed with a little knowledge, to find acceptable cousins or cousins-twice-removed from the fringes of the area, that retain some characteristics of the best burgundies.

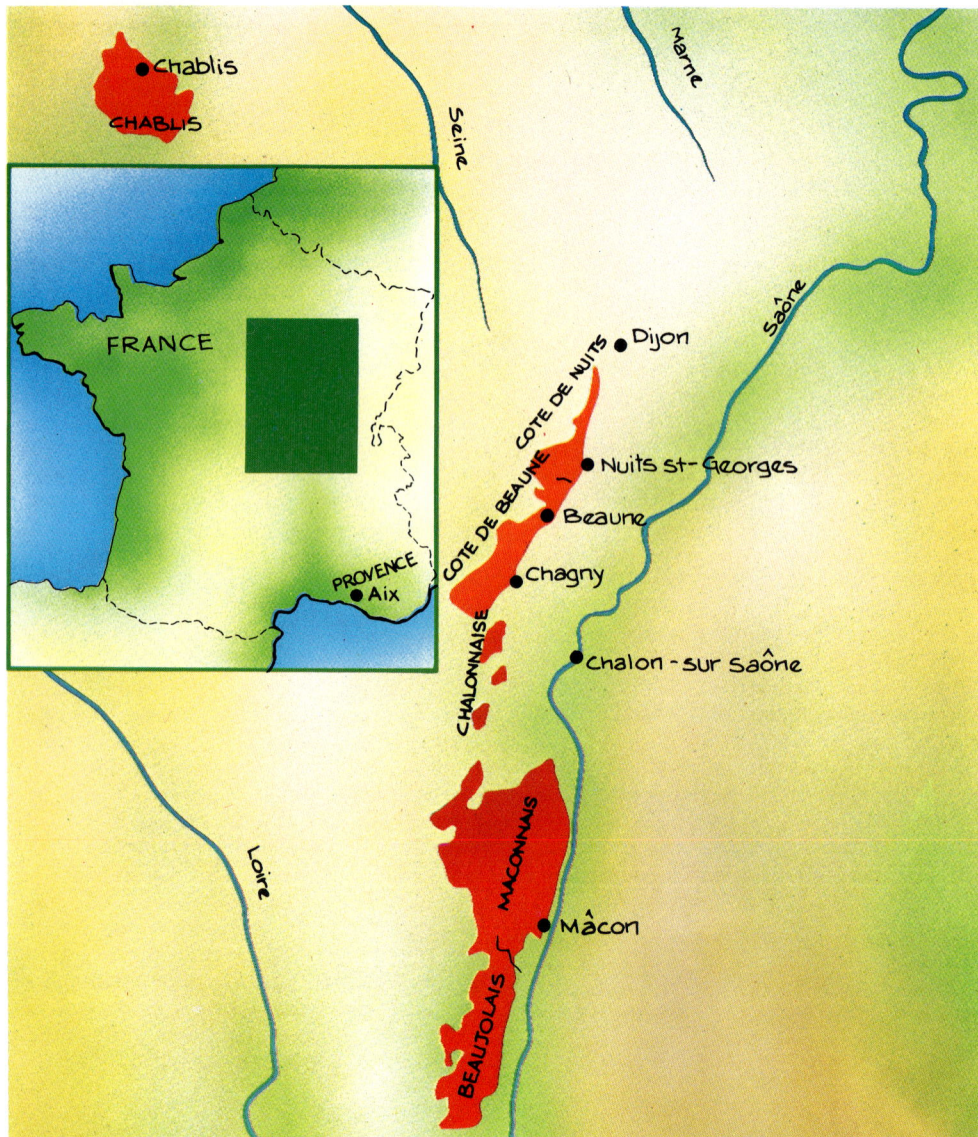

What are the characteristics of a good burgundy – red or white? The incomparable whites make up less than a quarter of the area's total output. As a rough description they are firm and balanced and are powerfully suggestive of the noble Chardonnay grape. They can be laid down for several years, as they have exceptional staying power. Well-made reds are full in the mouth, fruity and emphatic, but not heavy or 'soupy'. The adjective most often used to describe red burgundy is 'velvety'.

Burgundy costs so much because the total area producing wine entitled to bear one of the 114 burgundy appellations is small. The best burgundies come from the vineyards of the Côte d'Or. They lie along a south-east facing strip of gentle hillside no more than 50 kilometres long and often as little as 200 metres wide. The very best vineyards, which produce the *grand crus* (best growths), lie in the centre of this strip. Some of these vineyards, with world-famous names, are no bigger than large gardens. Romanée-Conti, for example, generally thought of as the peak of burgundy, covers a mere 1.8 hectares. Bad weather often dramatically reduces the potential yield, and then a large percentage of what is eventually produced is sold direct to individual buyers. In some years it is remarkable that any burgundy reaches the market at all and what little there is has to satisfy a burgundy-thirsty world.

Burgundy is said to be very variable in quality. In the past 'burgundy' was often doctored with heavy reds from Midi, or even Algeria, to give it the weight that the customers expected. Now, with the law tightened up, any wine with a burgundy Appellation Contrôlée label must be made entirely from grapes grown in the area.

Variability still remains, however, but this is partly because, unlike Bordeaux where large properties often belong to a single owner, burgundy vineyards may have dozens of owners, each responsible for a tiny parcel of land. Even wine made from grapes in adjoining rows may taste quite different because the grapes may have been differently tended and harvested. The grapes are then sold to different middlemen, *négociants*, each of whom will blend wines according to his own house style and bottling standards. The wines will then be marketed with his name on the label.

When buying great burgundy, a careful scrutiny of the label is the best guide. A top-ranking Gevrey-Chambertin or a Montrachet made and bottled by the grower at the property is the best choice; this is indicated by the words, *mise en bouteilles par le proprietaire*. Otherwise opt for a shipper whose reputation you can trust. Reliable names to look for on the label include Louis Jadot, Louis Latour, Joseph Drouhin, and Bouchard Pere et Fils. Beware the misleading '*mise en bouteilles dans nos caves*' ('in our cellars' means bottled almost anywhere.)

Grades of burgundy

The appellation system which governs the way Burgundy's wines are labelled and sold is complex. The most basic appellation is Bourgogne Grand Ordinaire. Next in price and quality comes the red Passe-tout-grains; this means 'all grapes included' and in practice the wine will be a mixture of two-thirds from the Gamay grape, the more prolific grape of the area, and one one-third the superior grape Pinot Noir.

The second grade for white wine is Bourgogne Aligoté; this is made from the Aligoté grape, the lesser of the two grapes used in the region for the white wine. AC Bourgogne comes next, the red made entirely from the noble Pinot Noir grape; the white from the Chardonnay. AC Bourgogne from a reliable shipper is often a good buy.

From the hilly countryside beyond the main slopes come two more basic appellations – Hautes Côtes de Beaune and Hautes Côtes de Nuits. These wines can also be very worthwhile, particularly in good years, when the grapes have plenty of sun, they will compare favourably with their aristocratic relatives.

From the Côte d'Or, the heartland of Burgundy come the three topmost appellations of the region. At the very top are the thirty grands crus, the best vineyards with famous names like Chambertin, Les Musigny and Le Montrachet. *Premier cru* is the grade immediately below. The third rank is *appellation communale*, in other words having the right to use the name of the commune. Examples are AC Vougeot, or AC Chambolle-Musigny. These are still fine wines, although not in quite the same exalted class as those from grand cru or premier cru vineyards.

The individual wine-producing areas will be discussed on the following pages.

Côte de Nuits

The Côte d'Or 'golden slope' stretching between Dijon in the north and Santenay in the south, has been producing legendary wine for hundreds of years. The narrow strip of hillside falls naturally into two parts, of which the northern one is known as the Côte de Nuits.

In the Côte de Nuits vineyards, the Pinot Noir grape produces the finest red burgundies, which all share a powerful family likeness but also display a rich variety of individual flavours and bouquets. Only a small quantity of white wine is made on the Côte de Nuits, but what there is, is of equally fine quality.

The main communes

There are eight important wine communes in this Côte and they take their names from the villages dotted along the length of the slope. For the commune appellation titles some proudly hyphenate the names of their most famous vineyard to the village name, giving resounding combinations like Chambolle-Musigny and Nuits-St Georges.

The two northernmost communes are Fixin and Gevrey-Chambertin. Gevrey-Chambertin is often described as the typical, red burgundy – rich, mouth-filling and long-lasting. Sadly, the description is the closest that most wine-drinkers can get while fine burgundy prices are at their current level. The commune has no fewer than nine *grand cru* vineyards including Chambertin, and Chambertin Clos de Bèze where the monks of the Abbey of Bèze were making wine in the seventh century. The *appellation communale* wine of Gevrey has a high reputation and therefore a high price. The wines from Fixin, north of Gevrey are dark red, strongly perfumed and age well, but the name is less famous and so they are a little cheaper.

Beyond Gevrey-Chambertin lies Morey-St Denis, another of the Côte's less well-known names where prices are still within the realms of possibility. Morey-St Denis wines are big and sturdy like the Gevrey-Chambertin wines, but they also have a trace of softness that makes them the 'bridge' between their northern neighbour and Chambolle-Musigny just to the south.

Chambolle-Musigny is elegant and perfumed, but very full-bodied. The great vineyard in this commune is Les Musigny which also produces a small quantity of white wine. Among the *premiers crus* (first growths) are the prettily named Les Amoureuses and Les Charmes. Next door lies the small commune of Vougeot. Almost all of it is taken up by the single vineyard Clos de Vougeot.

Within the stone walls of the Clos the problems that affect Burgundy as a whole can be seen on a smaller scale. Clos de Vougeot is the biggest vineyard in Burgundy, but it is divided up between sixty-odd separate owners, whose holdings are all at different levels. The best wine comes from the top of the slope and the poorest from the low land bordering the road. Each grower has different methods, and the wine may well be sold to négociants with different standards. Although there is no guarantee of consistency, all the wine still ends up on the market as grand cru Clos de Vougeot. There will also be a price to match the grand cru reputation, and the wine may be worth every penny of that price or it may be a sad disappointment. As a result criticism is often directed at burgundy as a whole, when it should in fact be directed at the multiple-ownership system. The only guarantee of quality for the ordinary buyer is the shipper's reputation.

Between Vougeot and Vosne-Romanée lies Flagey-Echézaux. Most of the wines from this commune are sold as Vosne-Romanée. The commune of Vosne-Romanée itself is almost hallowed ground. Amongst its five grands crus is Romanée-Conti, thought by some of those who can afford it to be the very greatest red wine of all. The other equally famous names here are la Romanée, Romanée-St Vivant, le Richebourg and la Tâche.

The last important commune of the Côte is Nuits-St Georges, centred on the town of Nuits. The wines of Premeaux, the neighbouring commune, are also sold as Nuits-St Georges. These are big wines, typically Côte de Nuits, firm and tannic and with a deep colour. They take time to mature, but are worth waiting for. Nuits has no grand crus, but the quality in general should be high although its reputation in the past has been damaged by the fraudulent passing off of 'Nuits-St Georges' that bore no relation to the real thing. Tightening up the appellation laws has ended this abuse.

Other wines

Certain inferior vineyards along the length of the Côte are only allowed to sell their wines as Côte de Nuits-Villages. (Remember that 'inferior' is a relative term when talking of the Côte d'Or.) These are still of a higher standard than AC (*Appellation Controlée*) Bourgogne, and are worth looking out for. Along the fringes of the busy main road, RN 74, marking the boundary of the Côte proper, are low-lying vineyards of a poorer standard. From these, and from the vineyards across the road comes the bulk of plain AC Bourgogne. However, this is still the Côte d'Or. An honestly-made AC Bourgogne embodies some – even if only a trace – of the great burgundy taste.

Large baskets of Pinot Noir grapes.

Côte de Beaune

Burgundy's southern half, the Côte de Beaune, is world famous for its white wine. To many people the white wine from this region is the greatest in the world, and the many classic wines from the area, with their distinctive dry but lusciously rich flavours command high prices.

The Côte de Beaune produces excellent red wines, as well as classic white. They differ from the wines produced by their neighbours on the Côte de Nuits to the north in that they are usually softer, lighter, and quick to mature.

White Côte de Beaune wines

The neighbouring communes of Puligny-Montrachet and Chassagne-Montrachet at the southern end of the Côte de Beaune are the best known. As in the Côte de Nuits, these communes take their names from the villages with the name of the most illustrious vineyards tacked on. Le Montrachet is the greatest of the white *grands crus* vineyeards. It is split between the two communes of Puligny and Chassagne, with its only marginally less illustrious grand cru neighbours – Chevalier-Montrachet, Bâtard-Montrachet, Criots-Bâtard-Montrachet, and Bienvenues-Bâtard-Montrachet – clustered around it. These wines are intense, succulent and golden and for most wine-drinkers are a once-in-a-lifetime experience. As even Appellation Contrôlée commune wines from this area are very expensive, it is wise to take a look at wines from the neighbouring commune at St-

Vineyards surrounding Meursault

Aubin. Its wines, white and red, are dependable and much cheaper while still providing an echo of the Montrachet distinction.

Next to Puligny-Montrachet lies the commune of Meursault, producing soft white wines with a distinctive flavour described as either 'mealy' or 'buttery'. The single-vineyard wines – les Genevrières, les Charmes, les Perrières – are excellent but the commune AC wines can be disappointing if they come from the low vineyards bordering the main road. As always, it pays to choose a reliable shipper – the Patriarche company is good in this area. Meursault is popular and sometimes overpriced; neighbouring Auxey-Duresses is a cheaper alternative. Red wines from Meursault are generally sold as Volnay, and Volnay's whites as Meursault.

Red Côte de Beaune wines

North of Meursault lie the famous red wine communes of the Côte – Volnay, Pommard and Beaune. Pommard is the most expensive and imitated. Volnay's reds are attractive, short-lived but with a delicate roundness and a fragrant bouquet. A cheaper

alternative to these red wines can be found in Auxey-Duresses or Monthélie.

Beaune is a large commune centred on the town of Beaune, the administrative centre of the Burgundy wine trade. It is a famous name and almost all the wines from the commune get *premier cru* rating. AC Beaune is the lowest appellation and tends to be overpriced for its variable quality – better buys are to be found amongst the reds of Savigny-lès-Beaune, or Santenay. The commune of Santenay is at the southern end of the Côte and produces lower priced wines. These may be either light and fruity, or powerful and long-lived - more like a Côte de Nuits red – according to the variability of the soil.

In the town of Beaune is the picture-postcard symbol of Burgundy, the Hôtel-Dieu or, as it is much more widely known, the *Hospices de Beaune*, a charity hospital for the elderly. Over the years, since the first bequest in the fifteenth century, Burgundian vineyard-owners have traditionally bequeathed land to the Hospices. The foundation now owns parcels of vineyards scattered through the Côte de Beaune and the wines of the Hospices are auctioned every November. They command high prices, partly because of the charitable tradition and a certain prestige, but also because they usually are well-made.

At the northern end of the Côte is the village of Aloxe-Corton with the hill of Corton rising above it. On the slopes of this hillside lie a wonderful concentration of grads crus vineyards, both red and white. The red wines of Le Corton rival the very best of the Côte de Nuits. Corton-Charlemagne – legend has it that this land was once the property of the Emperor Charlemagne – produces superb white wine. As prices for AC Aloxe-Corton are very high, AC Pernand-Vergelesses is a less expensive substitute.

The Côte de Beaune is much larger in area than the Côte de Nuits, so its basic wines are more plentiful and therefore cheaper. Immediately below commune level is AC Côte de Beaune-Villages, from several of the villages around the town of Beaune. Some of these villages are also entitled to their own individual appellations. Plain AC Côte de Beaune is the product of sixteen villages on the edges of the Côte proper. If the blending is done by one of the big *négociants* these wines can also be good value. Finally there is Bourgogne Hautes Côtes de Beaune, from the country over the hill beyond the Côte d'Or itself. If they are carefully made in a good year, generic wines like these are excellent and can provide the only really accessible burgundies for the average drinker.

The following Burgundian négociants have well established reputations. One of these names on the label of your bottle should provide a fair guarantee of the quality of the wine inside the bottle. Louis Jadot, Louis Latour, Patriarche, Bouchard Père et Fils, Chanson, Joseph Drouhin, Prosper Maufoux, Marcel Amance, J. Faively and Remoissenet. Remember, when ordering burgundy from a restaurant wine list, check for these names on the wine list.

Côte Chalonnais and the Mâconnais

After the classic names and prices of the Côte d'Or it is a relief to turn southwards to the humbler country of the Côte Chalonnais and the Mâconnnais, where you can find interesting everyday wines, that still have some of the characteristics of the finer ones from the Côte de Beaune.

Côte Chalonnais

The Côte Chalonnais is a tiny area lying to the south of the village of Chagny. It is really a continuation of the Côte d'Or although the countryside in this area is rougher and hillier and the vineyards are broken up between patches of farmland. The Côte produces both red and white wine, and its commune wines are good value especially when compared with the prices commanded further north.

The four Chalonnais commune appellations to watch out for are Mercurey, Montagny, Rully and Givry. Montagny's whites are particularly good, clean-tasting and with a tinge of greenish-gold colour that tells of their closeness to Mâcon. The reputation of these commune wines is growing fast, helped along by the presence of top *négociants* like Louis Latour. In fact a Louis Latour Montagny can command a price nowadays that wouldn't shame a top commune wine from the Côte de Beaune.

Rully is also beginning to be known for its whites. These are dry and quite full-bodied, with a certain sharpness due to the high level of acidity. Both Rully and Montagny are wines for drinking while they are still young and fresh, although a year or two in the bottle will do no harm.

Celebrating the end of a Mâcon harvest

The best known reds of the Côte are from the vineyards of Mercurey. They are light, but with a subtlety that can be reminiscent of a Pommard or a Beaune from a lightweight year. Givry and Rully also produce reds with slightly more body but less finesse than Mercurey; Givry is the better of the two. Do not leave any of these fresh wines lying about for too long, and be wary of any that are more than five years old.

Mâconnais

South of the Côte Chalonnais is the much bigger area of the Mâconnais, best known for its white wines – and for Pouilly-Fuissé in particular. In fact the villages producing Pouilly-Fuissé – Vergisson, Chaintré, Solutré, Pouilly and Fuissé – are so far to the south of the Mâconnais that they overlap with the Beaujolais area. They lie on an isolated pocket of soil that gives the wines a distinctive earthy character, known as the *goût de terroir*.

Pouilly wines are praised for being dry and full-bodied, as well as fruity and soft like a good white burgundy. Unfortunately Pouilly-Fuissé is a famous and fashionable name which has suffered from being too much in demand. When looking for the characteristic Pouilly taste, it would make economic sense to choose from one of the other three appellations in the area, Pouilly-Loché, Pouilly-Vinzelles or Saint-Véran. (Remember that Pouilly-Fuissé is not to be confused with Pouilly-Fumé, made from the Sauvignon grape at Pouilly-sur-Loire on the other side of France.)

Wine from the villages around Chaintré and Saint-Véran may also appear under the label 'Beaujolais blanc'. The appellations here are interchangeable, and the producers are presumably keen to take advantage of the booming fashion for beaujolais – whatever colour their wine happens to be.

The rest of the Mâconnais produces less distinctive but perfectly good, rounded white wines made from the noble Chardonnay grape. The reds generally do not reach the same standard because they are made from the prolific and not at all noble Gamay (the beaujolais grape). Both whites and reds are sold as Appellation Mâcon Controlée if they reach a certain standard.

Apart from Pouilly, where the individual grower predominates, Mâconnais grapes tend to be sold by the grower direct to the local co-operatives, who then turn the grapes into wine. There are about twenty co-operatives in the area, at village centres like Chaintré, Clissé and Viré. Once the wine is made it is sold to a shipper who arranges the bottling. So it is worth being aware when choosing a Mâcon that there are *two* factors likely to affect the quality – the co-operative as well as the shipper.

A cut above plain white AC Mâcon is Mâcon-Villages, from certain designated villages. About forty villages producing white wine of this standard are allowed to hyphenate their names on to the basic appellation title – the best known are probably Mâcon-Prissé, Mâcon-Viré and Mâcon-Lugny.

Another local appellation, and one that can sometimes be puzzling, is Pinot Chardonnay Mâcon. This is a so-called 'varietal' wine, named in the Californian style after two grape varieties, and it can be particularly good value. It may be made from the Chardonnay grape or from its close relative the Pinot Blanc, and it is so called to set it apart from the other Mâconnais whites made from the Aligoté grape. These poorer cousins, which can taste thin and sharp beside the rich depth of the Chardonnay, will be identified as such on the label. Quite large areas of the Mâconnais and Chalonnais are planted with Gamay and Aligoté which will find their way into AC Bourgogne Passe-tout-Grains (or AC Mâcon, of course) and AC Bourgogne Aligoté, or into declassified *vin de table*.

Most of the wines from these two areas (except the Pouillys and the products of the grand *négociants*) are cheap enough to allow room for experiment. Watch the liquor store shelves or your wine merchant's list for the lesser-known names. Once you have found a particular Mercurey, Montagny or Mâcon-Villages that you like it would be well worth investing in a supply to draw on over the next couple of years. They are not the kind of wines to lay down with a view to a profit in ten years' time, but they will benefit from a year or two resting in the bottle, and will then appear at their fresh and economically appealing best.

Beaujolais

Light and fruity, beaujolais is a popular and well-known red wine and a very versatile one – suitable for most social occasions and as an accompaniment for many dishes. It comes from an 80 kilometre stretch of country between Mâcon and Lyons, at the southern end of the Burgundy vineyards. The region is attractive, with rolling hills and small villages, which epitomize rural France.

Grape pickers in a beaujolais vineyard

Until the 1960s much of the 'Beaujolais' exported was a soupy blend of cheap red wines, concocted by blenders from a number of sources; it bore no relation to true beaujolais. Fortunately, the situation has changed: former blending practices are now illegal and there has been a tremendous surge of enthusiasm for the genuine article – a light, refreshing, fruity red wine made exclusively from the Gamay grape, grown within a limited area and intended to be drunk young.

This is not to say that the quality of beaujolais is uniform. It comes from a large area which produces, in a good vintage, over 150 million bottles of wine. A lot of this comes from the lower-lying area in the south of the region, known as the Bas Beaujolais. This area has been extensively planted with new vines in recent years but the Gamay vine here makes a less interesting wine than it does on the granite hills in the north of the region.

How to choose a good beaujolais
Generally speaking, the more precisely a bottle of wine is defined by its label, the better it should be. A wine described simply as A.C. Beaujolais is guaranteed to come from the area, to be made from the Gamay, and to contain at least 9% of alcohol.

Beaujolais Supérieur is the same, but 1% stronger, over 10% (though it is not necessarily better wine). In the heart of the Beaujolais country there is a group of some 35 communes, or villages, whose product is entitled to be known as Beaujolais Villages. This wine has the same strength as Beaujolais Supérieur but because it comes from a region where the conditions of the soil and climate are especially suited to the Gamay grape, it should have more character.

Moving on, in terms of quality, there are nine communes in the area, the Grand Crus, which are entitled to their own *appéllation*, that is, a special wine label of their own. Their names are St. Amour, Juliénas, Chénas, Moulin-à-Vent, Chiroubles, Fleurie, Morgon, Brouilly and Côte de Brouilly. These wines are undoubtedly the best beaujolais, and a beaujolais expert will tell you that each of them has its own distinctive qualities. As a general guide, Fleurie is perhaps the most immediately appealing – bright, translucent and appetizing. Brouilly and Côte de Brouilly are usually the fruitiest of the group. Morgon is harder and longer lasting and Moulin-à-Vent, the biggest and deepest in flavour, sometimes needs several years to develop its full potential.

As a general rule, even Grand Cru Beaujolais is at its best within 2 or 3 years of bottling. Beaujolais also breaks the other rule usually applied to red wine because it can be served slightly chilled, at 'cellar' rather than room temperature.

Merchants
Most beaujolais is bought from individual growers or co-operatives by local négociants or merchants. They will blend the wines according to the traditions of their firms and the name of the négociant will appear on the label. The Beaujolais of Piat is a well-known label marketed in a distinctive rounded bottle with a small lip at the top. Other merchants' names worth looking for are Antoine Dépagneux of Villefranche and Georges Duboeuf of Romaneche-Thorins.

Prices
Beaujolais is a more reasonably priced wine than burgundy, but it has become a lot more expensive in recent years. This is in spite of the great amount produced, as verified by the saying that three rivers flow into the neighbouring town of Lyons: the Rhône, the Saône and the Beaujolais. Among imported wines a good A.C. Beaujolais is not markedly more expensive than unnamed cheap plonk. A Beaujolais Villages will be slightly more expensive than an A.C. Beaujolais. A Grand Cru from a good vintage will be about twice the price of the A.C. Beaujolais which is considerably less than you would pay for a bottle from a limited area in other parts of France.

Beaujolais nouveau
Beaujolais nouveau is newly made wine which is rushed from grape to bottle within the space of about six weeks and traditionally appears on the market around 15 November. It should be drunk immediately. Opinions are divided on its merits. It is very light, with the purplish colour characteristic of young wine, and with a pleasant scent and fruitiness. It is certainly fun to drink, but until quite recently you would have been lucky to find it outside the region of origin. Suddenly, through a combination of shrewd marketing and the whims of fashion, it has become a cult.

'The Beaujolais race' is now a social event in countries near France with merchants trying to get the wine into shops and restaurants at the first possible moment and at the most competitive price. It is at best a six weeks' wonder – by Christmas the fuss is all over for another year.

No other wine is subject to such intense short-lived demand. The effect on the beaujolais market has been colossal. It can be relatively easily and cheaply produced, and the grower and négociant see a quick return on their investment. It is therefore hardly surprising that in 1983, 40% of all the A.C. Beaujolais produced was sold as Beaujolais Nouveau or Primeur, and producers throughout the region feel mounting pressures to jump on the bandwagon. This would be a pity, for beaujolais nouveau is made to be drunk within weeks rather than months, and when it is all gone there is less of the more worthwhile wine to go round.

Chablis

Chablis is the best known of the white burgundies, and could even be described as the most famous white wine of all. It is one of the most widely imitated and debased names in the wine world, and as a result the reputation of authentic chablis has suffered unfairly.

It is quite common to find undistinguished dryish white and sometimes pink wines cheerfully dignifying themselves with the Chablis label when they really come from almost anywhere in the world except the proper place.

Only a limited amount of genuine Chablis is made each year. Real Chablis comes from an isolated little pocket of northern vineyards, a mere 160 kilometres south-east of Paris. It is one of the smallest fine wine-producing areas, comprising only 2000 hectares of vines. The local conditions demand that the land has to be 'rested' from time to time, so that even this small area is not always under cultivation.

The area's geographical situation is a major factor in determining quantity produced. Damaging spring frosts are a recurrent problem, not entirely solved by the elaborate heating devices in the vineyards. In bad years, too, there may just not be enough sun to ripen the grapes and bring the wine up to the required strength to meet *Appellation Contrôlée* requirements.

Yet when the conditions are favourable, Chablis is a great wine that more than deserves its widespread fame. Although

The rolling countryside around Chablis

Chablis is made from the same grape as the great white burgundies, the Chardonnay, its taste is very different from a Côtes d'Or wine. The crucial factor is the mixture of chalk and limestone in the soil ('Kimmeridgian clay', to give it its technical name). It gives the wine a hard and stony taste which is sometimes described as 'flinty', or, in the French version, as having a '*goute de pierre à fusil*'.

Whatever the description, at its best Chablis is an elegant wine that combines fruitiness with a striking steely strength. The bouquet is fresh and clean but comparatively light, and the colour is particularly attractive, pale strawy gold with distinctively gleaming greenish highlights. Traditionally Chablis is paired with oysters or any shellfish, and with more plainly-cooked fish. It might be overwhelmed by heavy sauces.

Classifications

Chablis has its own fairly simple system of classification. The best (and very expensive) wine comes from the seven *grand cru* vineyards. These lie in the best position on the south-facing slope across the river Serein from the little town of Chablis itself. They are instantly recognizable from their labels, on which they will be described as

'Chablis Grand Cru' followed by one of the seven vineyard names: Bougros, Les Preuses, Vaudésir, Grenouilles, Valmur, Les Clos and Blanchot.

As with Côte d'Or wines, the level immediately below grand cru is *premier cru*. These wines will be labelled 'Chablis Premier Cru', which may or may not be followed by a vineyard name. After recent amalgamation there are now about a dozen premier crus, and the label may indicate that the wine is from just one of these, or it may be a blend from several of them. Amongst the better-known names are Les Fourneaux, Montée de Tonnere, Beauroy, Fourchaume, Vaillons, Vosgros, Vaulorent, Monts de Milieu and Montmains.

The Chablis appellation laws state that grand cru wines must reach a level of 11° of alcohol and premier cru must reach 10.5°, so premier cru Chablis will be just a little less powerful than its grander relative both in bouquet and flavour. It is still fine wine however, and is likely to be expensive.

The appellation laws also set out the maximum yield per hectare for grand cru and premier cru vineyards. It is a strictly limited output, so it is hardly surprising that there is not enough of the best Chablis to go round. Prices, of course, reflect scarcity. Because of the climatic problems, the quality of even the best of the region's wine varies radically from year to year. In bad years the wine may not reach the required minimum strength, in which case it has to be sold off as Petit Chablis, the lowest of the local appellations.

Fortunately plain AC Chablis is rather more accessible. This wine comes from the less well-placed slopes of any of the twenty communes in the region, and the bulk of it is handled by *négociants*. As always, it pays to choose a reliable one. To qualify for this appellation the wine need only reach a level of 10°, so it is relatively light, but it should still have the authentic Chablis steely 'bite'.

At the bottom of this classification ladder is Petit Chablis, mainly from the outer fringes of the area (except in bad years, when even the best vineyards' wine may only reach this standard). In general these are very light wines, often disappointingly colourless and thin. They need only reach a minimum strength of 9.5%, and so are a long way removed from the flavourful potency of the top Chablis. They still carry the big name, however, and can often be rather overpriced as a result.

The lighter wines of the Chablis region should not be left too long before they are drunk. A year or so in bottle is plenty for Petit Chablis and the ordinary AC wines. Premier cru wines are ready to drink after two years and most grands crus can be drunk after three years in the bottle. The best Chablis does have remarkable staying power, however, and can go on giving of its best for ten years, or even longer for the great years.

Chablis is never cheap but it is a remarkable and memorable wine. A good bottle might mark a special occasion or celebration meal, but for everyday white wine-drinking there are better and cheaper alternatives to mediocre AC Chablis or Petit Chablis.

Introducing Bordeaux

Bordeaux is the largest fine wine-producing area in the world – Burgundy may rival it for quality, but cannot compete with the wonderful quantity of wine that is produced by the 50,000 Bordeaux growers. Nor can such a wide variety of wines, from the cheerful and easily drinkable to the highest-ranking aristocrats, be found anywhere else in the world. Since there is no shortage of Bordeaux wine, prices are usually reasonable, for all but the great wines.

There are striking differences in the wines of Burgundy and Bordeaux and in the way they are made. While all the great red Burgundies are made from one variety of grape, the Pinot Noir, the Bordeaux reds are made from a blend of three main varieties: Cabernet Sauvignon, Cabernet Franc and Merlot.

Bordeaux wines generally have more finesse, a more individual bouquet and seem a little austere, compared with the fullness and opulence of Burgundy. Although they are quite recognizably from the same family, Bordeaux wines differ tremendously from one another. They range from the light, dry reds and whites, to the honeyed white dessert wines of Sauternes and Barsac, with all the subtle variations in between. The red wines are often referred to as claret – an wholly English term.

As well as the different grapes, the soil, too, accounts for much of Bordeaux's rich variety. It is poor soil, consisting largely of clay, sand, pebbles and gravel – just what the vines need to produce the best grapes.

The weather is equally crucial to the variety of wines available. Bordeaux is famous for its micro-climate. The area of St Emilion, for instance, is warmer than the Médoc area, so that the grapes flower earlier. A sudden hailstorm in one area, causing great damage to the grapes, may leave the rest of Bordeaux unscathed.

Labelling

If the wide range of Bordeaux wines sounds daunting, the clear and simple labelling of bottles is a useful guide. The top grades of all French wines are designated Appellation Contrôlée. In Bordeaux, about 70% of the wines come into this category, which gives some idea of the high standards of wine-making. Between these two words, you often find the name of a region. Appellation Bordeaux Contrôlée indicates an ordinary wine, but nevertheless deserving of the Appellation Contrôlée label. Appellation Bordeaux Supérieur Contrôlée still indicates an undistinguished wine, but it must have an alcoholic strength higher than 10.7%.

After these two lowest grades, successively higher-quality wines are labelled with a district name, then with the name of a precise area within that district, or with a village name. The more precisely the origin of the wine is pin-pointed, the higher the quality, for instance, 'Appellation Haut-Médoc Contrôlée' indicates that the wine comes from the great wine-producing area of Haut-Médoc in Bordeaux. Alternatively, a bottle may be labelled with one of the districts of the Haut Médoc, where giants such as Château Lafite are produced.

A little knowledge of the different areas that make up the huge family of Bordeaux wines comes in useful when you are buying.

The name of the château on a label, unless it is a famous one, does not mean very much. There are about 10,000 châteaux in Bordeaux. Anyone who owns a vineyard and a *chai* (cellar) can call his estate a château and give the bottle a fancy label. Of the 10,000 châteaux, about 200 produce a wine of special reknown, which will naturally cost more.

Classified growths

In 1855, an official classification was drawn up for the best Bordeaux wines. Each of the 60 Médocs and the one red Graves chosen, were solemnly graded in order of excellence: First, Second, Third, Fourth or Fifth Growth, or *cru*. The system gives a roughly accurate guide to the 60 top châteaux in Bordeaux, though many more, especially from St Emilion and Pomerol, would be included if the league table were ever brought up to date. When a wine is referred to as 'Fifth Growth' in Bordeaux, it does not indicate a fifth-rate wine, but a high-class one that was privileged to enter the old 1855 classification.

Classified growths can be very expensive, but below them is a huge range of wines known as *Cru bourgeois*, often wines of real quality that cost much less. Well-made wines from the less highly regarded parts of Bordeaux, such as Blaye, Bourg and Fronsac, can often give more pleasure than the wine of a well-known château in a poor year.

Vintage

When they are young, Bordeaux wines have so much tannin in them that they are not very drinkable. After a few years in bottle, however, they develop in a fascinating way, becoming smoother and more complex. Some are good after three or four years, others are better left much longer.

Vintage dates give the wine buyer some useful hints, but are not always infallible since the weather pattern, as already explained, differs widely.

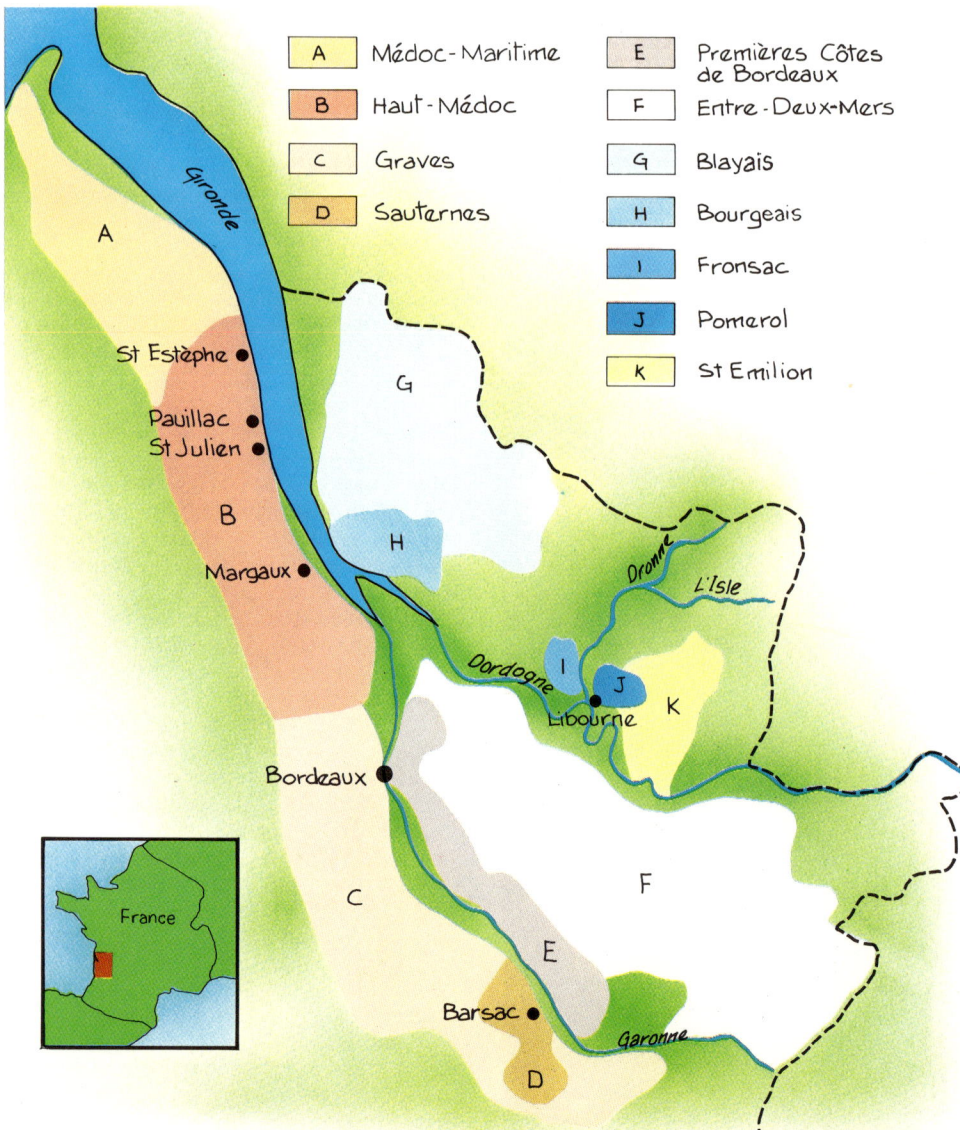

A	Médoc-Maritime
B	Haut-Médoc
C	Graves
D	Sauternes
E	Premières Côtes de Bordeaux
F	Entre-Deux-Mers
G	Blayais
H	Bourgeais
I	Fronsac
J	Pomerol
K	St Emilion

Haut-Médoc: St Estèphe and Pauillac

The Médoc is the most famous red wine district in Bordeaux. One-third of it, lying to the north, is known simply as the Médoc, or Bas-Médoc, and has a proliferation of small châteaux making sound wine at reasonable prices. The Haut-Médoc, to the south, is in a different league altogether – here the very greatest red wines are made.

Château Lafite

The countryside of the Haut-Médoc is not exciting. To the west, sand dunes and pine forests roll away monotonously; to the east the precious slopes are covered in vines which are beautifully trellised in straight, regimental lines. The overall effect is oddly undramatic.

The wines, too, are unassertive at first and almost have to steal up on you before you appreciate them properly. They are difficult to judge when young. They have to be allowed time to mature, especially a great wine, which should never be opened until it is at least five years old. But once you have begun to recognize the distinction and the depth of flavour of fine Médoc wine, you will be certain to return to it again and again.

A parish in Bordeaux is known as a commune and every commune in the Haut-Médoc has more world-famous vineyards and châteaux than there is space to mention here in this chapter.

St Estèphe

St Estèphe, the northernmost commune in the Haut-Médoc, has sturdy, slightly 'harder' wines than the other communes. They contain a great deal of tannin. Bought young, they need to be kept for 10–15 years before they are at their peak.

Anyone prepared to be patient can disprove the old 1855 classification (see page 26), which listed no St Estèphe wines as 'first growths'.

One of the best vineyards of St Estèphe is Château Cos d'Estournel, which has a series of cellars built in an eccentric Chinese pagoda style. The wine from here is a second growth wine. Following closely for quality are the dark-coloured Château Montrose (second growth) and Calon-Ségur (third growth). Even these lesser greats are better known than you might imagine when you consider the prices: only a very special occasion can justify the purchase of, say, the classic 1970 vintage.

However today's buyer can also find good *cru bourgeois* wines from the area to the north of the town of St Estèph itself. Many are produced in rambling, old-fashioned cellars. A knowledgeable wine merchant should be able to hunt out several that are reasonably priced and worth keeping.

From farther south, wine from Château de Pez, although humbly classed as *cru bourgeois supérieur*, is well worth looking out for. Every year Château de Pez makes 400 hogsheads (large casks) of excellent wine. There is also the *cru bourgeois* of Château Meyney, made in a beautifully kept farmhouse: this is a wine that seems to improve year by year.

Pauillac

Adjoining Cos d'Estournel in St Estèphe is the first growth Château Lafite vineyard in the commune of Pauillac, but the two wines have totally different characters. The sturdy, hard quality of St Estèphe gives way to a wine that has sometimes been described as slightly 'feminine'. Château Lafite has been classed, by some, as the greatest claret in Bordeaux; and when you realize that Pauillac also includes Château Latour and Château Mouton-Rothschild – the first two heading the 1855 classification, with Mouton-Rothschild joining their lead in 1973 – there can be no question that this is the greatest of the Bordeaux communes.

In Pauillac the country is hillier and the vines have to work harder to produce their grapes – leading to heightened quality. Even the landscape, like the wine, is a little more sumptuous, with whole hillsides belonging to one rich owner, instead of being confusingly sub-divided, as in Burgundy.

The great wines are all individuals in their own right. Château Latour, produced from soil full of egg-sized stones, is a really big wine. It is strong and full, compared with the perfumed finesse of Château Lafite wines. Château Mouton-Rothschild, on the other hand, is a wonderful, dusky red wine with great concentration of flavour.

Coming a little down the scale, but still in the realm of fine wines, there is Château Pichon Lalande, half in Pauillac and half in the commune of St Julien. Equally well known is the slightly heavier wine of Lynch-Bages. The attractive Château Pontet-Canet has a big production of 1500 barrels a year which means that the wines can sometimes be bought at reasonable prices. Farther inland are the much smaller Château Batailley and Château Haut-Batailley, the latter producing wine that is considered the better claret of the two.

All these châteaux in the Pauillac commune – and many others – cater for connoisseurs who have 'worked their way up' from lesser wines to the great gourmet bottlings. Luckily, there are ways of sampling Pauillac without distressing one's bank manager. Château Latour makes a second wine, Les Forts de Latour, as does Château Lafite, Moulin des Carruades; both make outstanding drinking. From Mouton, there is Mouton-Cadet, a popular branded Bordeaux. There is even a co-operative of some 200 farmers in Pauillac, bottling under the name of La Rose Pauillac. The quality of the wine remains consistently good.

Haut- and Bas-Médoc

Here we look at the well-known Haut-Médoc communes, St Julien and Margaux, together with the lesser-known Bas-Médoc.

St Julien is a small commune on the west bank of the River Gironde. It produces less than the other three great red-wine communes of the Haut-Médoc – Pauillac, St Estèphe and Margaux. There are no first-class growths in St Julien, if you go by the somewhat outdated 1855 classification, but it has a higher proportion of 'classed' growths than anywhere else – five second classes, two thirds and five fourths, although Pauillac has more fifth growths. There are so many good wines that you would be unlucky to buy a bottle of St Julien that fell below a high standard.

The experts tend to say that St Julien is a kind of breathing space between the brilliant but sturdy Pauillac wines to the north and the more refined and elegant offerings from Margaux. They are wonderful wines to lay down, maturing sooner than the Pauillac 'greats', and acquiring a gentle, smooth texture detected easily in the wines of Château Talbot or Gruaud-Larose.

Château Léoville Las Cases is the most revered name in St Julien, closely followed by two other famous châteaux, Léoville Barton and Léoville Poyferré. For sheer aristocratic finesse, Château Beychevelle is a wine to buy in a good vintage year, when it outclasses its rivals. But in a poor year, it can be a disappointing buy.

Château Ducru-Beaucaillou (named after the 'beautiful pebbles' that make up so much of the soil of these riverside vineyards) and Château Gloria are situated next door to each other. It used to be possible to buy the latter cheaply because it is only classed as *cru bourgeois*. However, if a new classification were made now, it would never be so overlooked. Indeed, even without this recognition, so many people seem to know about Château Gloria, with its splendidly dark colour and full taste, that it seems unlikely the wine will ever be sold at a bargain price again.

The two small villages of Moulis and Listrac, situated to the south of St Julien and farther inland, produce cheaper *cru bourgeois*. The well-respected Château Chasse-Spleen is in Moulis, while Listrac has the highly regarded Châteaux Fourcas-Dupré and Fourcas-Hosten. Other good *cru bourgeois* from nearby areas are Châteaux Dutruch-Grand-Poujeaux, Pierre-Bibian, Duplessis and Maucaillou.

Margaux

From farther south comes the magnificent fruity red wine of Château Margaux, a famous first growth of the Margaux area, which can boast another eleven in the hallowed classified list. Choose a Château Margaux from a good vintage year to get full benefit of the marvellous bouquet. Château Margaux also produces a dry, rather individual white wine, Pavillon Blanc, which is by no means over-priced.

You can even find a distinctive dry rosé from these parts, Rosé de Lascombes. This is made by Château Lascombes, whose fine second-growth claret is delicate and perfumed in typical Margaux style, like the sought-after wines of Château Palmer.

For classed growths that are at middle-range prices, but with sound quality, look for the Châteaux Cantenac-Brown, Brane-Cantenac, Malescot, Marquis d'Alesme and Kirwan. Watch out for Château Giscours, a wine that has improved greatly recently, thanks to an energetic proprietor.

Bas-Médoc

The Bas-Médoc has now officially been renamed Médoc-Maritime, because 'bas' suggests inferiority. Sadly, for those who hope to find some undiscovered châteaux selling their wines at giveaway prices, the flat country of the Médoc-Maritime produces only 25% of the wines of the Médoc – and most of these seem to be kept for local consumption.

Few are exported, with the shining exception of Château Loudenne. Apart from producing fine claret, this château also produces a good, inexpensive Appellation Médoc Contrôlée, La Cour Pavillon, made from a careful blend of local wines. Even their Bordeaux Blanc is crisper and fresher than many others in Bordeaux and is worth trying to find.

Two exemplary wines of the Haut-Médoc

Sweet wines of Bordeaux

The rich, sweet wines of Bordeaux are one of its greatest glories. The best of them, Sauternes and Barsac, come from the most southerly area of Bordeaux. They are probably the most undervalued Bordeaux wines, simply because of the recent trend to drink dry wine rather than sweet. But with a dessert or fresh summer fruit nothing can compare with a honeyed glass of Sauternes.

Sauternes

Sauternes is made by a few hundred growers centred on five tiny communes on the banks of a stream 30 miles south of the city of Bordeaux. The five communes are: Sauternes, Bommes, Fargues, Preignac and Barsac. Only they are allowed, under French law, to put the Sauternes label on their wines; Barsac, the largest commune, has the choice of calling its wines either Sauternes or Barsac.

The wine is made from the golden Sauvignon and Sémillon grapes, which are ready for picking by the end of September. However, for producing Sauternes, they are deliberately left on the vine until they are over-ripe and have been attacked by a mould known as the 'noble rot'. As long as October stays mild, the fruit will lose its colour, take on a reddish tinge, then fade to a wizened grey. Every morning the pickers take the grapes with 'noble rot' and press the tiny harvest that evening.

The wine that results from these specially picked grapes is naturally sweeter and has a more concentrated taste than any other in the world. In view of the risk of total failure if the weather fails, coupled with a very small yield and high labour costs, the wine is comparatively moderately priced. The only exception is Château d'Yquem, where the wine is in a class of its own and is highly prized. The château itself is one of the most striking in all Bordeaux, and is the only place where the entire wine-making plant is made of wood. No metal ever comes into contact with the wine in case it affects the taste.

Yquem is in the commune of Sauternes, which also has Châteaux Guiraud, Filhot and Lamothe. The commune of Fargues has just one great name, Château Rieussec, considered second only to Yquem, while Preignac has Château Suduiraut. Châteaux Rayne-Vigeau, Lafaurie-Peyraguey and La Tour Blanche are all in Bommes. All these wines keep beautifully and are worth laying down.

The largest commune, Barsac, makes a slightly different wine from the others. It is a fraction less sweet and not quite so rich. The two outstanding châteaux of Barsac are Climens and Coutet, both of which have changed hands in recent years. Châteaux Doisy-Védrines, Doisy-Daëne and Nairac, just a little lower down the scale, are correspondingly cheaper.

It is important to check that the label on a bottle of Sauternes bears the name of the commune. The term Haut-Sauternes means nothing at all. Any wine calling itself Sauterne, without the concluding 's', is not the genuine article. The best Sauternes should not be highly chilled, otherwise the wine will lose its intensity and depth of flavour.

Other sweet Bordeaux

A district to remember is Cérons, where the wines come halfway in sweetness between Sauternes and Graves. They are half a degree less in alcoholic strength than Sauternes and are more modestly priced. Those who find Sauternes too rich and heavy, should sample Cérons wine.

Equally inexpensive are the sweet wines of Ste Croix du Mont and Loupiac. Both are in the area of the Premières Côtes de Bordeaux, on the right bank of the Garonne river, opposite Sauternes and Barsac. The wines, a little heavier than Cérons are not easy to find because both are prone to frost and produce little in a poor year. In good years, however, they can be a wonderful buy.

Between the Garonne and Dordogne lies the attractively-named Entre-Deux-Mers, an enormous tract of land that at one time produced some quite drinkable sweet wines.

Nowadays, these wines tend to be dry, following the fashion. However, if a wine merchant has an acceptable sweet Entre-Deux-Mers, it might be half the price of a Sauternes.

Finally, there is Monbazillac, which is outside the Bordeaux area altogether. It lies near Bergerac, in the Dordogne valley. Its lovely sweet wines are reminscent of Sauternes and are fairly cheap. The principal difference is the taste of the Muscat grape.

There seems little demand for it which seems odd with prices so consistently low. Those who develop a palate for it can drink a quality dessert wine fairly cheaply.

Two delicious, yet very different, sweet white wines of Bordeaux

Pomerol and North East Bordeaux

Pomerol, situated to the north-west of St Emilion, is a relative newcomer as a wine area in Bordeaux — it is the place to look for undiscovered red Bordeaux wines. On the other hand, the areas of Fronsac, Bourg and Blaye, to the north-west of Pomerol, are well-established wine areas, offering a more modest, everyday type of wine.

Pomerol

The wines of Pomerol are often grouped with St Emilion, because the best wines of both areas are near their shared border. Yet there is a marked difference in the wines, which is attributed to the extraordinary soil difference. Pomerol consists of a large gravel bank, held together by clay, with the best wines growing on a mixture of quite deep clay and a thin layer of gravel.

The fact that Pomerol is a relative newcomer as a wine area is a great attraction: there is no official classification, nor is there a long history of buying and selling. The wine of Pomerol has an instant appeal, with its full, slightly exotic flavour that turns into a gentle richness in the mouth. The scent is very distinctive, with a faint earthiness.

A small château in Bourg

Even without any official classification, there is no argument about the top wines of Pomerol. They come from Château Pétrus, whose prices regularly fetch as much as the great first growths of the Médoc. This tiny vineyard produces a wonderfully fruity wine but it is very expensive.

Château Trotanoy is said to come second to Château Pétrus in reputation. Its name derives from the mixture of gravel and deep clay that becomes so hard in summer that it is '*trop ennuyeux*', or too much like hard work! Sadly, the vineyard is a tiny one, so demand greatly exceeds the supply of this velvety, fruity wine.

Vieux-Château-Certan, next door to Château Pétrus, is also held in high regard. Other good names include L'Evangile, Certan-de-May, La Conseillante, La Fleur-Pétrus and Petit-Village. Look too for Château Le Gay, Château Rouget, Château Plince, Château Clos René and Château de Sales — they are all reliably consistent.

Pomerol wines need not be hoarded for a great many years, like some of the great Médoc wines, before they are drinkable. Made mostly with the soft Merlot grape, they lack the tannin for laying down. Four or five years after the vintage, they make the most acceptable drinking.

Fronsac, Bourg and Blaye

Fronsac, Bourg and Blaye are situated on the right bank of the Dordogne and Gironde rivers, where the soil is a little too rich to make wines of real distinction. However, they are good enough for all but the grandest dinner party.

Of the three areas, Fronsac makes the liveliest wines with the Cabernet Franc grape much in evidence. There are two appellations here: Côtes de Fronsac and Canon-Fronsac, both producing big, fruity wines that slip down very easily.

Château Canon in the Canon-Fronsac area is a well-known château but is easily confused with a St Emilion wine of the same name. A great deal of Château de la Rivière finds its way abroad and improves with keeping as long as ten years, for a good vintage. Château Rouet, beautifully set high up in the village of St Germain-la-Rivière, makes good, honest wines. Others worth sampling are Châteaux Bodet, Junayme, Mayne-Vieil, Toumalin and La Valade.

The districts of Bourg and Blaye also supply good value wines which are at their best when young. Most are made with a blend of Merlot and Cabernet Franc grapes.

Bourg produces more wines than Blaye. The best of them, such as Château de Barbe and Château Guerry, come from the slopes near the Gironde river. Here the thinner soil produces rather better grapes. Other names to investigate include Du Bousquet, Guionne, Mille-Secousses, Tayac and Rousset.

In Blaye, it is difficult to go far wrong, now that so many small châteaux have improved their standards. Haut-Sociondo and Le Menaudat are châteaux of repute and so are Mondésir-Gazan and Segonzac. They produce a lighter wine than Bourg, that is mellower and even easier to drink. There are also some pleasant, dry, white wines that go well with fish.

St Emilion

St Emilion produces more claret than any other wine district in Bordeaux, simply because it is the largest district. The wines are richer and redder than most other clarets, falling halfway between the fullness and depth of Burgundy and the more usual dry, austere-style Bordeaux.

The wines of St Emilion have a different character from that of other Bordeaux wines for two reasons: the soil is richer and the grapes used are different from the other Bordeaux wine districts. The Cabernet Sauvignon, the king of Bordeaux grapes, is little used in St Emilion. It largely gives way to Merlot which is softer, ages sooner and imparts a certain richness.

The French make a distinction between the wines grown on the hillsides, known as Côtes-St-Emilion, and those grown on the plain, known as Graves-St-Emilion. Although these terms are not used on labels, they are worth remembering when buying a particular château wine. If you know the area it comes from, you will have a good idea of the character of the wine in the bottle.

Côtes wines are 'rounder' with more body and the great name here is Château Ausone. The cellars are cut from the solid rock of the hillside with pillars left to support the roof. The vineyards are situated under the brow of the hill, sheltered from the north wind. The wines of Château Ausone, together with those of Cheval Blanc, top the St Emilion classification list and are designated *Premiers Grands Crus Classés*. St Emilion was left out of the 1855 classification (see page 26), so it drew up its own league table 100 years later. Unfortunately, the classifications of the various districts cannot be compared because there is no agreed definition of *grand cru* or *cru classé*. The term may not indicate a wine that is up to a Médoc classified growth and, as the list is always being revised, it is best ignored.

The proprietors of Château Ausone also own Château Belair, a lesser wine that is widely distributed. Farther down the steep slopes are the vineyards of Château La Gaffelière-Naudes, while across the road and running all the way to the top of the plateau are those of Château Pavie. As these are well-known names, and priced accordingly, it is worth looking out for some of the lesser châteaux that are so often overlooked – for instance, Troplong-Mondot, Grand-Pontet, La Clotte, L'Angélus, Clos des Jacobins. These are still good value.

The 'Graves' wines (not to be confused with the Graves district) are mostly grown from vineyards standing partly on heavy clay, partly on light gravel. The velvety, aristocratic wines of Château Cheval Blanc, with their charming softness and perfume, are one example. Since Cheval Blanc is usually mentioned in the same breath as the Médoc first growths, it is best left to the wealthy buyer. However, again, there is a host of not-so-famous châteaux making good wine for much less, notably Châteaux Figeac, Latour-Figeac and Latour-du-Pin-Figeac, Croque-Michette, Corbin and Ripeau.

As if the choice was not already wide enough, the St Emilion name is also shared by seven small communes to the south and east, extending down to the right bank of the Dordogne. The winegrowers here are fiercely independent, making wine of widely different quality. The communes are St Christophe-des-Bardes, St Laurent-des-Combes, St Hippolyte, St Etienne-de-Lisse, St Pey-d'Armens, St Sulpice-de-Faleyrens and Vignonet. Sound château wines can be found in these much overlooked areas.

Finally, there are five more St Emilion communes to the north-east on slightly higher ground, namely St Georges, Montagne, Lussac, Puisseguin and Parsac. They make pleasant wines and stand in relation to St Emilion as Beaujolais villages does to Beaujolais.

Those who would rather not pick and choose from small growers could settle for one of the co-operative wines. The largest, with a total of 400 members, is the Union de Producteurs de St Emilion. Most of its wine is sold as Côtes Rocheuses or Royal Saint Emilion. No fewer than 20 members also have their own *Grand Cru* wines. They use the co-operative to dispose of good St Emilion that is over and above the legal production limit. This information is useful to bear in mind when buying St Emilion co-operative wines.

The town of St Emilion

White Graves

For most people, the name Graves conjures up a white wine, pale gold in colour and rather sweet. But things have changed in recent years and nowadays the Graves district offers a whole new range of lighter drier whites as well as several excellent red wines. On this page we look at the different types of white Graves.

The Graves district is a large flat area stretching from the city of Bordeaux along the left bank of the Garonne to the foothills of the Pyrenees in the south-west. The area takes its name from its soil which is a mixture of gravel and sand. Although many of the Graves estates make both red and white wines, it will be easier to look at them separately.

Only white wines may be called simply 'Graves', although red wines may have the appellation on the label. Many of these whites are full-flavoured, with a hint of vanilla in the after-taste which comes from ageing in oak casks. Don't be misled by the term Graves Supérieur on a bottle: it is no guarantee of quality, and simply means that the alcoholic strength is above 12%!

For some years now Bordeaux has been making a strong push with dry white wines from the Sauvignon and Sémillon grapes, sometimes with a little Muscadelle added.

Many growers from the Graves area have followed suit. As a result, the whole spectrum of tastes – from the very dry to the sweet – is available and the choice is wider than ever.

Starting at the top end of the range, there is Haut-Brion Blanc, rarely seen and extremely expensive. It is fresh and full-bodied and connoisseurs think it well worth the price. It comes from Château Haut-Brion, in the commune of Pessac in the suburbs of Bordeaux. One of its great rivals, Laville Haut-Brion, comes from the estate over the road, Château La Mission Haut-Brion. Laville Haut-Brion is another great treat for those who can afford it. If kept for a few years, it acquires an opulent and subtle taste. Another great white wine comes from the Domaine de Chevalier, a very modern establishment with a huge production of excellent wines. These wines have a clean-cut taste.

Choosing the right white Graves

Leaving Bordeaux to the north and travelling south, white wines seem to take over. Generally speaking, they are more difficult to make than the reds. There is an increased risk of oxidation, called *madérisation*, which darkens the colour of the wine and leaves a stale taste in the mouth. Sulphur is the best remedy, but it also leaves its traces which are particularly noticeable when you open the bottle and pour the first glass. The art of buying white Graves is to find the wines that avoid both hazards. It may mean choosing one of the new, drier, delightful wines that are more like Loire whites than traditional Graves. Try Château Carbonnieux – crisp, light, easy to drink, and made mostly with the dry Sauvignon grape.

The commune of Villenave-d'Ornon in the south east also produces several drier, lighter whites in the Loire style, even though this means giving up oak barrels and losing the traditional Graves taste.

If you want an old-fashioned Graves, with its traditional taste, try Graves de Portets. It is a medium dry white, with a fruity flavour which many people enjoy, especially during the winter months. The same goes for Château Millet, which is full of flavour, keeps well and sells briskly to Britain and the U.S.

Château Haut-Brion

Red Graves

Red wines from the Graves area are underestimated: less well known than the local whites, they have improved enormously since the 1960s and are usually good and sometimes excellent.

Graves reds are a good introduction to Bordeaux wines like St Emilion and they are much easier to get to know than any of the Médoc reds. If kept for a few years, they become satin-smooth, with great fullness and richness, and go very well with a creamy cheese. Many experts rate them above the whites of the area. In the official 1959 classification, 13 red wines had the right to call themselves Appellation Graves Controlée, compared to only 8 whites.

The best reds come from the north of the Graves area, very near the city of Bordeaux. The greatest is probably Château Haut-Brion, the only red Graves to be called a First Growth in the original classification of 1855. The vines are grown in very favourable conditions, on a thick layer of pebbly gravel that reflects the heat and allows rainwater to drain away rapidly. The Haut-Brion reds have a marvellously rich aroma, and a smooth velvety taste, with an intense concentration of different flavours. They easily compete with the best reds of Pauillac and Margaux.

Other excellent red wines from the area include Château La Mission Haut-Brion, and Château Pape-Clément, named after the pope who moved the papacy to Avignon in the 14th century. Château Pape-Clément is fragrant, earthy and full, and produced by one of the oldest vineyards in Bordeaux, in the commune of Pessac. Pessac is actually in the suburbs of Bordeaux: in the Middle Ages, the vines grew all around the city. They are now fighting a constant battle against encroaching roads and houses. The Château Pape-Clément vineyards were completely replanted in the 1950s. They now make what is known as a 'big' wine, a blend of Cabernet Sauvignon and Merlot grapes.

A few miles south of Pessac, the commune of Léognan produces extremely fine reds: Château Haut-Bailly, Château Carbonnieux, Domaine de Chevalier and Château Malartic-Lagravière, with its fresh and spicy wines.

Next to Léognan is Martillac, which is the home of a number of well run estates, including two chosen for the 1959 classification: Smith-Haut-Lafitte and La Tour-Martillac. The Smith-Haut-Lafitte wines offer good buying opportunities for people who want to enjoy the classic Graves taste – elegant and full of flavour. A little further south is another Château worth remembering, Château La Garde, which produces a soft red wine, with a pleasant dry finish characteristic of red Graves.

Most of the wines just mentioned are expensive. A more reasonably priced but still good red Graves is Château Bouscaut, well known in the United States as a result of having had an American owner. The Château Bouscaut vineyards have been largely replanted since World War II and produce sound red wines, which are supple, easy to drink and with good lasting qualities, just like their whites.

Red Graves wines are well worth looking for: they have a distinct character, and they are robust and generous.

The satin-smooth reds of the Graves region are a good introduction to claret.

Dry white wines of the Loire

The Loire is the longest river in France and for much of its length it is flanked by vineyards producing a great variety of wines. Few have the distinction of fine Burgundy or Bordeaux wines, but they have more immediately appealing qualities of charm, delicacy and freshness, with the additional advantage – in most cases – of being good value for money.

The chateau of Azay-le-Rideau

The majority of wine produced in the Loire valley is white and most of it is dry. The best known comes from two distinct areas, the region of Sevre et Maine at the Atlantic end of the valley near Nantes, and the area to the East of Orleans, about half-way up the river, around the towns of Sancerre and Pouilly. The district of Touraine in the middle of the Loire also produces some dry white wine.

Sevre et Maine

The best wine from the Sevre et Maine district is Muscadet, named after the grape from which it is made. Pale gold, very dry and slightly acidic, it is traditionally thought of as a 'fish' wine. In fact it is more versatile than this; its refreshing qualities make it the ideal thirst-quencher for hot summer days and it can be a pleasant aperitif.

The reputation of Muscadet outside its own home area is a comparatively recent event. With the greatly increased demand, vineyard area has doubled in recent years and this can mean variable quality. Even the best Muscadet is not expensive by French standards and you would be advised to look for a wine from a single estate or château, which will usually be bottled by the grower. Some good names are Château de la Galissonière, Château la Noë and Château de l'Oiselinière.

Another variable factor, and one which applies to the whole of the Loire, is the weather. Frost, rain and lack of sunshine are obvious enemies, but a very hot summer like 1976 can produce an uncharacteristic wine with too little acidity. The qualities which make Muscadet attractive and appealing will not improve with keeping. It is essentially a wine to be drunk young, certainly within two or three years of bottling.

Some growers do not filter and bottle all their Muscadet immediately after fermentation, but leave some in the vats for another few weeks in contact with the deposit known as the 'lees'. A wine which has been treated in this way will have the additional description *sur lie*. It is considered to have a little extra body and flavour and will also pick up a slight tingle resulting from retained carbon dioxide.

Another rather coarser white wine from the same area is Gros Plant. This is again named after its grape and is sold almost exclusively as the local *vin de pays*.

Sancerre and Pouilly

The most distinguished, and expensive, dry white wines of the Loire come from around Sancerre and Pouilly. These are made from the Sauvignon Blanc grape. Somewhat confusingly, a wine described as Pouilly-sur-Loire will contain at least a proportion of the inferior Chasselas grape; the Sauvignon is known locally as Blanc Fumé and the best wine from Pouilly is called Pouilly Blanc Fumé.

Both Sancerre and Pouilly Fumé are slightly fuller bodied wines than Muscadet. They have a characteristic bouquet usually described as 'gun-flint', because it is reminiscent of the smoke from struck flints. They have been widely adopted as alternatives to Chablis and other very expensive white burgundies. However, the production area is small, demand has recently raced ahead of supply, and this state of affairs, particularly in the case of Pouilly Fumé, has been reflected in much higher prices. The district is also very susceptible to poor weather. Both quality and quantity of vintages have been badly affected by frost and hail in the past. Like all dry Loire whites, Sancerre and Pouilly Fumé should be drunk young; the delicate balance of fruitiness and acidity which gives them their charm will be lost after a few years in bottle.

The seriousness with which Sancerre and Pouilly Fumé have come to be regarded in recent years is really a little inappropriate in wines which used to be considered the white equivalent of Beaujolais. There are good Sauvignon wines produced at a more reasonable price in the neighbourhood of Reuilly, Quincy and Ménétou-Salon to the south-west of Sancerre.

Middle Loire

Sauvignon Blanc is also grown widely in the middle Loire district of Touraine – Sauvignon de Touraine is a good bargain, if you can find it. The main white grape of Touraine is the Chenin Blanc, and the best-known dry wines made from this grape come from the towns of Vouvray and Montlouis. Vouvray is generally reckoned the better.

The Chenin Blanc is chiefly used for producing sweet wines, so the dry Vouvrays tend to have a distinct fruitiness of flavour, but this is balanced by refreshing acidity. They are wines for swigging rather than sipping and have all the straightforward, easy appeal which has made Loire wines so popular.

Other dry white wines from the middle Loire which you may be able to find outside France are Touraine-Azay-le-Rideau and Touraine-Amboise.

Other Loire wines

Although the Loire is best known for its dry white wine, the area is large and productive and a great diversity of wines is to be found there. Unfortunately, it can still be a problem obtaining the lesser known wines outside France.

Rosé

Rosé is one Loire wine that is widely available. The most basic is called simply Rosé de la Loire. More specific, but familiar, names are Rosé d'Anjou and Rosé Cabernet d'Anjou. The latter is made from the Cabernet grape and is generally drier and slightly more scented than plain Rosé d'Anjou. Both are light, attractively pale in colour and ideal summer picnic wines.

Rosé wines are also made in the region from the Pinot Noir, especially in the area around Sancerre and Ménétou-Salon. Some of these, especially those from single estates, are more than just a pretty glassful, but they are correspondingly more expensive. Good examples are the Gold Medal winning Ménétou-Salon of Georges Chavet and Sancerre Clos du Chêne Marchand.

A light Rosé d'Anjou and a sweet dessert wine, Moulin Touchais

Red wine

The main centre of red wine production is the region of Touraine. A variety of grapes are grown here, producing wines of contrasting character. The Gamay, the grape of Beaujolais, yields a pleasantly light red wine for early drinking. It has rather less fruitiness and higher acidity than Beaujolais itself; some is even marketed within a few weeks of harvest as *Touraine primeur*.

Other red wines are mainly made from Cabernet Franc–known locally as Breton, probably because it was introduced to the region from Bordeaux via the Breton port of Nantes–Cabernet Sauvignon and Malbec, known in the area as Cot. These are all grapes traditionally associated with claret, but in the Loire the wine which results is softer, less tannic and faster maturing, with only a relatively brief spell in barrel.

The towns chiefly connected with red wine are Chinon, Bourgueil and St Nicolas de Bourgueil. Some growers aim for a more robust and long-lasting wine in the Bordeaux style. These wines will usually be from a single estate, called a *domaine* or *clos*, which, strictly speaking, is a vineyard enclosed by a wall to give added protection from wind and frost. These wines are also frequently bottled by the grower, in which case the words *propriétaire récoltant* will be on the label. They will be a lot more expensive than wines labelled simply 'Chinon' or 'Bourgueil', but will have more body and distinction. A good vintage may develop for up to twenty years.

Sparkling wines

Another increasingly popular Loire wine is the sparkling wine or *vin mousseux*. Made mainly from the Chenin Blanc or Sauvignon Blanc grapes, sometimes with the addition of Pinot Noir, these are true *méthode champenoise* wines which have undergone their second fermentation in bottle. The best of them have a good rich flavour and, as they are much cheaper than champagne, they must be considered quite a bargain. Saumur and Vouvray are the main centres of production. There is also a lighter, less fizzy sparkling wine from the region called Vin Crémant de Loire.

Sweet dessert wines

Sales of the popular wines, the sparkling wines of Touraine and the rosés of Anjou, enable growers in these areas to continue small-scale production of the wines they consider their greatest achievement, the fine sweet dessert wines. The Chenin Blanc gives a naturally fruity wine and, if the grapes are allowed to ripen through a long fine autumn, they will eventually become affected by a fungus called the noble rot, or *pourriture noble*. The fungus attacks the skins, shrivels the fruit and concentrates the natural sugars. It is difficult to make this process sound attractive, but it is responsible for all the world's greatest sweet wines, the Château d'Yquem of Sauternes, the Trockenbeerenauslen of the Rhine and the Tokay aszu of Hungary. The grapes for such wines have to be carefully selected when they have reached just the right stage of ripeness and a large quantity will yield relatively little juice. These factors, and the long storage period needed before the wines reach full maturity, inevitably make them expensive.

Traditionally these sweet wines are drunk at the end of a meal, though in France it is the current trend to drink them as aperitifs. Ideally, they should be drunk on their own and simply enjoyed for what they are, a glorious mouthful of flavour. It you feel like indulging yourself in one of these luscious wines, the best names to look for are Bonnezeaux, Quarts de Chaumes and Moulin Touchais from the Côteaux du Layon. The vineyard of Moulin Touchais was the only one on the Loire to escape the phylloxera plague of the last century, and until 1959 this extraordinary wine was made only from pre-phylloxera stocks. Look too for the Vouvrays described as *moelleux*, especially those from good growers such as Gaston Huet and Marc Brédif.

Champagne

Champagne has a happy reputation as the wine to drink when it is time to celebrate a memorable occasion or at a romantic moment.

There are good reasons for the high price of champagne—it is not mere snobbery. The quality of the grapes themselves, the length of time the wine must be kept before it can be marketed, the skilled labour involved throughout the making, all contribute to the final cost. However, the quantity produced is never sufficient to satisfy world-wide demand.

The name champagne can only be applied to a drink produced by the *méthode champenoise* in the Champagne area near Reims in France. Wine has been made there, northeast of Paris, for centuries, but until the 17th century the best known wines of Champagne were still reds and whites, not sparkling wines. These wines were highly thought of and rivalled those of neighbouring Burgundy.

The art of making sparkling wine was perfected in Champagne by Dom Pérignon, a Benedictine monk, cellar-master of the Abbey of Hautvilliers. It was seen that sometimes in the spring, wine bottled after the harvest began a second fermentation; warmer weather restarted the fermentation of the sugar—giving the bubbles to the champagne. The second fermentation resulted in many broken bottles and lost wine. Dom Pérignon originated the use of corks to stopper the bottles—rags had been used before—and stronger bottles were made. Dom Pérignon also devised a system of blending wines from different vineyards to produce the fine balance essential to champagne. The champagne produced then was delicious to drink but not pretty to look at. A side-effect of secondary fermentation is the breaking down of yeast particles, which form a sediment and make the liquid cloudy. To hide this, champagne was served in glasses which were frosted.

In the 19th century, Madame Cliquot, founder of the firm Veuve Clicquot in Reims, was responsible for finding a practical way to make champagne clear and bright, as well as sparkling. Holes were cut in tables and the bottles placed in the holes, necks downwards. To make sure that all the sediment moved to just behind the cork, the bottles were moved carefully – a process known as *remuage*. The sediment was removed (*dégorgement*) by opening the bottle, taking the deposit out and topping up, then re-corking, very quickly. These processes have been refined over the years and now the sediment which collects is removed by freezing the neck of the bottle. When the cork is removed the sediment pops out and the wine is topped up with a small amount of wine and sugar. All the sugar in champagne is used up in secondary fermentation, so the sugar added now will give the champagne a dry or sweeter character. Less

than 2% is added for Brut; 1.5-2.5% for Extra Dry; 2-4% for Sec; 4-6% for Demi-Sec and over 6% for Doux. Although most champagne is white, it is usually made from a blend of black and white grapes, with black predominating. The grapes used are Pinot Noir, Pinot Meunier and Chardonnay. During the vinification process the black grape skins are carefully separated from the juices when pressing begins.

Vintage and non-vintage

On wine lists champagne is classified into Non-Vintage (NV) and Vintage. Non-vintage champagnes have to be matured in the cellars for a legal minimum period of 18 months and are blends of wines from several different years. In fact, the NV champagnes exported by the leading champagne houses are usually 3 years old. When allowed to mature longer in a cool cellar or cupboard NV champagnes will improve greatly.

Vintage champagnes, selected from a particularly good year, must by law remain in the producer's cellars for at least three years, often more, and may mature well for up to ten years. The leading champagne houses are known as Grande Marques and all are proud of their individual house styles, which have been evolved over many years of production.

Serving

Most important—never try to pull the cork from the bottle. Remove the foil and wire from the cork. Then lever the cork upwards with your thumbs, turning the bottle, as you gain leverage. When the cork starts to loosen, cover it with a cloth and with the other hand gently turn the bottle away from the cork. The cork should be held back against the escaping gas, to avoid a loud pop, and gush of wine. If opened correctly the only noise should be a soft sigh!

Depending on the temperature at which the bottle has been stored, it will only need an hour or two in the refrigerator.

Styles of champagne

Bollinger: deep, golden colour with an intensity of flavour, dry with great finesse

Charles Heidsieck: traditional, full-bodied and fruity, not very dry

Georges Goulet: a racy, youthful wine, very fruity, medium dry

Krug: subtle bouquet and flavour, silky and well-balanced, dry

Louis Roederer: great elegance, pale golden with a delicate flavour. Notably dry

Laurent Perrier: light gold, brisk and youthful with a 'leafy' bouquet

Mercier: slightly flowery bouquet, dry with a good finish

Moët & Chandon: straw gold in colour, light, well-balanced and not very dry

Mumm: pale and sprightly with a nice finish, medium dry

Pol Roger: very light gold in colour, with an extremely fine bouquet, dry and elegant

Veuve Clicquot: pale, nicely balanced, dry, bright and lively to taste

Removing the sediment from champagne in the Veuve Clicquot caves, Reims

Alsace

Alsace is the French wine region geographically closest to Germany, and as a result the wines from the area have characteristics of both countries. Although a small amount of light red and rosé wines are made here from the Pinot noir grape, almost all the wine produced is white – fragrant, full-bodied and dry.

Although Alsace is in France, it has spent long periods under German control. Between the Franco-Prussian War and the First World War, Alsace was treated as a poor relation of the great Rhine and Mosel vineyards, planted with inferior vines and used mainly for the bulk production of lower grade wine. A period of recovery during the 1920s and 1930s was halted by the Second World War when some towns were almost totally destroyed. But others were hardly touched – Riquewihr and Kaysersberg for example have an authentic medieval appearance – and enough grapes were still grown to make a memorable vintage in 1945. Since then the reputation of Alsace as a producer of quality wines has been firmly established, though even now the area has no appellation more specific than 'Alsace', and this was only granted in 1962.

The best vineyards lie in a narrow strip on the lower slopes of the Vosges mountains, looking East towards the River Rhine. Growers and merchants may sometimes use village or estate names on their wine labels, but these have little significance outside the area, if at all, because the wines are traditionally 'varietal'. This means that they are labelled with the type of grape used not by the place of origin.

The finest wines, Riesling, Gewürztraminer, Tokay (or Pinot Gris), Muscat and Sylvaner are made from one of five grape types, known as *cépages nobles*. If these are blended the result is known as *edelzwicker* (noble mixture). Although there are about 50,000 individual growers in Alsace, most belong to co-operatives or sell their grapes to the handful of famous merchants in the area, such as Hugel, Dopff, Trimbach and Schlumberger, whose names on a label should guarantee quality.

The wine most usually associated with Alsace is Gewürztraminer; *gewürtz* means spicy and Gewürztraminer is known for its remarkably powerful and spicy flavour, coupled with a strong-scented nose. It is a big wine, designed to complement the rich foods of the region such as *choucroute* (sauerkraut) and *foie gras* (goose liver pâté). But in spite of its fullness it is a dry wine, as the French winemakers prefer strength and dryness to the delicate sweetness of residual grape sugar which is so characteristic of German wines. Gewürztraminer is memorable and attractive, but it lacks subtlety.

The local growers, like their German neighbours, will usually claim pride of place for the Riesling, a vine which never bears heavy crops and also presents more of a challenge to the winemaker. In a good year it is well worth the extra effort; what it lacks in power it makes up for in elegance and delicacy of flavour. The Tokay, or Pinot Gris, from Alsace is a full-flavoured wine more in the style of the Gewürztraminer but without its pronounced fragrance – do not confuse this with Tokay from Hungary, which is a rich sweet dessert wine.

The Muscat has a heady aroma usually associated with that grape but without its usual sweetness of taste. The Sylvaner, the least interesting of the five, is a reliable but rather bland medium-dry wine, and is now produced less and less.

Unlike most French quality winegrowing areas, Alsace has room for further expansion and in recent years new plantings have been made, particularly with the Pinot Blanc grape, which in 1984 accounted for over 17½% of the total acreage under vines – this should be an interesting wine to watch out for in the future.

Because the French prefer wines suitable for drinking with food rather than on their own, many of these wines are purposely made less sweet than their German counterparts. The merchants and co-operatives do sometimes produce rich wines in the style of German *auslese* (selected bunches) or *beerenauslese* (selected grapes). These are made from late-gathered grapes whose juice, even after fermentation, retains a high sugar content. These are described in French as *vendage tardive* and *sélection de grains nobles*. They are full golden wines with great depth of flavour and repay laying down for a number of years.

Conditions are not suitable for these sweeter wines to be made every year; 1977, for example, was a year of late flowering and a poor, rather chilly summer in which the grapes had no chance to achieve the necessary over-ripeness. The previous year on the other hand, with its prolonged dry heat, produced record levels of natural sugar in many of the grapes and some outstanding late-harvest wines were made which will have a life of at least 20 years.

In general, like other dry whites, Alsace wines should be drunk fairly young. Compared with other French wines of quality, they still represent good value and also offer a variety of distinct flavours to try from dry but fruity to richly sweet.

The wines of Alsace are immediately recognizable in their slim green bottles.

Northern Rhône

The wines of the Rhône Valley include some of the most distinguished in France but, surprisingly, many of them are little known outside France. Most are red, although whites and rosés are made, mainly in the southern region.

Most Rhône wines are full-bodied and improve considerably with age. They are produced by over 100 parishes or domaines under the general label of Appellation Contrôlée Côtes du Rhône. Côtes du Rhône-Villages is only applied to 14 specific communes in the southern part of the valley. Fifteen areas have their own appellations. Here we discuss the main appellations in the northern Rhône Valley, which stretches from Vienne to Valence. On the next page the southern Rhône Valley will be discussed.

Rhône wines fall into two quite separate regions of north and south, but the same robust characteristics apply to both.

In the northern Rhône Valley the sharp, granite-based hills press against the river and the vines are grown on both banks on almost vertical, steep hillsides. The plots are very restricted and the long low walls of each plot retain the soil of the sharply-angled slopes. The climate is ideal for vines: the summers are long and hot and, as the weather is consistent, the vines have a head start. The relentless Mistral wind blows down the valley from the north but it serves a purpose, often drying the grapes after rain, lessening the chance of any mould developing. The red Syrah grape is predominant in the northern Rhône Valley.

The top appellations

On the Côte Rôtie the Syrah grape is mixed with a little wine from white grapes. This rare red wine contains 80% Syrah, which gives it a deep and powerful flavour, and 20% of perfumed Viognier grapes, which softens the flavour. The result is a big gutsy wine rarely at its best before ten years.

The Côte Rôtie, or 'Roasted Hill' has two well-known slopes, the Côte Brune and the Côte Blonde. A blended wine labelled Brune et Blonde can also be found occasionally, but you are more likely to find straightforward Côte Rôtie. The biggest growers are Vidal-Fleury and Chapoutier, with Côte Rôtie Les Jumelles of Paul Jaboulet Aîné, a wine of great distinction. Just south of Côte Rôtie are the vines of Condrieu, a dry white wine made from the Viognier grape. Considered one of the best white wines of the Rhône Valley, it may reach its peak after five or six years of bottle age. Not much is made because of the nature of the terrain on which it is grown.

Within the Condrieu vineyards is a small vineyard, Château Grillet, which has its own appellation contrôlée. It is the smallest individual appellation in France. There are not more than 2 hectares of vineyards and the very few bottles produced have to be rationed out among a few fortunate wine merchants. Château Grillet is a white wine, full and subtle with great finesse.

Hermitage

Hermitage is another of the main appellations further down the east bank of the river. Here on the Hermitage hillside both red and white wines are grown on granite slopes which catch the sun all day. The reds are burly and deep, and last a long time. A fine old Hermitage is for buying and keeping, as they are rarely drinkable in less than ten years. Some will go on improving for 30 years, with the bouquet becoming fuller and the wine softening.

Hermitage la Chapelle, grown on the top of the slopes, is a rich intense red wine that goes well with game or pheasant, and should be kept for special occasions. White Hermitage, excellent with salmon, is made from two grapes, Marsanne and Roussanne. Chante Alouette is one of the best-known wines. It is full and golden and often more powerful than a white Burgundy.

Around the Hermitage hill are the vineyards of Crozes-Hermitage. These wines are not so concentrated as Hermitage and do not last as long but, as they are considerably cheaper, they are often the best buys of the Rhône Valley. Those from Gervans, a small village with the best and steepest slopes, are especially good buys.

On the other side of the river are the St Joseph vineyards. On the bank, opposite the Hermitage vines the St Joseph vines encircle the castle terraces of Tournon. Here there is another range of outstanding red and white wines. The reds have a pleasant earthy flavour and are almost mauve; the whites are fresh and fruity.

Further south are the vineyards of Cornas, where a fine selection of red wines from the Syrah grape are made. These wines take 10–15 years to mature.

St Peray is the most southerly of the northern Rhône vineyards and it produces a sparkling white wine made by the méthode champenoise, excellent as an aperitif.

Sparkling wines are also made at Die, where the production of Clairette de Die has increased rapidly to meet demand. Clairette Brut is made solely from the Clairette grape and is an ideal thirst quencher on a hot day. Clairette de Die Tradition is a blend of Clairette and Muscat. These wines are less dry and sometimes are semi-sweet. It is difficult to be sure of the degrees of sweetness, since the ideas of many individual growers vary, but some Tradition wines are sweet enough to drink with desserts.

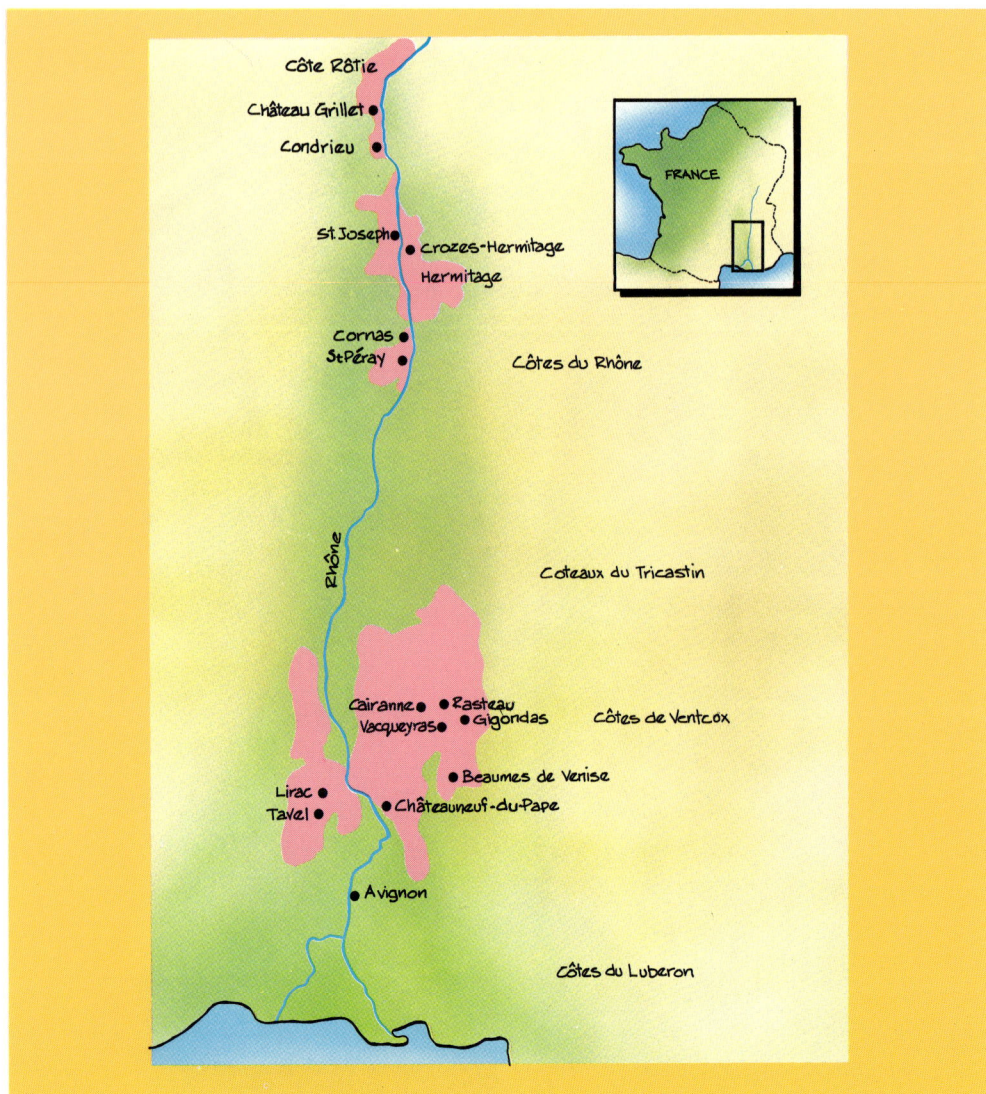

Côte Rôtie
Château Grillet
Condrieu
St Joseph
Crozes-Hermitage
Hermitage
Cornas
St Péray
Côtes du Rhône
Rhône
Coteaux du Tricastin
Cairanne
Vacqueyras
Rasteau
Gigondas
Côtes de Ventcox
Beaumes de Venise
Lirac
Tavel
Châteauneuf-du-Pape
Avignon
Côtes du Luberon
FRANCE

Southern Rhône

Wine from the hot, sunny southern part of the Rhône Valley could be described as bottled sunshine. It is ideal for drinking in a cold climate to warm the deepest winter.

The most famous of these southern Rhône Valley wines is Châteauneuf-du-Pape. This is a dark and glorious red wine. It is strong and fruity and matures faster than the wines of Côte Rôtie to the north. Châteauneuf-du-Pape is usually full-bodied with a powerful bouquet and has a higher alcoholic content than any other unfortified wine in France.

The vineyards where this wine is grown are covered with pebbles and stones which, like the slate in the German Rhine vineyards, reflect the sun's heat long after sunset, while the rich soil beneath them stays cool and moist. Unusually, for a great wine, Châteauneuf is made from many different grapes. As many as 13 varieties are permitted, but individual growers know the blends most suitable to their vineyards. The key varieties used for Châteauneuf are Grenache, which gives alcohol and roundness, and Syrah for body and deep near-purple colour.

Châteauneuf is produced under some of the strictest wine quality controls in the world. The best, such as La Solitude, Château de Fines Roches, Domaine du Mont Redon and Château Rayas are usually domaine-bottled.

To the east of Châteauneuf-du-Pape is Gigondas, the southern Rhône's other full-bodied, single appellation wine. The vineyards march up the jagged Dentelles de Montmirail hills and the wine produced is rich and mellow. A good bottle of Gigondas has great depth of flavour and a strongly recognizable bouquet that is nicely earthy. It reminds some drinkers of the scent of blackberries and others of black truffles. It is a very assertive wine, but not always well balanced. It is at its best drunk between eight and nine years old, when the flavour is at its peak.

Near to Gigondas is the area which produces Beaumes de Venise, a delicious, heavily sweet Muscat wine. It is halfway between a dessert wine and a liqueur. There is no escaping the potency of the Muscat, which makes a wine of ample flavour with a long, rich aftertaste. It can be a great after-dinner treat with raspberries or a ripe peach.

Across the Rhône from Châteauneuf is Tavel, where the best-known rosé of France is produced. Tavel is a clear, reddish-pink wine, drier than most rosés and with more backbone. It is made largely from the Grenache grape, which changes character depending on whether it is grown on sandy, chalky or stony soil. Many growers blend wines grown on three types of soil to get a balanced wine.

As the vineyards here are small, most of the grapes go to a modern co-operative, so there is little to be gained by looking for vineyard names. Tavel is Tavel, a sound, all-round wine to be drunk with most white meat and poultry, or served, well-chilled, as an original summer aperitif.

Lirac, next door to Tavel, has a pleasant rosé, which is delicious drunk young. It is just as versatile but much cheaper than its famous neighbour, Tavel. Lirac also produces some noteworthy red wines, with plenty of fruit in them. They are at their most beguiling after six or seven years in the bottle.

Côte du Rhône Villages

This appellation covers 17 communes or villages, not including Gigondas, which now has a full appellation of its own. Of the 17, there are several southern Rhône village wines that are well above average and worth looking out for. Vacqueyras is one of the best with a fine red wine that achieves both depth and balance.

Many of the Vacqueyras vineyards share a border with Gigondas. It is no surprise that in the area there are more private bottlers, making their own individual wines, than in any other of the Rhône villages. Two outstanding domaines are La Fourmone and Pascal Frères.

Cairanne is another southern Rhône name to remember. This hilltop village has a modern co-operative, one of the best in the Rhône Valley, that bottles all the local wine. Half the Cairanne vineyards are planted on clay slopes and the rest on stony slopes. The wines are blended together to make a warm, sturdy red that lasts well in the bottle, up to six or seven years.

Rasteau is famous locally for its fortified white Vin de Liqueur, mostly made from Grenache grapes. Drunk young, this is rather crude and a bit too heavy for most palates. A sweet wine is also made which is usually left in cask for a year or two and improves noticeably with age.

Another village wine to remember is Chusclan rosé. The pinky-orange Chusclan rosé, made from Grenache and Cinsault, should be drunk young to appreciate its fruitiness and pleasant dry aftertaste. The best of them can equal Tavel and Lirac.

A village called Laudun makes red, white and rosé wines. The white is quite outstanding. Fresh and full, it is a natural partner for a fish dish. At Rochegude, the red produced has a softness not usually associated with Rhônes. The red wine from Vinsobres has a great length of taste and lasts in the bottle for eight years but is high in alcohol.

The bigger, more generous Rhône wines are always at their best with hefty, well-flavoured or spicy dishes, such as game, pâté and rich stews.

Making wine in the Rhône

Tricastin, Ventoux and Lubéron

The wines from Tricastin, Ventoux and Lubéron, newer Rhône vineyards, are rarely for serious wine connoisseurs, but are cheap and cheerful wines of the warm south, ideal for holiday and home drinking.

Tricastin

One of the fastest-growing wine areas is Côteaux du Tricastin. In the 1960s little more than pines, bracken and gorse grew here. The new vineyards are south of Montélimar, with the village of Les Granges-Gontardes as the centre. The area was derelict until the early 1960s when the French settlers, expelled from North Africa, set up their base in the village.

Many of the returning French had been wine-growers in Algeria. They found the parched Tricastin terrain very similar to Algeria. They uprooted the existing vegetation and planted huge vineyards which, like those of Châteauneuf-du-Pape, are covered with smooth round stones, that reflect the sun's heat.

Tricastin is red wine country and the grapes which are grown here, Grenache, Cinsault and Syrah, are well able to withstand the heat. Harvests last from the end of September to the end of October and the wines are vinified quickly. Many go to huge co-operatives such as Cellier des Dauphins or Cellier des Templiers. Most Tricastin reds are dark in colour, full-bodied, smooth and eminently drinkable. The better wines, such as Domaine de Grangeneuve, are kept in modern, water-cooled vats that control the temperature of the fermenting wines.

Domaine de Grangeneuve is a wine which has improved from being graded Vin de Table, to VDQS (Vins Délimités de Qualité Supérieure) to Appellation Contrôlée in the course of 15 years. It is a fruity and soft wine.

Equally rapid progress has been made by wines of Pierre Labeye of the Domaine de La Tour D'Elyssas. The high quality of his wine made from recently planted grapes is only just becoming apparent. Try the Cru de Meynas and the Syrah.

Other Tricastins worth noting are Domaine de St. Luc which is very fruity and bold, and Domaine de Bois Noir, which has a velvety smoothness. Domaine de Serre Rouge is slightly perfumed and very drinkable. A little Tricastin rosé is made though the rosés do not match up to the reds. They are best drunk young and well chilled.

Côtes du Ventoux

Côtes du Ventoux is another relatively new wine area which gained its Appellation Contrôlée status as recently as 1974. Its wines are mainly red and rosé, with a little white.

Ventoux wines are very different in character to any other Rhône wines. They are light and summery, low in alcohol and at their most attractive when drunk locally. The vineyards are dotted around the south flank of Mont Ventoux and the wines produced are pale in colour.

Most Ventoux wines are processed by co-operatives but there are several private growers making individual wines of higher quality. Those from the Domaine des Anges and Domaine St. Saveur are fragrant and stylish, with a great deal of charm. The Domaine de Champ-Long makes a rather ordinary rosé and an outstanding Cuvée Speciale red that would well repay keeping.

Lubéron

Whether the wine from Lubéron, a very beautiful area of rolling hills and gorges, inland from Marseilles, counts as Rhône or Haute Provence is a matter of debate. For most wine lovers it is simply a happy hunting-ground with a number of new wines that are proving to be remarkably good value for money.

Lubéron has Vin de table and a VDQS rating, which accounts for its low prices. The 17 co-operatives in the area have a complete wine-making monopoly. They send their wines to the huge new Union des Vignerons de Lubéron for final bottling and packaging. Luckily for the discriminating drinker, the wines are not standardized. The Union des Vignerons treats them all individually so that they have a varying appeal.

One of these, the Vin de Pays de Vaucluse, both red and white, is pleasantly dry and unassuming, with an aromatic bouquet. The ruby red Côtes du Lubéron has a bit more weight to it and lasts longer in the mouth.

The best co-operative wine is Cellier de Marrenon, which is a VDQS wine. The red has an ample bouquet and just the right amount of fullness and depth. The white is flowery and quite subtle, a perfect accompaniment to a bouillabaisse.

The Lubéron wine most likely to attract serious wine drinkers comes from Domaine de L'Isolette, near the town of Bonnieux. These wines are red, white and rosé, and are not cheap, but the red especially, with its depth, subtlety and concentrated flavour is well worth its price.

Wines from the new Rhône vineyards of Ventoux, Lubéron and Tricastin

Languedoc and Roussillon

The vineyards of the Languedoc-Roussillon are to wines what the Middle East is to oil! From this huge wine-growing area, which consists of 35% of the area under vines in France, comes almost a billion gallons of wine a year – enough to provide every man, woman and child in Britain, France and America with a dozen bottles each annually.

The vineyards of the Languedoc-Roussillon, or Midi area of France, stretch from the French Pyrenees inland from Banyuls on the Spanish border, in a broad band to the mouth of the Rhône. If the wines from this area are not well known, it is because more than 95% of them are not of Appelation Contrôlée status. They belong to the ordinary table wine category.

However, the number of wine shippers and merchants listing a selection of wines from the Midi demonstrates the growing interest in these wines.

In the Midi there are four *départements*, from which the ordinary *vins de pays* come: the Gard, Hérault, Aude and Pyrénées Orientales. You may find these wines labelled according to the commune in which they are produced. The exact zone of production is not of great importance to the buyer looking for a cheap and cheering wine.

For wines one grade up on the quality scale look out for the VDQS (Vins Délimités de Qualité Supérieure) wines which come from four areas in the Midi. Try the reds, rosés and dry white wines from Corbières, Costières du Gard, Côteaux du Languedoc and Minervois districts.

Grape pickers in Carcassonne

Languedoc area

Corbières: in the middle of the Corbières district is Château Les Palais. The vineyards here are hemmed in by the Pyrénées Orientales to the south and the valley of the Aude to the north. This VDQS wine, which is fermented by a process called *macération carbonique,* is well up to dinner party standard and goes well with rich dishes like cassoulet or roast duck.

The grapes, including stalks, go straight into the vat without being crushed. Fermentation starts naturally within the grape and then is continued in a process in which carbon dioxide is retained under slight pressure. This helps to produce a wine which needs a shorter maturation period. Château Les Palais is a big and fruity wine with a vivid deep colour and powerful bouquet. It is at its best a year after the vintage, but after three years begins to fade.

Costières du Gard: the wines from this area, around the Roman Pont du Gard, are strong red wines of VDQS level, although some whites and rosés are produced.

Coteaux du Languedoc: Vins Delimites de Qualité Superieure come from a large area between Nimes and Beziers. There are no fewer than 13 communes entitled to add their own names to the overall title. One of them, Faugeres, makes a fine, assertive red wine, while St Chinians's red is well made with a scented bouquet.

St Saturnin is another commune name to remember. It has a good co-operative wine and a Vin d'Une Nuit, a light, fruity red wine, which is achieved by the overnight maceration of the grapes. St Saturnin also has a delicious rosé, which is pleasant chilled and served as an aperitif.

Minervois: there are no Appellation Contrôlée wines in this area. All the wines from the Minervois area are classified as VDQS. The reds which form the bulk of the production are vigorous and sometimes slightly peppery. They are strong in alcohol and much of it is sold in the typical occitan bottle, which is half way between a Burgundy and a Champagne bottle in shape.

Vins des Sables: from the Camargue there are the Vins des Sables, which are neither VDQS nor Appellation Contrôlée but are cheap and drinkable.

Roussillon

Roussillon is the eastern part of the Midi wine area. In the northern part of Roussillon is Latour de France, part of the Côtes d'Agly, whose wines have AC status. Latour de France is full-bodied and strong and is a good choice for rich meat dishes.

Other Roussillon appellations are Côtes du Roussillon, Côtes du Roussillon Villages and Collioure. The best commune names to look for are Maury, Estagel, Rasiguères and Caramany. The reds are bold and straightforward while the whites are mostly dry and fresh. Both should be drunk young. Look out for Vin Vert, a notable white, made from early-picked grapes. It is a lively wine with a pleasant degree of acidity

Other AC wines and muscats

Fitou is an AC area of note producing a red wine made mainly from Carignan and Grenache grapes, with up to 25% of other varieties added. Fitou spends at least nine months in wood before being released. Château de Nouvelles at Tuchan is a good Fitou red. The best white of the region is probably the sparkling AC Blanquette de Limoux. Made by the Champagne method from the Mauzac grape, it is every bit as good as the best sparkling Loire wines.

Do not overlook AC Clairette de Bellegarde from just south of Nîmes. It is a dry white wine made entirely from the Clairette grape and will make a good accompaniment to starters or fish dishes. Another sweet white wine is AC Clairette du Languedoc from west of the Costières du Gard area.

To crown the versatility of Languedoc-Roussillon wines, there are the fortified, *Vins-Doux-Naturels*, which are all AC wines. These wines are made either from the Grenache or Muscatel grapes. From Banyuls, Rivesaltes, and Maury, these wines, lush and honeyed on the palate, are the perfect choice with dessert or fresh fruit to round off a good meal.

Provence

Provence is one of the happiest hunting grounds for lovers of rosé – an uncomplicated and easy wine, which can be drunk at any time and with any food. A small amount of red and white wine is also produced in Provence, so a trip through the area will produce some good drinking.

Côtes de Provence is a wine area which was promoted to *Appelation Contrôlée* status in 1977. It covers an area stretching for 80 kilometres like a half-moon across the Maures plateau, from Toulon to St. Raphael. Within this area is a coastal zone between the Massif des Maures and the sea, with a wide inland strip between Toulon and Fréjus. Here there are particularly good reds to be found at Pierrefeu, Puget-Ville and Cuers. Further inland, there are sound white wines round Correns and reds near Cotignac.

St. Tropez is thought of as the wine capital of the area and is the natural centre for many of the best rosés. The wines are cultivated along the seaward slopes of the hills, where they are sheltered from the fierce mistral winds which blow from the north. These rosés are eminently drinkable and of direct, simple appeal. Just behind St. Tropez is Château de Minuty, with its expensive Cuvée de l'Oratoire, sought after by connoisseurs.

Otherwise the range of tastes and individual bouquets is not very wide. Most growers concentrate on the primary appeal of cheerful, clean, refreshing wines, made to a standard formula in a highly reliable climate, where vintages barely differ from one year to the next.

With so many growers and so many names jostling for attention on the shelves, one can only pick out a few for special recommendation. Châteaux de Selle and de Roseline, Clos du Relais and Domaine de Saint-Martin are well-known for all-round consistency. So, too are Domaine de l'Aumerade, Clos Mirelle, Côte au-du-Ferrage, Domaine de Noyer and Domaine de Mauvanne. The Domaine de la Croix is highly regarded as are Domaine des Féraud, Domaine de la Clapière, Castel-Roubine and Château Grand 'Boise.

Just outside the Côtes de Provence area is Côteaux d'Aix-en-Provence, a VDQS wine area. One outstanding property here is Château Vignelaure, 30 kilometres northeast of Aix, at Rians. From here comes a highly palatable red wine made from a blend of Cabernet Sauvignon, Grenache and Syrah grapes. The soils here are chalky and the wines, made without any chemical treatments, are refined and elegant.

Some other above-average wines in this area include Domaine de la Crémade, the Mas de la Dame, Château La Coste and Château de Calisanne.

AC Palette

To the south of Aix is the tiny appellation of Palette, which enjoys a micro-climate all its own. The only name of note, but a good one, is Château Simone, famous for red wines that are aged in wood until they acquire all sorts of subtle nuances. The rosés and whites are also of fine quality.

Clinging to the coast near Marseilles is the tiny appellation of Cassis. Its white wine is a perfect partner for *bouillabaisse*, the delicious fish stew of Marseilles. Names to note in this area are Château de Fontblanche, Clos Ste-Magdeleine and Domaine du Paternel.

Further along the coast from Cassis is Bandol, the best-known specific AC wine area in the region. There are 200 growers making as much red wine as rosé and the red is usually the better choice.

Domaine Tempier's reputation for making a rich red wine of depth that ages well, has never been surpassed. Domaine du Val d'Arenc and Château des Vannières and the Mas de la Rouvière are not far behind. Some of these reds can take three to six years in the bottle before they are ready.

In general, when buying Provence rosés, avoid those exported in fancy bottles bearing florid labels. They have often been sweetened up for easy marketing and in the process may lose much of their original charm and vigour.

These wines are unbeatable for drinking at picnics, barbecues and other outdoor meals, where they will almost certainly bring to mind the Mediterranean.

Typical village vineyard in Provence

South-West France

Apart from the renowned wines of Bordeaux, the south-west of France also has an extraordinarily wide range of relatively unknown wines for delicious drinking, at reasonable prices.

Wines from south-west France

Inland, to the east of Bordeaux, and in the districts to the south are produced a number of modest drinkable wines.

Bergerac and Cahors

Bergerac produces pleasant, fruity red and white wines, reasonably priced and best drunk when they are young. The dry white Bergerac Sec is made from a trio of grapes: Sauvignon, Sémillon and Muscadelle. These same grapes are used in different proportions to produce the sweet white wines of Monbazillac. A Monbazillac is a first-class choice to serve with a dinner party dessert or with fresh fruit and cheese at the end of a meal. Similar to Sauternes, which is at least double the price, Monbazillac has its own fragrance, lusciousness and peachy charm.

Cahors, further west, used to produce 'the black wine of Cahors' before the days of quality control. This was used to fortify poorer Bordeaux wines. Made largely with the Malbec grape, it is now recognized as a delightful red wine in its own right, and is not as heavy a wine as it once was. Cahors wine goes well with casseroles and red meat, and is a warming winter red. It has the ability to age for many years. Quality varies depending on the grower, but Château de Cayrou, Domaine de Pailhas, Domaine du Cèdre and Clos Triguedina have all proved their worth in the past. A big co-operative, Les Caves d'Olt at Parnac, makes a sound Vin de Cahors, worth trying.

Marmande and Buzet

From the Côtes du Marmande, up the river to the south of Bordeaux, come soft and beguiling red wines, made with a blend of Merlot, Cabernet and Malbec grapes. There is also a delicious rosé. Most Marmande wines come from co-operatives, and carry a VDQS rating.

Côtes de Buzet wines are AC. The reds, made from the usual Bordeaux blend of Cabernet Sauvignon, Cabernet Franc and Merlot, are aged in oak and will improve for a year or two, if left in the bottle. Cuvée Napoleon is the best co-operative wine from the area, while Château de Padère at Ambrus is always a reliable buy.

Gaillac and Madiran

AC Gaillac district lies in the Tarn valley to the south and is a good source of bargain-priced sparkling white wines. Some are made with the local grape, Len de l'El, and some with the Mauzac grape, which is also used for the traditional Gaillac sweet white wines. Red Gaillacs are made from Gamay, the Beaujolais grape, generally blended with Syrah or Merlot to make agreeable wines, suitable for casual drinking.

For serious red wine drinkers, Madiran is the name to remember. It is a rich, full-bodied wine that rates as one of the best reds from the Pyrenees. The local Tannat grape is mixed with Cabernet to make a wine of real staying power. Château de Peyros always seems to have the blend of red grapes absolutely right. Vignobles Laplace, Domaines Barréjat and Lalenne are well regarded Madiran reds.

West of Gaillac, to the north of Toulouse, is a local red wine, Côtes du Frontonnais, which is now being exported and is worth looking out for. It should get better and better, as the new vines mature. Château Bellevue-La Forêt is particularly good.

Jurançon and Béarn

Jurançon, from the foothills of the Pyrenees, is sweet and spicy, and drinking it is an acquired taste. These wines are made from a wide selection of unusual grapes with Courbu, Petit Manseng and Gros Manseng, the most important. Because of the climate, which is affected by the Pyrenees and the sea, these impressive sweet wines are not harvested until mid-October. At this time the effects of the sunshine and night frosts combine to concentrate the sugar in the grape juice, raising the resulting alcohol level to 16%.

The taste of Jurançon wine is sometimes compared to carnations, honey or grilled hazelnuts – all these comparisons, like the wine, are highly individual. Little of this wine is made and it is strictly for the connoisseur. Plenty of Jurançon dry white is made but apart from Clos de la Vierge, it is rather undistinguished.

To the north of the Basque country is Béarn, whose wines are good enough to gain an Appellation Contrôlée. Most of it is red and rosé and much of it comes from the co-operative at Bellocq. A few kilometres nearer the sea than Béarn is the tiny appellation of Irouléguy, which has a light rosé version of typical Pyrenian foothill wines that goes with almost any food.

GERMANY

The most northerly of the world's great vineyards lie in Germany – in the complex of valleys made up by the Rhine (or Rhein) river and its tributary the Moselle (or Mosel). The wines produced vary from light fruity whites to rich, golden dessert wines.

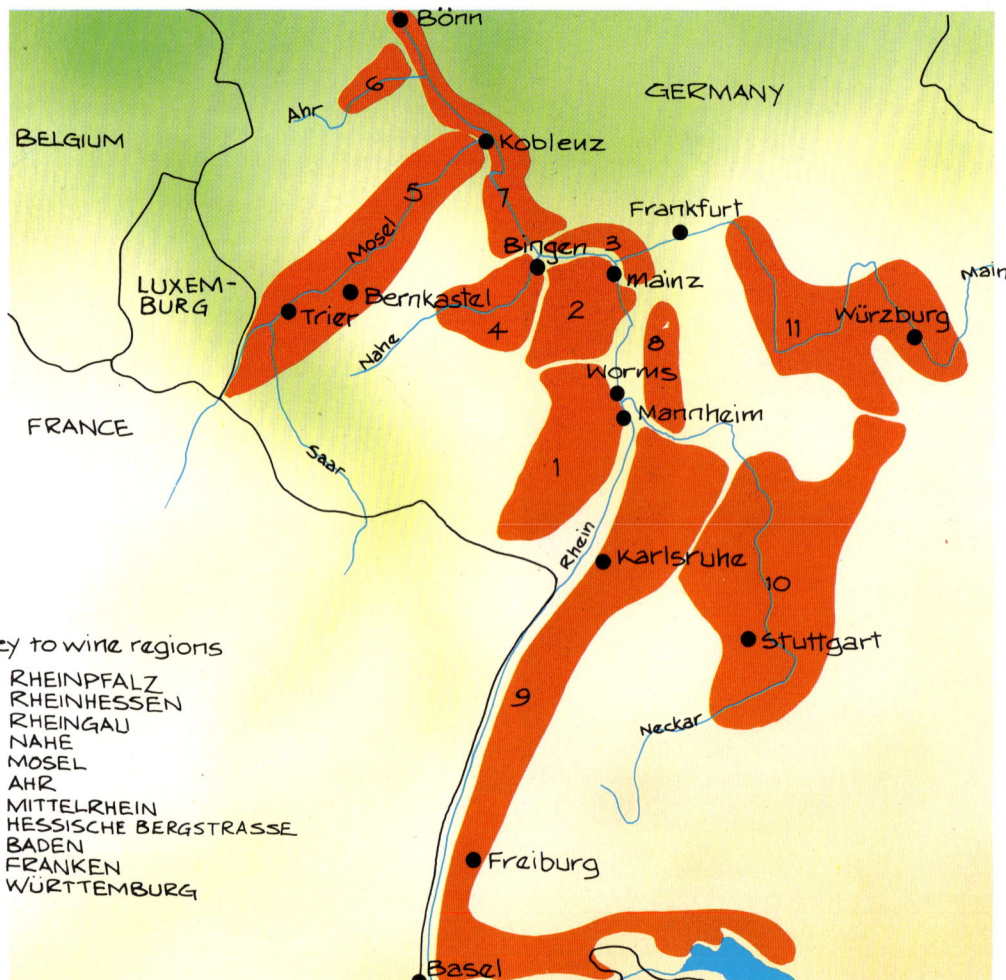

Key to wine regions

1. RHEINPFALZ
2. RHEINHESSEN
3. RHEINGAU
4. NAHE
5. MOSEL
6. AHR
7. MITTELRHEIN
8. HESSISCHE BERGSTRASSE
9. BADEN
10. FRANKEN
11. WÜRTTEMBURG

Known once as 'Rhenish', and more recently as 'Hock', the white wines of Germany have been appreciated in Britain for centuries. We are still the greatest drinkers of exported German quality wines, taking over one third of the total, mostly in the form of Liebfraumilch.

Liebfraumilch is one German wine that everybody knows. But what exactly is it? The name is imprecise by the rigorous standards of German wine law, which will usually see to it that you have an almost embarassing amount of information about what you are drinking. It was originally called after the Liebfrauenkirch, or Church of our Lady, in the Rheinhessen town of Worms. It means literally 'Our Lady's Milk', though it is possible that the 'milch' is a corruption of 'minch', the German word for monk, as the vineyard used to be in the care of the local monastery. Be that as it may, the picturesque title was soon being applied to other Rhine wines, and there is still a certain vagueness about it today, though it must originate from one of the four main Rhine regions, Rheinhessen, Rheinpfalz, Nahe and Rheingau – and be made chiefly from one or more of the three main grape types – Riesling, Sylvaner and Müller-Thurgau. It must also have been tested to the standard of German quality wine, and will therefore have the letters Qba on the label. This is roughly the equivalent of the French AC and Italian DOC designations. All quality wine must also have a control number to prove that it has passed the rigorous tests required; this number is printed on the label.

As a general description, Liebfraumilch is a light, fruity wine, with a pleasantly fragrant bouquet, but the regulations leave some scope for the individual producer to create his own style. Most is sold under a brand name associated with a particular company; two of the better known ones are Blue Nun from Sichel and Hans Cristof from Deinhard.

All wines from the Rhine are traditionally marketed in brown bottles; German wine in a green bottle will come from Moselle. Some blended wines from Moselle appear under brand names; the best known is Moselblumchen. This does not have to satisfy the same quality testing as Lieb-fraumilch and is of the lower Deutsche Tafelwein status, but it can still be a very pleasant drink; Moselles are generally slightly drier and fresher-tasting than the Rhine wines and often have a penetrating flowery bouquet.

The practice of blending is sometimes regarded by the layman as a slightly suspect activity, but in fact it is an essential part of the winemaker's skill. German wine has a reputation for sweetness, but the main problem in many vintages is a lack of natural sugar, as the vineyards are among the most northerly in Europe and do not always have enough warm sunshine to ripen the grapes. The German Wine Institute at Geisenheim has developed sophisticated techniques for making the most of what is available. For any wine up to and including Qba status, it is permitted to add small quantities of grape sugar – *süssreserve* – after fermentation is complete. But for the very best wine – labelled Qmp – this is strictly forbidden, as the grading of wine is closely linked to the amount of natural sugar in the unfermented grape juice. It is a temptation – not always resisted – to break this law, as the top wines command much higher prices; hence the recent scandal concerning diethylene glycol, which can give a very ordinary wine a deceptive sweetness and viscosity. Fortunately only a handful of unscrupulous producers have been involved, but the publicity has been disproportionately damaging.

In spite of the best efforts of the legislators to bring order and simplicity to the German wine scene, there are still some terms in use which may be misleading. For instance, a wine which is labelled simply 'Tafelwein', as opposed to 'Deutsche Tafelwein', will almost certainly come from more than one country within the EEC; this label information is likely to be in German and is often inconspicuous. Then there is the word 'Bereich'. This means 'district', so that a wine named Bereich Bernkastel will come from the small neighbourhood of Bernkastel in the Moselle. But Bereich Johannisberg, for example, can come from anywhere in the 7000 acres of Rheingau. Again, vineyard names can refer either to 'einzellagen', individual vineyards, or to 'grosslagen', vineyard areas, and there is no way of telling which is which, except by carrying a reference book around with you or learning from experience. Finally, there is the description 'erzeugerabfullung' which means 'estate-bottled' and was once almost a guarantee of a fine wine in the same way that 'mis en bouteilles au Château' is indicative of good claret; under the new wine law, this can be used not just by individual growers, but by wine co-operatives, for any wine, however cheap.

All of which may make you feel that you would sooner forget the whole business of getting to know the better German wines and just stick to Liebfraumilch. But this would be a pity. As we shall see, German wine labels do give a great deal of genuinely helpful information and can point you in the direction of some very enjoyable drinking.

German wine labels

To fully appreciate German wines you will need to understand the German labelling system. German wine is actually easier to choose than its French counterparts, since the label of a German bottle tells you, in simple terms, how good the wine is.

The German labelling system is strictly controlled according to a major reforming law passed in 1971. This defines exactly what the label must and must not say about the wine. Any indication of the quality of the wine must fall into strict categories and a wine may only be proclaimed as of a certain standard and type after rigorous official testing. There are two basic categories: *Tafelwein* and *Qualitätswein* – table wine and quality wine.

Table wine
To even use the word Tafelwein, the wine must come from one or more E.E.C. countries. Deutsche Tafelwein (German table wine) must be a blend of wines of German origin only – there are five German Tafelwein areas. A Deutsche Tafelwein is likely to be inexpensive and suitable for everyday drinking. Much Tafelwein for export is sold under general brand names.

Quality wine
Qualitätswein is another matter, although it will not necessarily be more expensive. Here, the producer of the wine in one of 11 specified traditional wine growing areas has applied for the wine to be given official approval. This involves the scientific testing of the wine to see if the levels of sugar, alcohol and acidity are correct and that there is no foreign matter in the wine indicating improper cellar techniques.

A great part of the German wine that is sold abroad comes into this category, bearing the designation *Qualitätswein bestimmter Anbaugebeite* (usually QbA on the label) – quality wine from a registered region. The region will be named prominently on the label, together with the registered place of origin, vintage and perhaps the grape type and shipper or bottler. QbA wines are sometimes exported under brand names, like Tafelwein. Look out for QbA on the label – it is an adequate guarantee.

All Qualitätswein is also allocated an official coding – the A.P. number, which gives, in 11 digits, a full record of what it is and when and where it was tested.

Special distinction wines
If a producer feels his wine is of even higher quality, he may submit it for a further level of testing before a panel of experts representing the growers, the state and the wine trade. To be awarded the designation *Qualitätswein mit Prädikat* (QmP – quality with special distinction) the wine must be accepted as having reached a high state of excellence, without the addition of sugar in its fermentation. It will still not be necessarily expensive.

Tafelwein, Kabinett and Auslese labels

There are five categories of QmP:
Kabinett: the basic QmP category.
Spätlese: the grapes were late picked and fully ripe, indicating a rich wine.
Auslese: grape bunches were selected as ripe and in perfect condition. The sweetness and quality of the wine will be high.
Beerenauslese: the grapes were picked only after the 'noble rot' fungus had begun to attack the grapes on the vine. The wine will be even more concentrated in flavour.
Trockenbeerenauslese: wine of superlative quality, made from grapes that had begun to dry to sultana form on the vine.

A final category is Eiswein, a rare and expensive wine made from grapes pressed during a severe frost so that the water in them, still frozen solid, can be separated.

Place of origin
German wine labels are very precise about the place of origin. About 3,000 place names are included in the official list, the *Weinbergsrolle*. The most significant names are the five Tafelwein areas and the 11 Qualitätswein areas. The Tafelwein areas are Rhine, Mosel, Main, Neckar and Oberrhein. Of the 11 Qualitätsweins, seven are in the region covered by Rhine in the Tafelwein classification: Ähr, Hessische Berg-strasse, Mittelrhein, Nahe, Rheingau, Rheinhessen and Rheinpfalz. The others are Mosel-Saar-Ruwer, Franken, Württemberg and Baden, each again occupying the central portion of a larger Tafelwein region. The most important areas are Mosel-Saar-Ruwer, Nahe, Rheingau, Rheinhessen and Rheinpfalz, and most good wines will have one of these names on the label.

The remainder of the 3,000 registered names are villages and parcels of land, from whole areas down to just single vineyards. Generally the first part of the wine's name is most useful – indicating the village from which the wine comes. Bernkastler Doctor, for example, means that the wine comes from the Bernkastel area and from a smaller parcel of land signified by 'Doctor'.

Other information
Vintage: the year in which a quality wine was produced will always appear on the bottle. Refer to vintage charts if you want to know whether a year was good or bad. The categorization system helps here.

Grape types: German wines use many different types of grape and the type will often be mentioned on the label. There are three to look out for among white wines: Riesling is the best; Müller-Thurgau is a newer type, growing in production and reputation; and Sylvaner is grown more in southern regions.

Shipper and bottler: because the German government has taken such a positive role in protecting the reputations of its wines, you will need to rely less on the good names of the traders involved than formerly. But the established shippers do have some of the best growers on their books.

Rheinpfalz – the Palatinate

It is the most productive area of all Germany, home of the most northerly of the world's great vineyards. From its vines come many quality wines – and some of the country's greatest ones.

Riesling grapes in a Rheinpfalz vineyard

The wines of Germany are predominately white. They are sweet in character, but balance their high sugar content with a clear fruitiness that makes the term 'sweet' wholly inadequate. Simple, fresh wines share the market with the traditional giants of German viniculture, much of which comes from the rocky-topsoiled land of the Rhine.

The most productive area of all, making almost 25% of German wine, is the Rheinpfalz – the Palatinate. Wine has certainly been produced here since Roman times. The Rheinpfalz is the warmest and driest area in Germany, hence the huge scale of its wine yield. The other great wine districts of the Rhine valley perch on the slopes of the valley itself, but the Rheinpfalz to the south occupies a strip of land some 15 kilometres to the west of the river, running for about 80 kilometres from north to south. From the French border to the south west, towards the town of Worms in the north, winds the famous *Weinstrasse* – the wine road. Along its twisting course through the Haardt hills it is thickly lined with vineyards.

In the central portion, known as the Mittelhaardt, lie some of Germany's most famous vineyards. And in the south is the Oberhaardt, which does not have the pedigree of the Mittelhaardt but is growing in reputation. To the north of the Mittelhaardt, is an area known as Unterhaardt. Its wines are not highly regarded and not often sold outside Germany.

The Oberhaardt

The southern area, known as the Oberhaardt, is responsible for the greater quantity although it is not renowned for great wines like its neighbouring region, the Mittelhaardt, to the north. In the past, almost all the wine produced here was drunk locally, as carafe wine or as the heady, milky *Federweisser* (feather-white). This is drunk when so young that it is still half grape juice. The better wines that were not drunk by local farmers were often used in blended wine – Liebfraumilch, for example – and this was the only way it was likely to be drunk outside Germany. Now, however, the region is changing and many wines are bottled with the name of their particular places of origin and reputations are being established. Many quality wines are produced, and *Spätlese* and even *Auslese* can be found proudly inscribed on the label.

One reason for this is the growing popularity of the Müller-Thurgau grape variety, gradually replacing the older Sylvaner in the area. While Sylvaner vines ripen early and produce high yields, their wine has none of the character of the Rieslings from which all the great German wines are derived. Müller-Thurgau, however, is a cross between the two types, and combines the efficient qualities of Sylvaner with some of the richness of Riesling. Wines from this vine are often identified on the label. The vine is grown in the southern part of the Rheinpfalz and these wines are an ideal way to become acquainted with German wine style. Pale, fruity and light, they make a better accompaniment to food than the more powerful wines of the Mittelhaardt.

Names to look out for are Rhodten Ordensgut and Berzaberner Kloster Liebfrauenberg – these are the very best.

The Mittelhaardt

To the north of the town of Neustadt, on the *Deutsche Weinstrasse* proper, are a group of villages producing some of the greatest wines of all. Three large owners have properties in the district and their names often appear on the labels of these esteemed products: von Buhl, Bürklin-Wolf and Bassermann-Jordan. These names all indicate superb quality. The four most distinguished villages are Deidesheim, Forst, Ruppertsberg and Wachenheim. Königsbach nearby is also highly thought of, although its output is small. Any wine bearing one of these names (as the first part of the wine's name, as in Deidesheimer Hohenmorgen) will be fine indeed, and will be quite expensive. This area favours the Riesling grape and the wine is much deeper in colour than those from farther south.

The wine from Forst is reputedly the sweetest in Germany. Near the village is an outcrop of black basalt, a rock rich in potassium which contributes to the fine character of the wine. In consequence stone from local quarries is crushed and spread on the vineyard of other districts to impart some of the quality of Forst wine to their products. Next to the church at Forst, almost in the centre of the village, are two of the most famous vineyards in Germany – Jesuitengarten and Kirchenstück. A short distance away is Deidesheim, a charming little village surrounded by famous vineyards such as Grainhübel, Hohenmorgen, Leinhöhle and Kalkofen. Wachenheim, too, has its famous names – Böhlig, Gerümpel, Goldbächel and Rechbächel among others. But these are truly great wines, hard to come by and to be reserved for a special occasion.

To the north is the small town of Bad Dürkheim, Germany's largest wine commune. Here, the famous *Wurstmarkt* (sausage fair) is held annually in September. This fair is a marvellous celebration of wine and sausage. A few local place names, including Bad Dürkheim itself, signify good wine, Kallstadt and Ungstein, in particular.

Rheingau

The Rheingau is the outstanding wine-producing area of the Rhine valley. On the right bank, roughly between the bridges across to Mainz and Bingen, it produces the rich dessert wines for which Germany has no rival.

The site of the Rheingau is unique among the Rhine regions, in that the river, which generally flows from south to north, at this point turns, blocked by the Taunus mountains, and flows slightly to the south. The slopes of the Taunus hills face to the south and receive the maximum amount of sun making them ideal for vines. Furthermore the thickly wooded Taunus mountains form a natural wind-break, keeping off the cold winds from the north and east. It is also believed that the river, with its broad surface, reflects the sun back up on to the slopes, increasing their warmth – an especially important factor when the grapes are ripening. In addition, the great size of the river imparts moisture to the air, favouring the growth of the vines. In autumn the damp mists gathering over the river help the 'noble rot' which attacks the grapes and helps create the fine Auslese, Beerenauslese and Trockenbeerenauslese wines.

The soil is also a contributory factor. On the high slopes, there is quartzite and weathered slate, and closer to the river there are clays, loess and loam. All these advantages make possible the predominant use of the Riesling grape: in Rheingau 83% of the crop is Riesling with 9% Müller-Thurgau and under 5% Sylvaner.

Rheingau produces only 2% of the total German wine production, but because much of this is of the highest quality, the name Rheingau on a wine label will often suggest that the product is amongst the aristocrats of German wine. The good wines from Rheingau age remarkably well.

Rüdesheim and western Rheingau

Lorchhausen and Lorch, the villages furthest downstream and furthest west, are the least distinguished in the region. Some good wine is made, but it has more in common with the lighter, more commonplace wines of neighbouring Mittelrhein. The next village, Assmannshausen, is also an exception. Here, red wines are produced from the blue Spätburgunder (or Pinot Noir) grape.

Just beyond Assmannshausen, on the bend in the river, is Rüdesheim – a town producing characteristic and excellent Rheingau wines. The hill to the west of the town, the Rüdesheimer Berg, produces much of the very best wines – golden in colour, strong in alcohol and in flavour. Paradoxically, the great years for the rest of the Rheingau are not necessarily always the best here, because the soil of the higher slopes tends to dry out in long, hot summers, with the result that the wines, already strong in flavour, become overpowering. Great vineyard names to look out for are Berg Roseneck, Berg Rottland, Berg Schlossberg, Bischofsberg and Klosterberg.

East of Rüdesheim on the river is Geisenheim, and the revered Johannisberg a short distance inland. The official German school of winemaking is at Geisenheim, and the wines of the area are good. Johannisberg, however, is in another class and is perhaps the greatest of Rheingau, or even of Rhine, areas. Schloss Johannisberg is incomparable, immensely subtle in flavour – and very expensive. Other Johannisberg vineyards are Goldatzel and Hölle.

Next along the river, come Winkel, Mittelheim and Östrich, with Hattenheim and Hallgarten in the hills behind. At Winkel is Schloss Vollrads, rivalling even Schloss Johannisberg. Its wines are said to be beyond praise. At Hattenheim is another famous estate, Steinberg, with the monastery of Kloster Eberbach, where wines have been made for at least 700 years.

Eltville and eastern Rheingau

Erbach, along the river from Hattenheim, has another famous vineyard. Named Marcobrunn, the vineyard has been the subject of a legendary dispute between the villages, but it is now officially in Erbach.

Eltville, next along the river, is one of the larger vineyard towns of Rheingau, providing a centre for the wine trade and the manufacture of sparkling Sekt. Its wines are good, and may be less expensive than the more famous villages in the hills behind: Kiedrich, Rauenthal and Martinsthal.

Wiesbaden and Hochheim

On the bend in the river that marks the end of the Rhine part of Rheingau lies the major town of Wiesbaden. Although an attractive old spa resort, its own wines are not up to the high standards of its illustrious neighbours flanking its east and west sides. There are four groups of Wiesbaden vineyards: Wiesbaden itself, Schierstein, Frauenstein and Dotzheim.

Just beyond Wiesbaden, the river Main joins the Rhine. About 3 kilometres up the river Main is the town of Hochheim, forming the eastern edge of the Rheingau. Although not on the Rhine itself, it has given its name to all the wines of the Rhine regions in English usage – 'hock'. Hochheim's wines are certainly Rheingau in character, and are among the first rank in quality. The best vineyards, Kirchenstück and Domdechaney, are close to the centre of the town. Less good, although as famous, is Königen Viktoria Berg, named after Queen Victoria, who showed an idiosyncratic taste in wine by naming it her favourite vineyard on a visit in 1850. The best Hochheim wines are excellent, soft and fruity, but experts complain of an earthy taste in the less than perfect ones.

Rheingau is an area for those who want to start at the top. Its wines are fine indeed – and famous. There is almost no such thing as a bargain, for its products are carefully graded and bought at auction by those who know precisely which wines are the best. This, of course, makes it easier for the beginner. If you want to sample Rheingau, find a good wine merchant and choose a wine at the price you want to pay.

Vineyards around Assmannshausen

47

Rheinhessen

Rheinhessen produces some of the most famous wines in the world, as well as huge quantities of pleasant but undistinguished table wines. Bingen and the Rheinfront are two centres which export wines of unassailable quality.

Up to 300 million litres of wine are produced in the Rheinhessen annually. Rheinhessen is situated in the bend in the River Rhine known as the Rheinknie (the Rhine knee). Three of the roughly square-shaped region's corners are marked by towns on the river: Bingen, Mainz and Worms. To the west lies the River Nahe and to the south the Rheinpfalz, both areas of quality wines. Rheinhessen has a mild climate and is protected from cold winter winds by hills of the western Black Forest. The rolling, open countryside is not the prettiest in Germany but, because it is so fertile, is known as 'God's garden'. The different sedimentary soils here account for the difference in stature of the wines. The best wines come from grapes grown on the red sandstone along the Rhine, particularly to the south of Mainz. The poorest – in quality if not in quantity – come from the fertile clay soils in the centre of the region.

The Sylvaner grape was for a long time the dominant type in the region. Ripening early and giving high yields, Sylvaner produces wine with a light fragrant character. Recently, Sylvaner has been pushed into second place by the Müller-Thurgau grape – at present about 27% of the production to Sylvaner's 15%. To the grower, Müller-Thurgau has the advantage of high efficiency with a fuller flavour. Other, newer grape varieties are also gaining ground, but it is the most traditional of grape varieties that is grown on the best sites and yields the most famous wines. The Riesling grape is used to produce only 5% of the region's wine, but it has great depth and spiciness.

Bingen

Behind the town of Bingen rises the Schalachberg or 'scarlet hill', although it is brick-red rather than scarlet. Here is the famous chapel of St Rochas, from which the collective name for the vineyards of the area comes – Sankt Rochuskapelle. The best wines from this region are strong and full of flavour, with a smoky taste imparted by the soil. The famous vineyards are Schlossberg, Schwätzerchen and Scharlachberg.

The Rheinfront

The town of Mainz is one of the main centres of the German wine trade, although little wine is actually grown here. To the south is the Rheinfront. Red sandstone soils cover the east-facing slopes of the river banks which are packed with vineyards. The first Rheinfront village, Bodenheim, produces mild wines, known for their bouquet and quality. Nackenheim does not produce much wine, and is not well known outside Germany, but to wine experts, this is a special place. Its wines are now largely sold under the village name and not used in blends. The best vineyard is Nackenheimer Rothenberg; producers to look for are Gunderloch-Lange, Gunderloch-Usinger and the state-owned Staatsweingut.

Further south is Nierstein, important for the quality and quantity of its wine. The sun reflecting off the Rhine on to the vineyard slopes is said to help ripen the grapes. Nierstein's wine production is massive, and less than 20% is bottled as wine of high quality under the name of the place where it was produced. The majority goes into the well known blended wines. However if the wine is labelled 'Niersteiner' with the name of the vineyard it must be a great wine. The most famous Niersteiner vineyards are Floss, Glock, Hipping, Orbel, Pettental and Rehbach. There are also producers of considerable fame whose names will appear on the label, including Freiherr Heyl zu Herrnheim, Rheinhold Senfer, Franz Karl Schmitt and, again, the Staatsweingut.

Oppenheim, the next village up the river, produces wine almost as good as Nierstein. The best vineyards include Daubhaus, Herrenberg, Kreuz, Sackträger and Steig.

The Rheinfront ends with the village of Dienheim. The wine is still good, although not of the superlative quality of Nierstein or Oppenheim. Watch for these vineyard names: Goldberg, Guldenmorgen, Kröttenbrunner and Rosswiesse.

The Worms region

In the ancient town of Worms is a church called Liebfrauenkirche (the church of Our Lady). Though the small vineyards nearby produce average wine, the huge reputation of Liebfraumilch (Our Lady's milk) started here. Now, of course, the name Liebfraumilch is applied to wine produced all over Rheinhessen, and Rheinpfalz as well. The fertility of the soil and the skill of the growers have led to this being one of the most exported wines of all. Liebfraumilch is pleasant, sweet, and reliably fresh, but totally lacking in the distinction of the wines of Nierstein or Oppenheim, or even the individuality of less well-known local types.

Rhine red wines

One final wine of importance comes from Ingleheim, a village situated between Bingen and Mainz. Made from blue Spätburgunder grapes, this is a red wine – one of the best made in Germany. Other Rheinhessen reds are made from the Portugeiser grape, but these are as well left for local consumption. Ingleheim wines, however, are worth looking out for – but little is produced and they are not often found outside Germany.

The Nahe

Situated on a tributary of the Rhine, the Nahe region is less well-known than the other famous Rhine wine regions of Germany, but it ranks very highly since it produces some of the greatest dessert wines as well as good quality wines for everyday drinking. The region is small and only provides about five per cent of the total amount of German wine produced each year.

Although officially Nahe wines are categorized as Rhine wines (hocks), these wines unjustifiably suffer from the reputation that they fall midway between Moselles and hocks. The truth, however, is that the Nahe produces wines of quite individual character, combining the clarity and liveliness of Moselles with the strength and fruitiness of hocks. Its wines vary from place to place and from soil type to soil type. The best Nahe wines rank very high indeed, and the region fully qualifies among the five greatest areas of the eleven officially classified. Because the wines of the Nahe are often underestimated, this means that its better products are available at more acceptable prices than its illustrious neighbours.

The river Nahe is a tributary of the Rhine, flowing in from the west at the town of Bingen, which is in the Rheinhessen wine region, with Rüdesheim in the Rheingau opposite. Many of the Nahe vineyards are on the slopes of the Nahe valley itself, but they also stretch up the tributaries of the Nahe, the Glan and the Alsenz. Some vineyards are also scattered far back into the hills, particularly to the north and west of Bad Kreuznach, the region's central town. The vineyards are protected from the frosts by the range of forested hills – the Soonwald – to the north.

The soils are varied; the best for wine is the sandstone of the central portion of the river valley. The loams and weathered clays found mixed in with the sandstone around the Bad Kreuznach area also produce good wines. Over 80% of the grapes grown are Müller-Thurgau, Riesling and Sylvaner – Germany's great white wine grapes – though Riesling tends to produce the best wine.

This is not an area of great aristocratic producers like the Rheingau and alongside the important state domains there are numerous small and medium estates. The co-operatives which market about 20% of the wine maintain high standards. The Nahe typifies the care and industry with which German wine is produced, combining tradition with the most modern methods. This approach enables German wine production to keep pace with the huge growth in demand for fine wines.

Bad Kreuznach

The most famous centre of the Nahe is Bad Kreuznach, a picturesque old spa with a 600 year-old bridge. Roman artifacts and mosaics found in the area support the claim that viniculture was started here by the Romans, although it may go back even earlier. Some vineyards are quite close to the town centre – Rosengarten, Kahlenberg, St. Martin and Brückes, are names worth looking out for. Bad Kreuznach

wines are typical of the Nahe area and are of very good, although not exceptional, quality. There are some good vineyards across the river, notably Höllenbrand, Galgenberg and Rosenberg.

To the north and west, scattered back into the hills, there are a number of well reputed wine villages. Roxheim, Windesheim and Bretzenheim are particularly famous, but there are other lesser-known villages. The best of these produce wines with strongly individual character and a distinctively powerful fruitiness.

Schloss Böckelheim

The most significant name in Nahe wine production is Schloss Böckelheim, which lies further upstream from Bad Kreuznach. Between the two centres are a number of villages on the left bank of the river. Just south of Bad Kreuznach is the huge red rock of the Rotenfels with the village of Bad Münster below. Vineyards clustering at the foot of this giant sun trap (such as Rotenfelser im Winkel, Höll, Steigerdell and Bastei) are also on ideal soil. They produce some of the best Nahe wine, especially Bastei. Opposite Bad Münster, the Alsenz, a tributary of the Nahe, enters the river. Several good wines come from this valley, particularly from the villages of Ebernburg and Altenbamberg.

A little further along the Nahe is Norheim, again producing wine of the first rank. Vineyards include Dellchen, Kafels and Kirschheck, all close to the river, with Klosterberg and Sonnenberg behind. The next riverside village is Niederhausen. Vineyards such as Felsensteyer, Kertz, Rosenheck and Steinwingert cover the slopes leading down to the river and produce fine wines.

The next section of the river front belongs to the village of Schloss Böckelheim itself, beginning with the most famous Nahe vineyard, Kupfergrube or 'the copper mine'. Copper was indeed mined here and the traces in the soil give the wine a strong flavour – its taste has been compared to blackcurrants. The neighbouring Felsenberg, Mühlberg, Königsfels and In den Felsen vineyards also produce excellent drinkable wine.

There are scattered vineyard areas further up the Nahe valley and in the hinterland, many producing notable wines. Village names to look out for include: Waldböckelheim, Monzingen, Martinstein and Merxheim. All these produce above-average wines that are well worth trying.

Left: a Bad Kreuznach wine, and Right: a wine from the famous Schloss Böckelheim region

Moselle: Saar and Ruwer

Moselles are among the most highly prized of all wines. Their very individual style is as recognizable as the slim green bottles the wine comes in. Moselles are paler in colour than the wines of the Rhine.

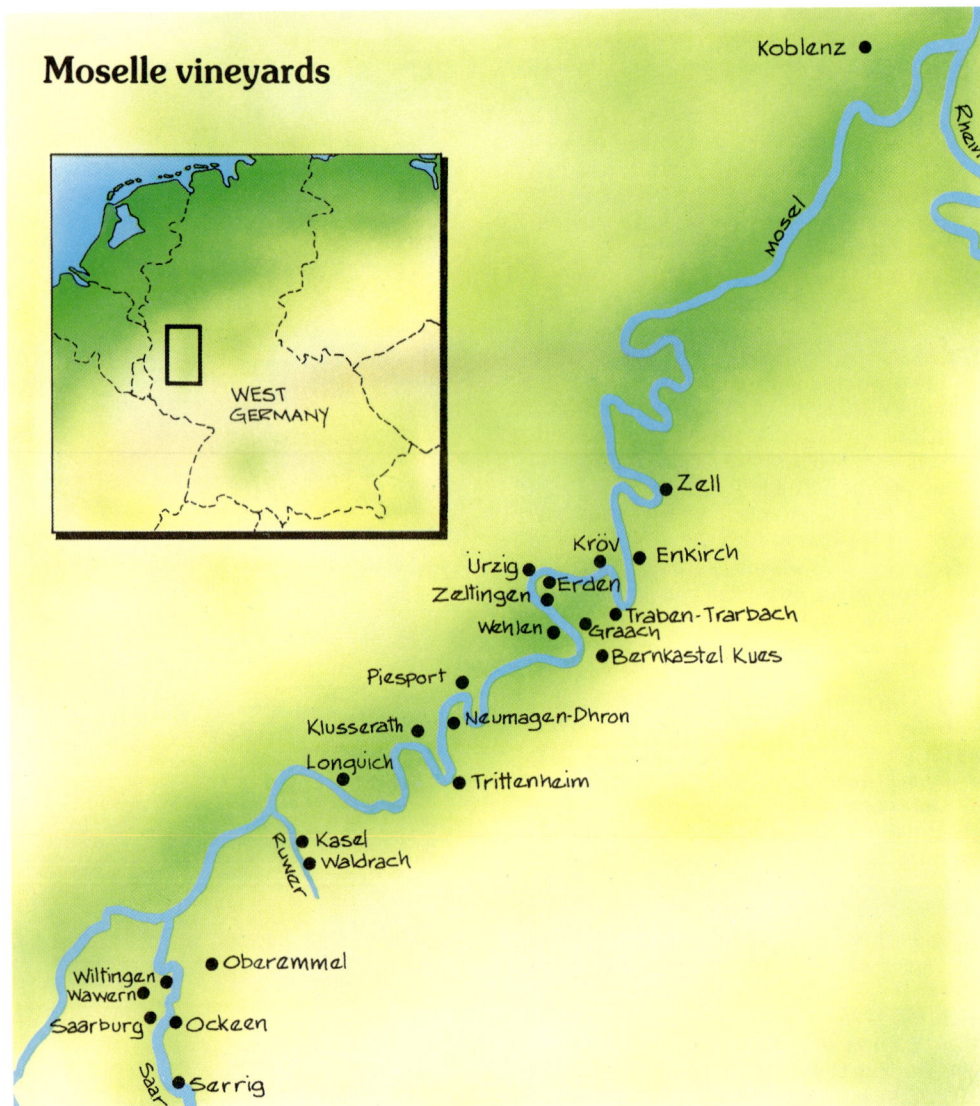

Moselle vineyards

(Map showing: Koblenz, Rhein, Mosel, Zell, Kröv, Enkirch, Ürzig, Erden, Zeltingen, Wehlen, Traben-Trarbach, Graach, Bernkastel Kues, Piesport, Klusserath, Neumagen-Dhron, Longuich, Trittenheim, Ruwer, Kasel, Waldrach, Oberemmel, Wiltingen, Wawern, Saarburg, Ockeen, Serrig, Saar; inset map of WEST GERMANY)

Whether you are new to German wines or already know them well, you can be sure that every bottle of Moselle holds the promise of a delightful discovery. Moselle wines have a fresh aroma, rich with the perfume of grapes, which is combined with a crisp light flavour.

Moselles are instantly recognizable among German wines by their tall and slender green bottles. The main Moselle characteristic of crispness is the result of the combination of grape type and the soil on which it is grown. Riesling vines are planted on the steep, slate-covered slopes that line the valley of the River Mosel.

The Moselle area is of course, included in, and protected by, the precise but complicated German system of wine laws. If you see the word *Mosel* printed alone on a label

it means that the wine is a *Deutsche tafelwein*, a blended German table wine, from the Moselle region. Mosel-Saar-Ruwer on a label signifies a quality wine, a Qualitätswein, from the same region. QbA is the basic quality grade while QmP indicates even better wines. Both QbA and QmP wines need not be expensive and Moselles of this standard are likely to be very pleasant.

Moselblümchen or 'little flowers of the Moselle' is sometimes used on labels to describe tafelwein. Other blended Moselles are sold under proprietary names. Dienhard's Green Label, for example, is an excellent and inexpensive introduction to the charms of Moselle wines. It is widely available and is preferable to the cheaper Qualitätsweins with complicated names.

There are actually over 500 Moselle

vineyards that can be declared on labels, so it may take a while to discover them all! The key to understanding names is that the first word, ending in 'er' is the possessive adjective from a registered village. The second word is the name of the vineyard, which may be a tiny and famous plot or a major collective which means that the wines are blended from a particular area. The important names to look out for are in the central area of the Moselle or in the valleys of its tributaries, the Saar and Ruwer.

The Mosel rises in France and then flows into Germany near Luxembourg. It then flows north-east from Trier to join the Rhine at Koblenz. The river follows a twisting course past towns and villages, with castles topping the hills that slope down to the water. On the south-facing slopes, with sunshine at a maximum, vineyards are planted precariously, often so steeply that ladders have to be laid on the ground to work the vines. The river is best considered divided in two around the town of Trier, where the Romans first began cultivating the vine in Germany. On either side of Trier are the tributaries, the Saar and the Ruwer. Downstream, to the north-east are the Middle and Lower Moselle areas discussed on the following page

Upper Moselle and Saar wines

Wine is made on the French Moselle and in Luxembourg, but none of it offers the splendour of the German product. It is thin, pale and of local interest only. The Upper Moselle in Germany is similar and the wine from here is drunk locally or used in the manufacture of the sparkling wine Sekt.

To the west of Trier are 30 kilometres of the Saar, included in the Mosel-Saar-Ruwer and in good years its wines are reckoned to be the best in Germany. In bad years they can be disappointing. There are seven great Saar villages and a number of famous vineyards, given in brackets: Serrig (Vogelsang), Saarburg (Klosterberg), Ockfen (Herrenberg, Bockstein), Ayl (Herrenberger, Kupp), Wiltingen (Rosenberg, Scharzhofberg), Wawern (Goldberg, Herrenberger) and Oberemmel (Rosenberg). The name given to wine blended from the whole Saar region is Wiltinger Scharzberg, which is confusingly close to the most famous individual vineyard in the area, Wiltinger Scharzhofberg.

Ruwer wines

The Ruwer, to the east of Trier, is more like a stream than a river. Like the Saar it has wines which are good and very popular. The quality is again recognized to be variable depending on whether it is from a good or bad year. The most famous villages and vineyards, given in brackets are: Waldrach (Krone, Muisenberg, Jesuitengarten), Kasel (Herrenberg, Nieschen, Hitzlay) and Mertesdorf (Felslay).

Trier

Several good wines are made around the town of Trier, east of the confluence of the Saar and Moselle. The most famous vineyards here are Thiergarten, Rotlay, Hammerstein and Kupp.

Middle and Lower Moselle

From the narrow, winding, steep-sided river valley of the Middle Moselle come some of the finest and most famous Moselle wines.

Here the river cuts between the Hunsrück and Eiffel mountains and begins its meandering course to the east of the ancient wine town of Trier. The area known as the Middle Moselle ends at the village of Zell. In between Trier and Zell is a valley of incomparable loveliness, centring on the small town of Bernkastel, which is as important to German wine as Bordeaux is to France.

The great wines from the Middle Moselle are exquisite and expensive and should be reserved to enjoy on exceptional occasions. However, there are wines from this area to suit all tastes and from every price level. Many are cheap enough for everyday drinking but still good enough to give great pleasure.

The first stretch of the Middle Moselle consists of a broad valley as far as the town of Klüsserath. Here the vineyards are set well back from the river. The wines are worthwhile but undistinguished. Longuich is the main village and Probstberg is the designated name of the collective. Longuicher Probstberg is a wine you will encounter often but do not expect too much from it.

After Klüsserath, the valley begins to narrow and the slopes overlooking the river, warmed by the sun reflecting back from the river, produce better wines. Klüsserath, Trittenheim and Neumagen-Dhron are the main village names and the collective vineyards enjoy considerable reputations especially in good years. Look out for Klüsserather Bruderschaft, Trittenheimer Apotheke or Altärchen and Neumagen-Dhroner Hofberger.

Next the river takes a long slow bend with steep south-facing slopes above the village of Piesport. This is one of the main centres and wines from here are sought after. Goldtröpfchen, then Falkenberg and Günterslay are the best vineyards. The collective vineyard is Michelsberg, so if you buy a Piesporter Michelsberg, the wine will be from a wide area and will not have the outstanding quality of the great vineyards, although it may be good.

After a sharp bend at Minheim the river flows down to Bernkastel. On the way are Wintrich and Kesten, Brauneberg and Lieser. These villages all make good wine, but it is not in the highest class. These wines are softer than other good Moselles and do not have their unique piquancy.

At the next large bend of the river is the town of Bernkastel-Kues. Here in a single 7 kilometre slope the greatest Moselles of all are produced. Bernkastel-Kues, Graach, Wehlen and Zeltingen-Rachtig are the villages, and all produce fine wines. Bernkastel is the name given to the whole of the Middle Moselle, so Bereich Bernkastel means wine blended from any part of the area. Wine labelled Bernkastler Kurfürstlay signifies wine from the Bernkastel region rather than from a particular famous vineyard. It could be a perfectly acceptable wine but should not be too expensive.

Just above the town of Bernkastel-Kues are the slopes of the most famous Bernkastel vineyards: Doktor and Graben. Other vineyards with good reputations are Johannisbrünnchen, Bratenhöfchen, Mattheisbildchen and Lay. Further downstream are names just as well known: Gracher Domprobst or Himmelreich, Wehlener Sonnenuhr and Zeltingen-Rachtiger Sonnenuhr or Himmelreich. On the opposite bank is the less good but still worthwhile vineyard of Nonnenberg. Gracher Munzlay on a label indicates a cheaper wine from this stretch of the river in general. Beyond Zeltingen the river turns east and another series of south-facing slopes producing good wines begins. These wines are highly recommended as they are less expensive but as good as their Bernkastel counterparts. The villages are Ürzig, Erden, Lösnich, Kinheim and Kröv. The name given to wine from the area is Ürziger Schwarzlay. Beyond here there are good wines from Traben-Trarbach and Enkirch.

Lower Moselle

The Lower Moselle from Zell to the junction with the Rhine at Koblenz, produces wine from vineyards scattered along its whole length. Most are used in the blending of Moselblümchen or other lesser wines of the region and are unlikely to be encountered in named form.

Watch tower at Zell on Lower Moselle

ITALY

Italy is a wonderful hunting ground for the newcomer to wine, since it offers a vast range of different types of wine – from full-bodied reds to sparkling whites. The wines are generally extremely good value for money, making them perfect for the enthusiastic wine drinker who has a limited budget.

Most areas of Italy produce wine. In fact, Italy now produces more wine annually than any other country in the world. Her finest wines are powerful reds, but Italy is also the source of lighter fresh reds and clean young whites. These lighter wines make fine every-day drinking.

The great benefit of drinking Italian wine is that it is still possible to taste widely and compare different wines without spending large amounts of money. Italian wines, except the very finest, remain cheap. This is partly because of their abundance, and the Italians' attitude to wine as a happy drink, to be drunk with food and then forgotten about. It is also partly a legacy of the days when 'Italian wine' all too often did mean coarse, heavy reds from the far south, or tired oxidized white from almost anywhere.

Today, production standards have improved to the extent that almost any bottle of Italian wine will be acceptable. It might possibly be dull, in which case the answer is to move on and try something else next time. But the days of the very rough are past. Yet, luckily for the consumer, Italian producers still cannot command the high prices expected by France, for example.

Unfortunately, the very abundance and variety of Italian wine is also its major drawback for the drinker. Confusion reigns: the grading system is, as yet, much less organized than the neat system that applies in France and the many names that appear on the labels are baffling. As a start to penetrating the jungle, the opposite page explains the DOC grading system and Italian label-language in general.

SWITZERLAND

YUGOSLAVIA

Bardolino
Valpolicella
● Verona
Soave

Asti
●

Barbaresco
Barolo

Lambrusco

Chianti
● Firenze

Verdicchio

Orvieto

● Roma
Frascati

● Napoli

● Palermo
● Marsala

Italian wine labels

Italy is the world's biggest wine producer, turning our some 8 billion bottles of wine a year, varying from tiptop quality down to the everyday blend. There is such a profusion of Italian wine names, labels, producers and styles, that at first the Italian wine buyer can feel baffled when trying to penetrate the jungle. There are however some basic guidelines that are easy to remember, and as always the label provides almost all the clues.

Names

The name of the wine itself is the first pointer to look for when reading the label. Confusingly, an Italian wine may take its name from its geographical home area, from historical tradition or from folklore connected with neither of these. Lacrima Cristi (meaning 'The tears of Christ') is a good example of the latter. Many wines, particularly the best, take their names from their grape variety. Among these are the long-established Italian names like Barbera and Sangiovese, as well as the more familiar European ones like Merlot and Riesling.

Classification

Once past the name, the next most important clue is the classification. In theory, the best ten percent or so of Italian wines are 'DOC': in other words, bear the official quality guarantee *Denominazione di Origine Controllata*. This is roughly equivalent to the French *Appellation Contrôlée* system. Unfortunately the theory is more clear-cut than the reality. The 200 or so DOC zones produce just over 450 types of wine, amongst which are some indifferent ones. So although the letters DOC appear on the label, the wine may still be disappointing.

At the same time, a handful of Italy's very best wines go to market with only the words *vino da tavola* (the lowest official category) on the label. This may be because, as a result of a production technicality, they do not qualify for the local DOC. Alternatively, the producers may simply have decided not to participate in the system. Some of these fine wines – for example Sassicaia and Tignanello – stand on their reputation alone and need no other classifying. They are recognizable by the price they command. Others, less well known, are cheaper and can be excellent bargains.

It is difficult to give specific examples, but it is worth remembering that DOC and *vino da tavola* are indications of quality, not infallible guidelines. You may encounter some *vini da tavola* with a geographical label tacked on too, and these tend to be of higher quality than the basic wine.

DOCG (*Denominazione di Origine Controllata e Garantita*) has now been introduced for a limited selection of the best wines, including Vino Nobile di Montepulciano, Barolo, Barbaresco, Brunello di Montalcino, and – most recently – Chianti. *Vino tipici* is being introduced for table wine. Both new categories are not fully operational. Standards are, however, rising all the time, as the big co-op wineries (watch for *Cantine Sociale* on the label) and large-scale private organizations take over from individual producers.

Vintage

Yet another factor to be considered is the vintage date – the *vendemmia*. It is difficult to be specific when discussing such a variety of wines, but if you follow the golden rule of choosing the 'youngest white and oldest red' available – with the notable exception of the light reds such as Valpolicella and Bardolino – you should not go far wrong.

Some fine red wines may be labelled *vecchio*, *riserva*, *riserva speciale* or *stravecchio*. These terms are legally controlled and relate to specific lengths of time that the wine has been aged in barrel.

Other terms

Superiore is another frequently-met term which appears on the label. It means that the wine conforms to certain production methods and standards, has a higher alcohol level and has been aged for a required amount of time.

If a wine is described as *classico* this means that it comes from the central, and so usually best, area of that particular wine region. Chianti Classico is an example. The terms *superiore* and *classico* are generally a reliable mark of quality.

Many bottles of Italian wine also carry an exuberant profusion of colourful information, pictures and extraneous decoration. All this is fun but is more an indication of the producer's enthusiasm than his wine-making skills. Take everything but the legally-defined terms with a pinch of salt. Remember too that *Imbottigliato . . . all'origine* means bottled by the producer, and *. . . nella zona di produzione* means that the wine was not estate bottled.

Quick wine terms guide

Bianco: white
Rosso: red
Rosato: pink
Spumante: sparkling
Secco: very dry
Asciutto: dry
Amaro: bitter
Abboccato: semi-sweet
Amabile: sweeter than *abboccato*
Dolce: sweet
Liquoroso: strong, and usually very sweet
Gradi: degrees of alcohol

From the left, good-quality chianti, straight DOC and vino tavola labels

Chianti

Chianti appears the most Italian of Italian red wines. The familiar straw-covered flask is a symbol of Italy in 'Italian' resturants all over the world and one sip of a fresh young Chianti instantly brings back the memory of Florence for anyone who has ever visited the city.

The changing face of Chianti

Surprisingly, Chianti's image is changing fast, and the present time is one of the most interesting in the wine's long history. Almost all the changes are for the better, but they do mean that the 'traditional' Chianti is fast being left behind. To begin with, the evocative, straw-covered bottle is becoming less and less common. It is labour-intensive and costly to make, and some producers, anxious not to seem too traditional and with an eye to the up-market appeal of Bordeaux, have opted for a high-shouldered claret-style bottle.

Modern technological advances throughout the process mean that the wine is more reliable and there is less chance of buying a bad bottle. The introduction of the DOCG system has improved the quality too, since it ensures that wine labelled Chianti actually comes from Chianti country. In the past, Chianti producers have taken advantage of the rule that allows them to add up to 15% of grapes from outside the region to add a strengthening dose of heavy southern wine.

This often resulted in a sweetish and rather dull brew, but it was thought to be what the customer wanted. However, the practice is less common now and the correction is made with good-quality grapes that do not detract from the characteristic vigorous Chianti flavour.

How Chianti is made

The main Chianti grape is the red Sangiovese, but it may be softened by the addition of 25% of other grapes, including some white. The exact blend is up to the individual winemaker. This flexibility in the make-up means that different Chiantis can be surprisingly varied in style. As a mark of this, the colour can vary from a light, bright ruby-red to a rich deep crimson.

Wine making methods can be very different too. To make a broad generalization, there are two main types. One group is fresh and fruity, rather in the style of a young beaujolais. These wines often have a slight refreshing 'prickle' that is the result of a secondary fermentation known as *governo*.

The other type is barrel-aged wines. These are not usually subjected to *governo*, are distinctly perfumed, powerful and subtle. The wines marked *riserva* have been aged for at least three years in oak barrels while those marked *vecchio* have been aged for at least two years. The best of them benefit from further ageing in bottle, and a ten-year-old Riserva can be a very fine wine indeed.

Again the style of wine that is made is the choice of the producer. Happily, many of them make both kinds.

Types of Chianti

Perhaps the best-known name in the area is Chianti Classico, the senior Chianti from the heart of the beautiful Chianti countryside. The black cockerel on the neck label is the trademark of the 700 members of the Chianti Classico consortium and is one of the most reliable guarantees of quality in the area. Classico Riserva must reach at least 12.5% of alcohol as against the 12% of Chianti Riserva from outside the central region.

It is important to remember, however, that Classico is not necessarily superior to every other Chianti. Chianti Putto is the mark of another giant consortium of growers from outside the central Classico zone. It is recognizable by the pink and white cherub on the neck label. The wine is often of high quality, and the growers have wisely set themselves the same standards as those of the Classico consortium. Other reputable growers choose not to belong to the consortia at all, yet still produce admirable, individual wines. Encircling the Classico zone are six other Chianti regions, together making up the biggest DOC group in Italy. The names to look out for are Montalbano, Colli Fiorentini, Colli Aretini, Colli Senesi, Colline Pisane and Rufina. Rufina is the smallest of the six, but it makes some of the finest wines; Marchesi de' Frescobaldi and Spalletti are the most important names here to remember.

Vintage

In vintage terms, ordinary Chiantis are cheerful, straightforward wines made for drinking young in much the same way as beaujolais. The wines you are most likely to encounter in wine shops will probably be two or three years old and this is quite mature enough. Riserva, of course, has already been aged in oak and a reputable wine of this category deserves a little longer in bottle.

Drinking Chianti

Chianti makes an excellent partner with all kinds of not-too-elaborate food. It is a suitable choice for any meal that requires a vigorous red. Whatever you eat with it, do not treat Chianti with too much ceremony unless it is a very aged and special one. It is basically a reliable red-wine standby that is cheap enough to experiment with, but is still varied enough to be interesting and rewarding.

A familiar Italian sight – Chianti in a straw-covered flask

North-West Italy

North-west Italy is best known for its powerful red wines that are the perfect partners for rich meat dishes. Piedmont is the largest wine region; apart from producing the best reds, it is also the home of the famous, sparkling white Asti Spumante.

Barolo and Barbaresco

As a region, Piedmont has more DOC and DOCG zones (thirty six in all) than any other in Italy. The noble wines of this prosperous corner of Italy are the twin reds Barolo and Barbaresco. At their best, these are complex wines that are fine enough to hold their own with the big names of Bordeaux, Burgundy or anywhere else.

The acknowledged prince is Barolo, although it is admittedly a difficult wine for the beginner, with its high level of alcohol and tannin bite. Made from the intense purplish Nebbiolo grape, Barolo is said, variously, to have the flavour of truffles, violets, raspberries and even tar. Whatever taste seems appropriate to the individual judgement, there is no doubt that wine of this strength may need as much as ten years ageing to make it sufficiently mellow and inviting. A good Barolo is an unforgettable wine and the Piedmontese are justly proud of it. It is not for everyday drinking however.

Barbaresco, Barolo's peer, is also made from the Nebbiolo grape under very similar conditions, but it is a subtly different wine. It has a lower minimum alcoholic content – 12.5% against 13% – and under DOC rules it requires a year's less ageing in barrel. The real effect of these differences is to make a wine that is smoother and more delicate than the intense Barolo. It is an easier introduction to the great Piedmontese reds.

The finest Barolos and Barbarescos are by no means cheap, but fortunately they do not command anything like the dizzy prices of a tiptop claret or burgundy. Both Barolo and Barbaresco should be brought gently to room temperature before serving. The cork should be removed at least a couple of hours beforehand too and the wine may even need to be decanted gently.

Other red wines

Sometimes, perhaps because of overproduction or failure to meet the minimum alcoholic levels, wine from the classic regions of Barolo and Barbaresco does not qualify for the big names on the label. In this case it goes on sale as *Nebbiolo vino da tavola*. This is often good-value drinking if you can find it. Some progressive wine-makers have been experimenting recently with Nebbiolo as a young wine, rather in the Beaujolais style. This known as *da pronta beva*. Interestingly, the result can be a refreshing fruity red that makes palatable drinking as little as a few months after the harvest.

In contrast to Barolo and Barbaresco, the everyday drinking wine for the Piedmontese is Barbera, named after the widely planted grape variety. When it is coupled with a place name, as in Barbera d'Asti, it implies a limited production area and, probably, superior quality. The trend now is to make Barbera dry, light and fresh, definitely for drinking young. Yet, typically for Italy, the wine can still vary dramatically according to the area and the wine-maker responsible. Since Barbera is widely available and cheap, the best way of testing it is to sample a range of bottles.

Another red that may be encountered from this north-western corner is Dolcetto, not a sweet wine despite its name, but a dry red wine with a touch of bitterness. Carema is another wine to watch out for. This is a softer version of Barolo, from the Valle d'Aosta at the fringe of the Alps. The Nebbiolo grape (confusingly also called Spanna locally) also makes easier wines from the north-east of Barolo heartland under the names of Gattinara and Ghemme. Any of these wines are well worth tasting if you come across them.

Harvesting grapes in Piedmont

The white wines

The white wines of the north-west are far less numerous, but they include one of Italy's most famous wines, Asti Spumante – literally meaning foaming wine of Asti. In the past, Asti has been regarded as a sweet budget alternative to champagne, but this is not justified now. To begin with, it is no longer particularly cheap. Although it is not usually made by the classic *méthode champenoise*, its successful production still calls for expensive technology and a great deal of care to preserve the elusive quality of the Moscato bianco grape. Secondly, the almost universal demand for drier wines has meant that its makers have turned their attention to creating a more elegant, fresh wine with a sweet tinge. This is often a less demanding drink than a heavyweight champagne. For these reasons Asti should be regarded as a pleasing sparkling wine in its own right.

The interest in drier sparkling wines has led to the production of other spumantes, made from the Pinot and various other grapes. For some reason, these are more widely exported than drunk in Italy itself.

Asti and its relatives apart, there are few notable wines from the area. Three names that just might be encountered though are Cortese di Gavi and Erbaluce di Caluso from Piedmont and Cinqueterre from Liguria (a region which is more familiarly known as the Italian Riviera).

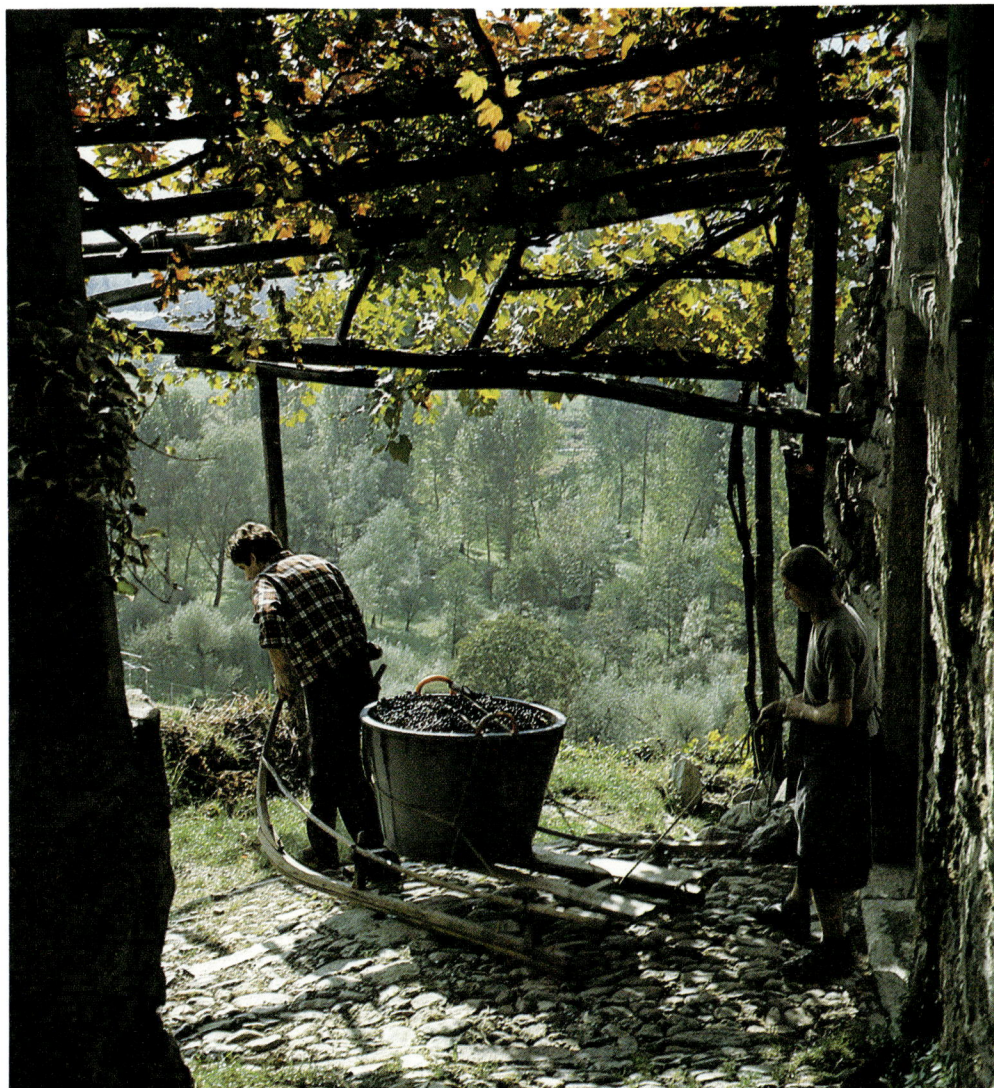

North-East Italy

The north-eastern corner of Italy follows a pattern that is familiar throughout Italy – it produces a huge volume of wine of all degrees of quality. In fact , many of Italy's best known wines, such as Soave, Bardolino and Valpolicella are from this area.

Sorting grapes in the north-eastern region of Italy

The Veneto

The Veneto region stretches from the shores of Lake Garda eastwards in a wide arc to Venice and beyond. It produces good, abundant wines at accessible prices. Among them are three of Italy's most famous wines – Soave, Bardolino and Valpolicella.

Soave, from the hills around Verona, is the archetypal Italian white. The slim green bottle is a familiar sight on the shelves of many wine merchants and it remains popular for its reliability and low price. If Soave is drunk young enough – anything more than two years old is too old – it is almost always fresh and crisp with a pleasing hint of almonds. The worst criticism that could be made of Soave is that it can be a shade characterless.

Another local big name is Bardolino, which is mainly red although some rosé is produced too. It is made from a combination of different grapes and is another uncomplicated wine to be drunk young. Serve it cool, too. Cellar temperature is best, and most flattering to the hint of bitterness that is characteristic of the wine. *Superiore* means that the wine is aged longer

and has a higher alcoholic strength, and consequent depth, but *classico* is not necessarily any better than straight Bardolino.

The third famous name is Valpolicella. The grape combination is the same as Bardolino's, and it is still a light, fresh wine. However, Valpolicella tends to have more colour, depth and taste, particularly the *superiore*. Some producers also make Recioto della Valpolicella, a strong sweetish wine which may have some sparkle. Another type is Recioto Amarone della Valpolicella in which all the sugar in specially selected grapes is fermented into alcohol. The resulting dry, powerful wine may have up to 16% of alcohol, but it is surprisingly easy to drink when compared with the other big Italian reds, such as Barolo.

Two white wines that make a change from Soave are Gambellara and Bianco di Custoza. Other wines from the Veneto region may be named after their more familiar-sounding grape variety. Merlot is the most widely planted, but Cabernet,

Pinot Bianco, Sauvignon and Chardonnay Riesling also hold their own.

Friuli-Venezia Giulia

Positioned right up in the north-eastern corner of Italy, bounded by Austria and Yugoslavia, this region has begun to be of interest only recently to Italian wine exporters. Now, however, it is gaining a reputation for interesting and reliable varietal wines. It is refreshing too, amid the confusion of Italian wine designations, to find six well-defined geographical DOC zones. Collio, Colli, Orientale del Friuli and grave del Friuli are the best-known zones.

From Collio come the wines labelled by the grape variety Cabernet, Merlot, Pinot Bianco and Sauvignon, and Tocai (no relation to the Hungarian Tokay). Colli Orientale has its varietals too, but its first claim to fame is Picolit. Picolit is a fine dessert wine sometimes (unhelpfully) described as Italy's Château d'Yquem. The most popular grape choice for the growers of Grave is Merlot, which makes soft red wines that are perfect for drinking young under undemanding conditions.

Wine from any of these DOC zones, or the neighbouring Isonzo, Aquilea and Latisana, are likely to have been carefully chosen for export. They often provide rewarding and interesting drinking at close to bargain prices.

Trentino-Alto Adige

The northern position of another region, Trentino-Alto Adige, is reflected in the German names on the wine labels. Even the region itself has the alternative name of the Süd Tirol. Confusion is increased, for the wine buyer, by the fact that the same wines may be labelled in either Italian or German, according to the maker's choice. One of the best known local products, for example, is a widely exported fruity red that may appear as Kalteresee or Lago di Caldaro.

More interesting is Santa Maddalena, once ranked by Mussolini as one of the top three Italian reds. The wine's popularity declined with its admirer's, and while it is not in the same class as the big Piedmont reds, it is a fragrant and supple wine that is frequently undervalued.

White wines make up only a quarter of the Alto Adige output, and those that do appear are most likely to have German names like Sylvaner or Weissburgunder.

Emilia Romagna

From the vineyards of the flatlands around the river Po come huge amounts of wine, much of it low grade for blending, vinegar making and industrial use. True to Italian form, some good wine is made, but Emilia Romagna is best known for one of America's favourite wines, Lambrusco. This purplish red wine froths up in surprising pink bubbles when it is poured: it is sparkling and usually sweet to taste. The Italians themselves belittle it as a wine for non-wine drinkers, and it is true to say that it is a wine that is either liked or immediately disliked. Yet a well made Lambrusco, in one of its drier versions, is a partner with a difference for robust and uncomplicated meat dishes.

Central and Southern Italy

In the area that stretches from Florence down to the toe of Italy, the dominant wines are white – Orvieto, Verdiccho and Frascati are perhaps the most famous names. There are red wines of course, among which are some of Italy's finest wines – Chianti is the best known.

White wines

Orvieto is the most famous wine of Umbria. Classically, this is a smooth, rich wine, golden in colour with a fragrant delicacy that offsets the natural semi-sweetness. Because of this lightness, Orvieto is not a dessert wine, even in the old *abboccato* versions that are slowly being replaced by the more fashionable *secco*. The dry wine the producers prefer to sell nowadays is crisper and paler than the old country wine. It is still perfectly palatable, but less interesting than it once was. However, whether it is secco or abboccato, Orvieto should be drunk young to make the most of its freshness.

Verdicchio is another famous white wine with a long history. It is produced in the region of the Marches, on the Adriatic coast of central Italy. The wine is easily recognizable by the shape of the bottle, a tall vase reminiscent of the two-handled vessel of classical times – it is claimed that the ancient Etruscans enjoyed the delicate Verdicchio

The terraced slopes of Umbria – the region that produces the famous Orvieto

wines. Whatever its illustrious history, this light wine is now a reliable accompaniment to fish or poultry. Many producers do not state the vintage date on the label, and this is because Verdicchio is at its best a year, or at most two years, after the harvest. For this reason you should distrust cobwebby bottles from suppliers who might not have a high turnover of stock.

Frascati, another deservedly popular wine, comes from Rome and its country environs. DOC regulations have brought the end of an era when any flask of cheap white wine from somewhere around Rome could call itself Frascati. Now anything labelled as such is likely to be a pleasantly reliable, golden white wine with a strong taste of the whole grape. The extra grapy flavour is achieved by keeping the must (the grape pulp in the process of fermentation) in contact with the skins, and is distinctive among Italian whites. Frascati is usually dry now, labelled either *asciutto* or *secco,* but it may also be found in softer, sweeter styles called *amabile* or *cannellino* (the latter is the sweetest). Frascati *superiore* has a higher level of alcohol. Thanks to heavy investment in new vines and equipment by both large and small-scale producers, this wine is remarkably consistent in quality. Frascati is definitely a wine for drinking young – six months is fine, but two years old is the maximum.

Est! Est! Est! from Lake Bolsena, to the north of Rome, is yet another famous white, as renowned for its name as for its taste. Legend has it that a bishop sent his servant ahead to mark the doors of inns serving good wine with the word *Est!*. When he stopped at an inn in Montifiascone, he was so impressed with the wine that he wrote *Est!* three times on the door. It is a soft white wine in the Orvieto style, once lush and golden but now, like its more impressive neighbour, fashionably drier and paler.

Other white wines: These household names apart, central Italy makes numerous other reliable white wines, usually from the Trebbiano grape. Trebbiano di Romagna is excellent value, and other name to look out for is Montecarlo, a splendid Tuscan white that is well balanced between dry and fruity. Contrary to the usual rule, it can stand several years' ageing.

Vernaccia di San Gimignano is a highly-flavoured white that is supposed to have been Michaelangelo's favourite. It makes an unusual aperitif, or a partner for more robust fish dishes.

From the area around Mount Vesuvius comes the famous Lachryma Christi (meaning the tears of Christ). Most of it is an acceptable white wine; the best is dry.

Do not confuse Vernaccia di San Gimignano with Vernaccia di Oristano from Sardinia: Sardinian wines in general are a little too heavy and alcoholic, and sometimes too sweet, to appeal widely, but the Vernaccia has a sherry-like taste that is both unusual and interesting; the *superiore* has a hefty 15.5% of alcohol. Nuragus is another interesting Sardinian wine, lighter and more acid than most Sardinian wines.

Red wines

Chianti apart, there are some excellent red wines from the central region. There is the legendary Brunello di Montalcino from Siena, a long-lived red made from the Sangiovese grape. This wine commands prices as rarefied as any first-growth claret. Sassicaia is an unusual and excellent wine made from 100% Cabernet Sauvignon, and Tignanello is in the Chianti mould, but with more body, flavour and staying-power. These are all connoisseurs' wines. It is worth remembering their names, but for ordinary drinking Sangiovese di Romagna, from the most widely cultivated red grape of the region, is often a rewarding buy. The wine improves with age, so opt for the oldest bottle, within reason. Rosso Conero and Rosso Piceno are two more reds, also from the Adriatic coast, that are worth a try if encountered.

The wines from the far south tend to be strong and alcoholic, intended for local consumption. Some however are used for blending. One of the most interesting reds from this area is Aglianico del Vulture. Ravello Rosso is another red wine from the south worth watching out for.

SPAIN

Wine is very much a feature of everyday life in Spain, where it is looked on in the same way as the English look on their pint of beer – it is an agreeable way of quenching thirst, not a sophisticated experience.

Although Spain has the largest area under vines of any country in Europe, most of its produce goes into the making of ordinary table wine, *vino corriente*, the Spanish equivalent of *vin ordinaire*. The climate and the unsophisticated, easy-going drinking habits of the Spanish are the two main reasons for the high proportion of ordinary table wine.

The heat of the summer sun, especially in the south of Spain, produces grapes with very high levels of sugar. This ferments out to give wines which are strong in alcohol – sometimes up to 18% – but which are very unsubtle in taste.

This does not mean that Spanish wines of quality do not exist, though with the exception of sherry and Rioja they are not well-known outside Spain. In recent years Spanish authorities have taken determined steps to correct the impression that their country's produce is only fit for bulk export or blending. The *Estatuto de la Vina, del Vino y de los Alcoholes*, a Government Statute of 1970, laid down a strict code of practice for all connected with wine production and distribution. In the Statute, 18 limited areas entitled to a *Denominacion de Origen* (similar to the French A.C. and Italian D.O.C.) were defined and a network of local authorities – *Cosejos Reguladores* were set up to enforce standards within these areas.

Northern Spain

Penedés, a wine region on the north-east coast not far from Barcelona, seems most likely to follow the success of Rioja. In particular, the wines of Torres of Villafranca have been available outside Spain, and have a deserved reputation for honesty and good quality.

The wine which has brought them most prestige is the 1970 Gran Coronas Black Label, a fine red which at a grand wine-tasting occasion in Paris was judged superior to the 1970 Chateau Latour, a first-growth Claret from the Medoc – and at less than a fifth of the price!

At a less rarefied level, Torres of Villafranca market a number of sound red wines of varying fullness and alcoholic strength under such names as Tres Torres, Coronas and Sangre de Toro. They also produce white wines which are unusually fresh and dry by Spanish standards – their Vina Sol is particularly good value. Miguel Torres is a very skilful winemaker and in addition to the established Spanish growths he has introduced and acclimatized vines from France and Germany, to give wines a wide variety of flavours.

Penedés is also the centre of production of Spanish sparkling wine. It is forbidden by law to call this wine champagne, but that is what it is in all but name. The best of the *espumosos*, as they are called, are made by the *méthode champenoise*, which involves a second fermentation in the bottle and is a lengthy and labour intensive business. These wines are made from white grapes, chiefly Sumoll, and are similar to a French *blanc de blanc*. The quality is high, though unless you share the Spanish preference for sweetness, it is best to look for the bottles marked *bruto* or *seco*. The most famous wineries are Cordoniu and Freixenet.

Still in the North of Spain, but well to the West in the upper valley of the river Douro, is the estate which produces one of Spain's most remarkable and expensive red wines. It is called Vega Sicilia. The wine comes from the fruit of the native Spanish and acclimatized French vines. Like Rioja, it is made by traditional Bordeaux methods involving lengthy fermentation in oak barrels. A lesser but still excellent wine from the same estate, bottled after a shorter maturation period, is called Valbuena. Unfortunately, very little of each is produced and they are almost unobtainable outside Spain.

Other northern Spanish wines of quality are the reds from Navarre and both reds and whites from Galicia in the north-west. The Navarre wines, as might be expected, are rather similar to the fuller-bodied Riojas. Galicia produces some pleasant reds from Valdeorras and light, slightly pétillant (a faint fizz) reds and whites in the style of the Vinhos Verdes of Northern Portugal. Some very good still white wines are also made from the Albarino grape – tradition has it that the vines were brought from Germany many hundreds of years ago. The wines have been compared to Moselle in their delicacy and pronounced bouquet.

Central and Southern Spain

Across the great plateau of Central Spain to the wine-growing areas of the south, we are more definitely in 'bulk wine' country. La Mancha and Valdepeñas, and regions to the east as far as Valencia and the Levante, produce more wine than any other part of Spain and a good deal of it is exported. In earlier days, when the English had a taste for fortifying the light red wines of Bordeaux with something stronger, this area frequently supplied the necessary ingredient. Today, it appears under brand names in stores and supermarkets, and many people have probably drunk it at one time without being aware of its origins.

In the far south, the region around Malaga produces a sweet, fortified wine made mainly from the Pedro Ximenes grape. More interesting is the wine from the small region of Montilla-Moriles in Andalucia. The area has always lived in the shadow of Jerez, which has traditionally bought much of its produce for blending. Wines sold under the name of Montilla can be found, ranging like sherry from pale, delicate finos to full-bodied olorosos. Unlike sherry, they are never fortified but the method of production is quite similar and they are good value.

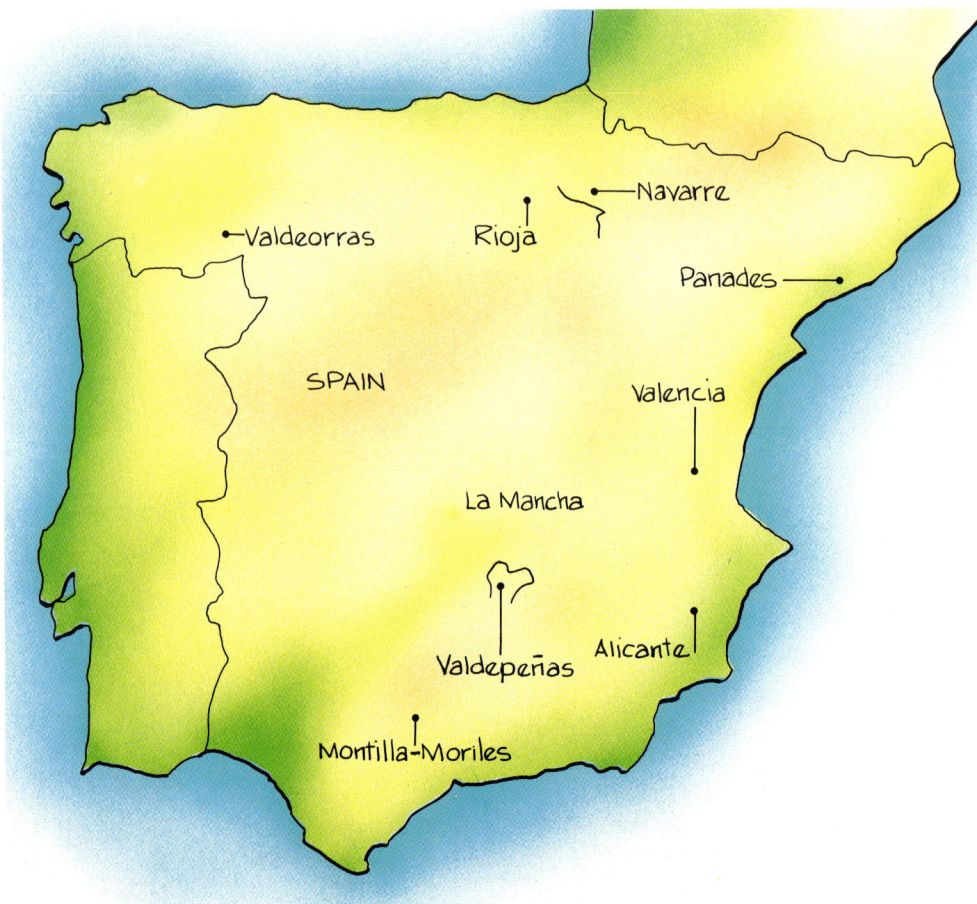

Rioja

Rioja is probably the best-known wine region of Spain – and a really good red Rioja compares very well with chateau-bottled claret – at half the price!

Two excellent examples of Rioja – white Rioja is less common than red.

Until recently, Spain was quite unfairly represented by just about the worst it had to offer – inky reds of doubtful parentage and imitation French whites such as 'Spanish Sauternes' or 'Spanish Chablis'. Unfortunately there is still some of this about, but Spain not only produces a lot of wine – the area under vines is, in fact, the largest in Europe – but a lot of very good wine too. As usual, the label is your best guide, so it pays to know a little about the names of regions and shippers.

The name Rioja is an abbreviation of Rio Oja, a tributary of the river Ebro, but the Rioja district extends along both banks of the main river for a stretch of almost 100 kilometres. It is where the wild mountainous country of the North meets the great plateau of central Spain, on the borders of Navarre and Castile.

The wines of Rioja have been praised in Spain for centuries, but it is only within the last hundred years that they have found a wider reputation. At the end of the last century the vineyards of France were attacked by a pest called phylloxera which for a time threatened the whole future of wine production. Many growers from Bordeaux, in search of new vineyards, travelled south and settled in Rioja where they added their own knowledge and techniques to native wine-making methods. As a result, Rioja wines are still being made today following the former Bordeaux methods with a lengthy period of ageing in oak which gives the red wines in particular a very distinctive bouquet and taste.

The French settlers found the area itself very different from home. The North and West, the Rioja Alta and Rioja Alavesa, are regions of upland valleys with plentiful winter rains and, sometimes, snow and frost as well. As the Ebro descends eastwards into the Rioja Baja, the country becomes more arid and summers can be fiercely hot. The vines too are different from the French vines, not only in variety but in the way they are grown. They are not trained on wires in ordered rows or hedges, as in France, but grow as individual bushes, sometimes alternating with other crops, sometimes covering whole hillsides. Nor are the wines named after individual vineyards. Instead the entire produce of the region is sold to the proprietors of the great wineries, or bodegas, who create blended wines with their own distinct character. These are then marketed under brand names.

Red Rioja

Most of the bodegas are to be found in Rioja Alta, in the stretch of country between the traditional wine centre of Haro and the provincial capital of Logrono 40 kilometres down river. This is also the area which produces the best crops of grapes, despite the more mountainous terrain and the more uncertain climate. Wines often give the best results when they have to fight a little against the climate.

Mediterranean countries can produce rather fat, bland-tasting wines, high in alcohol but lacking acidity, which would give them balance and interest. The red wines of Rioja Baja tend to be like this – very full-bodied with an alcoholic strength of 14–16% and a rich, rather sweet taste. The reds of Rioja Alta on the other hand are lighter, both in colour and body, have an alcoholic strength of 10.5–12%, and greater delicacy of bouquet and flavour.

The grapes grown in this region for the production of red wine are the Tempranillo, the Graciano, the Mazuelo and the Garnacho, which has a relation in the Grenache of Southern France. No wine made from one type alone would be satisfactory, so the Riojas we drink are the result of skilful blending in the bodegas, with Tempranillo being the dominant grape.

Red Riojas respond well to ageing. Most are given a minimum of 2 years in oak casks, whose size is limited to 225 litres so that there is satisfactory contact of the wine with the wood. This gives Riojas their characteristic 'oaky' nose and smooth texture. Wines from particularly good vintages are known as Reserva or Gran Reserva wines and are set aside for longer ageing of up to 8 years in cask. They will then spend perhaps an equally long period in the bottle before being ready to drink. At the end of this time they have the distinction of fine claret at less than half the price. There is no doubt that for a non-wine producing country like the U.K., Rioja currently represents one of the best wine bargains. Though as exports increased fifteenfold in the 1970s, it seems only a matter of time before demand exceeds supply, with the inevitable effect on prices.

Since around 40 different bodegas are now shipping wines abroad there is plenty of scope for shopping around to discover a favourite brand. Among the more widely available wines are the Banda Azul and Vina Vial of Federico Paternina, who also have Gran Reserva at an appropriately higher price. Marques de Riscal and Marques de Murrieta are other respected names. Bottles from the Marques de Riscal are usually covered in wire mesh (supposedly an extra insurance against illegal tampering with the wine). The finest old wines from the Marques de Murrieta are marketed as Castillo Ygay. There are also excellent wines to be found from the Bodegas Bilbainas, Berberana, Olarra and Domecq.

White Rioja

White wines are also made in more limited quantities in Rioja from the Malvasia and Viura grapes; the traditional methods, again involving ageing in oak, produce a mellow wine of 10–12% alcohol, but the flavour is not so popular abroad as it is in Spain. Most bodegas are now concentrating on the production of a fresher, lighter wine which has spent little or not time in wood; Paternina's Banda Dorada and the dry wines from Marques de Caceras and Olarra are good examples of White Rioja.

THE REST OF EUROPE

The wines of France and Germany, and more recently Italy and Spain, are known the world over. But wines from the rest of Europe are only just becoming familiar. Many countries offer reasonably-priced, good quality wines to the consumer – what they lack are enterprising merchants to bring them to our attention.

now widely available abroad. Bulgaria also produces good Chardonnay, not as distinguished as the great white wines of Burgundy which are also made from it, though they are recognisably of the same breed. One grape about which you need to take a little more care is Riesling; this produces marvellous wines in Germany and Alsace, but Eastern Europe Rieslings are usually made from a related but inferior strain, the

The blue-black grapes of the Cabernet Sauvignon promise rich red wine; the green Riesling grape of a light white.

Welsch or Laski Riesling, which is pleasant but unexciting.

Another way in which unfamiliar wines can gain notice is by competitive pricing. The Bulgarian wines have this to recommend them too, and so do those from Yugoslavia, Roumania (when you can find them) and especially Portugal. Their vinhos verdes, which although called green are actually red or white, are refreshing and increasingly popular, and the reds such as Dão, many of them well aged before they appear in the shops, can be very good value. The dessert Muscat from Setubal is also worth trying.

We must not forget that England too is now a wine-grower. There are a large number of commercial vineyards scattered about the country, and many of them welcome visitors, so what better way of increasing your wine knowledge than a trip to your very own local producer?

There are a number of reasons why the rich wine country of the rest of Europe has gone unappreciated for so long. Traditional methods have favoured small-scale production with few quality controls. People in countries where the grapes are grown tend to be eager drinkers of their own product, which leaves less for export, and it is not easy to sell strange names to a conservative market. Wine-drinking in England, for instance, is a comparatively new habit and people who have only just acquainted themselves with Pinot Grigio may be resistant to

the charms of Szurkebarat, though it is in fact the same grape.

A little knowledge of grape types can help greatly to guide you through unfamiliar wine territory, as many countries sell varietal wines, named after the grape variety rather than the region of origin, and although there will be subtle differences in flavour from place to place the basic character should remain the same. For example, Cabernet Sauvignon, the grape which is the basis of much fine claret, makes a full, dry blackcurrant wine in Bulgaria which is

Portugal

The abundant vineyards of Portugal, which cover much of the country's finest agricultural landscape, produce a variety of wines to suit every palate. They range from the frisky, slightly sparkling Vinho Verde of the north, to the voluptuous moscatels of the south. There are many styles of red wine too and of course Portugal is the home of the world famous rosé, Mateus.

Vinho Verde

As an aperitif, party drink or accompaniment to a summer buffet meal, Vinho Verde is incomparable. It comes from the Minho, the largest of all the country's wine regions, which extends from the northern frontier with Spain and spreads out beyond Oporto. The name literally means 'green wine' – it does not refer to the colour, which is usually almost platinum blonde, but indicates its youthful freshness. Nobody ever drinks a 'mature' Vinho Verde.

Vinho Verde is grown in an area where the vines climb along trellises, on pergolas and up branches of trees. It must be one of the few places in the wine world where grape pickers can be seen climbing trees to reach some of the grapes.

Although Vinho Verde is a delightfully frivolous wine, it is also one of a restricted number from Portugal which receive the EEC classification VQPRD (which means a quality wine from a designated region). It is now widely exported. If you prefer very dry wines, the Verdes which should appeal are those of 'classic' style. These are usually most popular in Portugal and are drunk with rich and spicy food. One of these is the delicious fruity Gatão: others to note are the very brisk and dry Casalinho and the deeper golden Alvarinho, which comes from the extreme north of the Minho. Look, too, for the more delicate, fruity Verdegar and the not so dry Ribalonga. Aveleda is another name to remember – this is medium dry, and very light on the palate.

On Portuguese wine lists tourists are often baffled to find 'Vinho Verde Tinto' – how can green wine be red, they may well ask! In fact it is a glorious light crimson, slightly sparkling like the white, with an astringency which comes as a shock at the first sip! It is a taste which can be acquired, for it goes very well with highly spiced meat dishes or even curry.

Dão wines

No contrast could be greater than that between Vinho Verde and the glowing rich reds for which the mountainous region of the Dão in the north has become famous. These, at their best, can fairly be compared with wines from the Rioja in Spain and from the Côtes du Rhone in France. The vines, which also produce good white grapes, flourish in rocky, granite-studded soil and produce wines of great stamina and character. When very young, they can be rough, but vastly improved methods of vinification and patient maturing tame their harshness. Among those to look for is the smooth, fairly light and dry Grão Vasco, the white version of which is golden, smooth and not aggressively dry.

Others to note are Terras Altas – the red is deep ruby and rather earthy, while the white is silky, golden and dry; Dão Ribalonga red is softer and lighter in colour; and Cavas Velhas red is subtle and long maturing. The Cavas Velhas white is dry, greeny gold and rather 'steely' – a characteristic of many white wines of this region. The 'steely' quality of the whites makes them particularly suitable to serve with all kinds of fish, while the reds go best with roast meat. Like the Vinho Verde, Dão is one of the larger demarcated regions in Portugal.

Douro

Although the Douro region in the north is best known as the home of port, its vineyards in the mountains and the foothills also produce good, generally full-bodied, red wines. It is also the home of the famous Mateus Rosé. This medium-dry, slightly sparkling pink wine is most popular as a versatile companion for many different kinds of food or as an attractive aperitif.

Another famous medium-sweet rosé is Lancers. This is made by the venerable house of Fonseca, whose original cellars date back to 1834. They are also producers of the rich and luscious golden Moscatel of Setubal. This wine's fame goes back many centuries. It was one of those beloved by Louis XIV of France, who served it regularly at state banquets. It is made in an unusual way – after the grapes are picked, they are pressed very quickly and the fermentation is halted by the addition of brandy. Some of the fresh grape skins are added to the must and are left in until the spring following the vintage. This greatly intensifies the perfume. Connoisseurs like to drink very mature Setubal wines, which are darker, richer and dryer than the younger version.

Bucelas

Another notable wine of Portugal is Bucelas. This comes from the area of that name, situated about 30 kilometres north of Lisbon. Sometimes spelt 'Busellas' on antique English silver wines labels, this used to be called 'Lisbon Hock' and was a favourite of the Duke of Wellington and his officers when they fought in Portugal during the Peninsular Wars. In those days it was a much sweeter wine; now it is a golden, dry wine with a fruity bouquet and a hint of honey. It makes a good aperitif and goes well with fish in rich sauces.

Grape pickers of Pinhâu

Hungary

Hungary has for hundreds of years produced one of the world's great dessert wines – Tokay Aszu – but many parts of the country make excellent red and white table wines, which are well worth trying. The description given to wines of quality is Minosegi bor – the equivalent of the French Appellation Côntrolée.

Hungary is a major wine-producing country, ranking eleventh in the world for quantity. Forty per cent of the production is exported and this goes mainly to Scandinavia and other North European countries.

White table wines

The Hungarian white wine known best outside Hungary is probably the Riesling, made from the Olasz or Italian Riesling grape. This grape is widely grown, especially in the Great Plain of central Hungary, and produces a pleasant, fragrant, medium-dry wine. A particularly good example is made around the town of Pecs in the southwest of the country.

The wines of Hungary taste as exotic as their labels look. Bottle shapes vary too.

More interesting wines, however, are made from native grape varieties, such as the Furmint, Harslevelu and Keknyelu. The wines produced from these native grapes tend to be full-flavoured, aromatic and spicy – the ideal accompaniments to the traditional foods of the country.

Good quality white wines are produced in the regions of Somlo and Mor and especially around Lake Balaton in western Hungary. On the north side of the lake, a range of hills slopes gently down to the water. Villages and towns on these favoured south-facing slopes have been making wine for hundreds of years. The town of Badacsony has the best reputation, producing fragant golden wines of varying sweetness from the Olasz Riesling, Rizlingszilvani (Müller-Thurgau), Keknyelu, Zoldszilvani (Sylvaner) and Szurkebarat (Pinot Gris) grapes.

Tokay Aszu

The Hungarians prize above all the sweet white wines. These are served with dessert, or on their own for they are a delicious drink in their own right. The supreme example of this type of wine is Tokay Aszu.

Tokay is a little town in northeast Hungary on the Bodrog river. The slopes of the nearby hills, with their volcanic soils and favourable exposure to the sun, are ideal sites for vine cultivation. Summers are hot, autumns long, and, in particular, the mists from the nearby river encourage the development on the grapes of a fungus known as the 'noble rot' (*Botrytis cinerea*) which penetrates the skin of the grape, shrivelling it and concentrating the natural sugars. The grapes may not look very attractive, but they produce spectacular results.

The 'noble rot' does not attack the grapes until late in the season and picking is delayed until the end of October, sometimes continuing into December if conditions allow. Grapes which are harvested earlier produce a more conventional white wine, described either by its grape type – usually Furmint or Harslevelu – or, in more general terms, as *Szamorodni* (which means 'as it comes'). Only the wine made from shrivelled grapes is known as Tokay Aszu.

The method of making Tokay Aszu is unique. The grapes are first loaded into tubs where they are allowed to stand while their own weight produces a rich juice known as *Tokay Eszencia*, or essence. This is drawn off from the tubs and used for blending; it has a very high sugar content and ferments extremely slowly. The compressed grapes are then added in varying measures to existing one-year-old wine. The measures – 32 litres /7 gallons each – are known as *puttonys* and the quality of the finished wine is assessed by the number of *puttonys* (up to five) which are used. After a few days this mixture is pressed and allowed to ferment in the usual way. It then matures in barrels in the town's ancient rock cellars. Traditionally brandy was added to Tokay Aszu to give it added stability; this is now achieved by 'cooking' the wine briefly at a high temperature. This is said to give the wine a slightly caramelized flavour.

Red Wine

Hungary does, of course, also produce red wine. Much comes from the warmer south, but the most famous is made around the town of Eger in the north. Called Egri Bikaver, or Bull's Blood – a name supposedly coined by invading Turks hundreds of years ago – it is a full-bodied rich red. It is made from a blend of Kadarka (Hungary's main red wine grape), Kekfrancos and Medoc Noir (Merlot), sometimes with the additions of Cabernet and Oporto. If allowed to mature and develop, it can be a fine wine, comparable to a good Chianti.

Yugoslavia

Yugoslavia is notable in the wine world both for the wide diversity of its products – the contrasting vineyard terrains reflect this variety – and for reaching tenth place among the producing countries.

White wines

The better quality white wines are a most important export of Yugoslavia, particularly to Britain. The finest white wines come from Slovenia, the northern province which extends to the Italian, Austrian and Hungarian borders.

In Slovenia, as in other regions, extremely well-equipped modern wineries have been built to receive the produce of many thousands of small growers, who continue to cultivate their vineyards privately. Much has been done to improve the quality of traditional wines, as well as introducing new varieties of vines and modern methods of cultivation and vinification.

The best Slovenian wines come mostly from the Drava zone in the north-east, near the borders with Austria and Hungary. Here the beautifully terraced vineyards not only yield excellent grapes from the Laski Riesling vine, but also from Rhine Riesling (known locally as Renski Riesling), Sylvaner, Traminer, Sauvignon and Pinot Blanc, among others. The finer mature wines are

often molten gold, voluptuous but never cloying. Some of the best come from the area called Jeruzalem. It is said that this area got its name from the Crusaders who, on halting there during their long journey south, imbibed so happily that they said they wished it were their journey's end!

The most notable of the white wines of Slovenia is the medium dry Lutomer Laski Riesling. The most popular of all dryish table wines exported, it is light pale golden, and fragrant with a slightly flowery bouquet. One of the finer versions is called Slamnak, named after its individual vineyard on the Lutomer estates. It is intensely fruity, yet dry with a lovely greeny gold colour. While Lutomer Laski Riesling is equally good as an aperitif, party or picnic drink, Slamnak goes well with fish, chicken or veal, especially in rich sauces.

Amongst the other Slovenian wines, the very pale blonde, dry Lutomer Sauvignon makes a delicious aperitif as well as being most suitable to serve with all kinds of fish. The Rhine (or Renski) Rieslings are more

stately wines – golden, dry and fruity. In total contrast there is the pale topaz, very flowery medium dry Gewürztraminer. This is made from the grape so famous in Alsace, but is much cheaper, and less flamboyant.

Some delightful white wines come from the Fruska Gora zone in the Vojvodina region of Serbia, north-west of Belgrade. The name Fruska Gora comes from the wooded mountain range, much visited by tourists for the ancient monuments and monasteries there. The Fruska Gora wines are made using the most advanced modern methods, and the platinum blonde, very dry, Sauvignon is worth seeking out. It is not so astringent as its French counterpart. They also produce a delicately aromatic Traminer, which is medium dry, with a very distinctive bouquet.

On the south bank of the Danube the town of Smederevo is a notable centre for viticulture and fruit. A famous native vine is the Smederevka, which produces an attractive dry white wine.

One of Yugoslavia's most distinctive whites is Žilavka, named after the grape which grows best in the vineyards of Hercegovina, near the historic old town of Mostar. It has a rather 'leafy' subtle taste, is greeny gold and dry. This makes it a good aperitif and compatible with smoked fish, pâtés or mousses, as well as with poultry or the more delicate cheeses.

Red wines

Serbia's most popular red wine is the powerful, deep ruby Prokupac, named after its grape variety. More likely to appeal to Western palates is the delightful Milion Cabernet Sauvignon. This dry, deep garnet-coloured wine is made in the fine cellars at Oplenac which used to belong to the last sovereign, King Peter.

Good Cabernet Sauvignon wines are also made now in the southern region of Kosovo, where viticultural tradition goes back to the era of ancient Greek colonists. Many vineyards are planted with a native vine called Burgundac Crni – the resultant wine is a deep rich dry red.

The smallest Yugoslav region, Montenegro, produces a very different red wine, called Vranac. This is fresh, brisk and as instantly attractive as a good young Beaujolais. It is best served slightly chilled. Nothing could be more different from the long-established Dalmatian favourite, Dingač, which comes from vineyards on the mountainous Pelješac peninsula. You need a strong head to drink Dingač – it is a powerful robust red, on the sweet side. From another Dalmatian holiday place, the island of Hvar, comes Faros. This rather perfumed wine is named after the Greek word for 'lighthouse' and refers to ancient Greek settlements there.

Brandy

It would be a pity to omit Yugoslavia's other celebrated drink – *slivovic*. This is a very potent plum brandy which the locals toss back with ease but novices should sip with respect. It is at its best with black coffee.

Two examples of Yugoslavian wine

Austria

Until a few years ago, Austrian wine was rarely seen outside its native country. However, wine production has now become a serious business in Austria. The recent scandal involving adulterated wine has dealt a blow to the market, but given time reputable growers should re-establish the reputation, particularly of the dessert wines.

There are four principal wine regions in Austria – Lower Austria, Styria, Burgenland and Vienna (probably the only capital in the world with its own vineyards). These regions are again sub-divided into fourteen different areas.

Most of the Austrian wines are sold labelled according to the grape from which they are made. Therefore, it is useful to get acquainted with important grape names.

The grapes and their wines

Grüner Veltliner: over 80% of the wine produced in Austria is white and of this by far the most popular grape is the Grüner Veltliner. It produces a typically Austrian wine, light and spicy with an almost 'peppery' taste – good both with food and as an aperitif. Grüner Veltliner is delicious, too, if drunk in true Austrian-style as a *G'spritzer*: half wine, half soda water. The colour of Grüner Veltliner was once described as 'light gold with green lights' and nothing could be more appropriate.

Müller-Thurgau is an early-ripening grape

From left: Beerenauslese, St Laurent, Grüner Veltliner, Traminer and Weisser Burgunder.

which produces a mild wine with a fruity bouquet and a surprising Muscat flavour. It has a lovely light, green-gold colour and although it has the general reputation of not ageing well, there are some notable exceptions, particularly in the Burgenland.

Rheinriesling: wine pressed from this grape matures slowly and usually reaches its peak only after two to four years in storage. It has a delicate fruity bouquet, faintly reminiscent of peaches.

The Neuburger grape is an Austrian speciality and the wines produced from it are full-bodied yet mild with a pleasant, fresh aroma.

Weisser Burgunder is an interesting wine with a deliciously fragrant bouquet and a flavour of fresh walnuts.

Traminer (or Gewürztraminer) produces an elegant wine which is golden in colour. The wine has a pronounced bouquet which has been likened to roses by some, violets by others. With a spicy, rich flavour, Traminer is usually rich in alcohol and is at its best when grown in Styria and Burgenland.

Muskat-Ottonel is a mild golden wine typical of the province of Burgenland, with an exceptionally strong bouquet of Muscat. According to where the grapes were grown,

the wine can vary from sprightly elegance to mellow fullness.

Welschriesling is not the real Riesling; 'Welsch' in this particular case meaning 'imposter'. However, it is a fresh, spicy wine which keeps well and can vary in colour from palest yellow to deep gold.

Zierfandler and Rotgipfler are two typically Austrian grapes, grown mostly in the Lower Austrian regions of Gumpoldskirchen and Baden near Vienna. They produce similar wines – rich and robust, with a fine fruity bouquet – which are often blended together and sold as Zierfandler/Rotgipfler. This wine is excellent if allowed to mature.

Blaufränkische produces the most popular Austrian red wine. Fruity and full-bodied it has a glowing colour which matures well.

Blauer Portugieser on the other hand, produces a red wine that should be drunk when young – it is velvety and mild with a faint spiciness.

St Laurent, named after St Lorenz because the grape usually starts to ripen around this particular 'saints day', produces a robust wine, deep red in colour. It has a slight, yet delicious, fragrance of raspberries.

Blauer Burgunder gives an elegant red wine, smooth, velvety and rich.

Special dessert wines

The Austrian Auslese, Beerenauslese, Ausbruch, Trockenberenauslese and Eiswein score very highly indeed. These 'special' wines are of truly superior quality, yet are still sold at prices well below those of similar wines from other countries. They have a mellowness about them – like liquid honey spiced with pine and scented with lime blossom – which can be wonderful.

Romania and Bulgaria

Though Romania and Bulgaria have claims to an ancient wine-growing tradition, until recently their wine-making techniques have bordered on the medieval. But a scientific approach and modern production methods have put the wines of these two countries into the forefront in the wine world. Both the red and white wines from these two countries are well worth seeking out.

The wines of Romania and Bulgaria tend to be underestimated because they do not have the hallowed reputations of France, Italy or Germany. In reality, the modern approach Bulgaria and Romania have taken towards wine production has made them the leaders of a revolution taking place in this field. The traditional wine rulers of the world have a tendency to sit on their laurels, benefitting too easily from increased prices for their products resulting from a much greater demand for quality wine around the world. There are many poor French wines, for example, selling in the middle price range purely by virtue of being French. A Bulgarian wine selling in a supermarket for half the price might be much better.

Romanian wine

Romania is situated by the Black Sea, sandwiched between Russia and the Danube. In the centre of the country rise the great Carpathian mountains, with the high Transylvanian plateau. Vineyards are dotted all over the country in pockets – in Carpathian valleys, in Transylvania and on the rolling plains stretching down towards the Danube and the Black Sea. A high proportion are still in private hands, despite a communist government, and are consequently varied, with old methods surviving alongside the new – the latter tending to be promoted on state properties.

Romania has an ancient wine growing tradition, but little reputation in the West. Its wine has historically graced the tables of Eastern Europe and much finds its way to the Soviet Union and East Germany. One light dessert wine, Cotnari, used to be famous world over. Cotnari comes from Moldavia in the north-east, but much of this land was ceded to Russia after the Second World War and the wine is now rarely seen. Although Cotnari is now fairly obscure, the Romanians are waking up to the possibilities of earning foreign exchange from wine exports. Wine production now features more importantly and more varied and better wines are appearing in our shops.

The whites are on the whole better, using some traditional grapes and some, famous from France and Germany, that have been introduced. Romanian whites are well worth trying, especially the Perla from the Tîrnăve region of Transylvania, which you will find labelled *Tarnave*. It is light and slightly sweet, with a hint of the German style, although really quite distinctive – a most pleasant wine for warm summer days and by no means expensive. Other cheaper whites are available, but tend to be sweeter.

A powerful red made from the Merlot grape is on sale from the Dealul Mare region in the Carpathian foothills. This is a hefty, slightly sweet (although that does not mean sugary) wine for drinking with roast meat or spicy casseroles. Again, it has more body and character than its price suggests, and should certainly be tried.

There are also good wines, red and white, from the Murfatlar region near the Black Sea and from Banat in the far west.

Bulgarian wine

Bulgaria, just south of the Danube from Romania, has a very different wine past – and present. Although claims are made of a tradition stretching back thousands of years to the ancient Thracians, 500 years of Muslim law when Bulgaria was dominated by the Turks have had more effect. During this period wine was outlawed and production survived only on a small and local scale. Since the Second World War, however, enormous strides have been made. Bulgaria is now a major wine producer in terms of both volume and quality.

The state monopoly, called Vinimpex, enjoys total domination and has brought the benefits of modern technology to bear in a big way. The vines are cultivated with the maximum mechanization, and viticulture is the subject of a great deal of research. The result is a substantial quantity of good wine to a consistently high standard, selling at astonishingly low prices in the West.

Like Romania, Bulgaria has widely scattered wine areas, although there tends to be a greater concentration in the central and southern plains, and again to the north. The vines are usually grown in flat terrain, facilitating mechanized cultivation.

Of the wines likely to be encountered, Cabernet Sauvignon is best known and often the best in quality. The great Bordeaux grape from which it gets its name seems to do well in Bulgaria, producing mellow wine with considerable body. It should be pointed out, however, that although the general standard is high it is not uniformly excellent. Look out for Cabernet coming from the northern Sukhindol region for a reliable introduction.

Another Bulgarian red, in a more expensive category but more individual with it, is Mavrud. It comes from the south and is darker, heavier and richer than the Cabernet. A currently available example comes from Asenovgrad. It should be drunk in small quantities with a good meal – the Cabernet is for drinking at any time that wine appeals.

Bulgarian whites, although good, are less impressive than the reds. A Pinot Chardonnay from the Shuman area in the north, using the great white Burgundy grape, is a worthy example. It is strong and fruity, but perhaps without the subtleties of the reds. The Misket from Karlovo in the middle of the country is worth a try. It is a lively Muscat and not particularly sweet.

Weighing harvested grapes

Switzerland

Swiss wines are fresh, lightish wines and reliably good. However, outside Switzerland, they are unlikely to be cheap. High production costs, due to the mountainous terrain and unpredictable climate, influence the export price. The Swiss' fondness for good wine also affects the price, in that they understandably keep the best for their own consumption.

A vineyard on the slopes of a Swiss valley

There are five principal wine-growing areas in Switzerland. The biggest and most important are the south-facing slopes of the upper Rhône valley, the area known as the Valais; the shores of Lake Geneva, known as the Vaud; and the environs of Geneva itself. The south-facing shores of Lake Neuchâtel are also under vine; lastly, there are large wine-growing areas in Ticino, in Italian Switzerland.

Rather confusingly, Swiss wines may be labelled in a variety of ways. They may be called after the village or area where they were produced or simply named after the grape variety. Alternatively, they may be given a legally-controlled name that does not relate to either the area or the grape. The profusion of growers and brand names also adds to the confusion. However, the most important wines are easy enough to identify; once you know a little about them, you can buy them with confidence.

Valais and Vaud

By far the largest proportion of the wine produced in the regions of Valais and Vaud is white. Most of it is made from the high-yielding Chasselas grape. The Chasselas is not regarded as a distinguished grape in France but in the Valais and Vaud it takes on a great deal of local character. In the Vaud the wine is known as Dorin, and in the Valais as Fendant, where it tends to have a riper, stronger flavour. Sion is the centre of the Valais region and produces Fendant of the highest quality. Both Dorin and Fendant are light and dry, and should be drunk young.

The red wine grapes of these areas are the Gamay of Beaujolais and the Burgundian Pinot Noir. Dôle is the red wine of Valais, made from either of the grapes or from a mixture of the two, rather like the Passe-tout-Grains of Burgundy. Dôle must reach a certain level of quality and alcoholic strength before it may bear the name. (Wine that does not reach the required level, is sold under the label of Goron.) The red Vaud equivalent is Salvagnin. Again these are light wines, although they tend to be sweeter than the whites. They should not be left lying for too long.

Another name that you may come across is Chablais, which is the area between the Vaud and Valais, where the Rhône leaves Lake Geneva. Look, too, for the name Aigle, the principal town of Chablais. Aigle produces dry white wine with some of the style of both Valais and Vaud. Other names to watch out for are Lavaux, which is the eastern section of the Vaud, and La Côte, the western shore of the lake, between Geneva and Lausanne. The wines from these areas will be pleasant, if lightweight, white Dorin and red Salvagnin.

A name well worth looking out for is Johannisberg. This is the local Valais name for the Sylvaner grape. Here it makes a soft but robust white wine with much more flavour to it than the Chasselas.

The interestingly named Vin du Glacier, a speciality of Switzerland, is sadly no longer made. This was a long-matured white wine, stored at high altitudes until it possessed heroic strength. Its modern equivalent is just an ordinary, branded white wine.

Geneva

The most significant wine-producing area around Geneva is the district of Mandement. This district produces very light reds from the Gamay grape, as well as white Perlan, which is from the Chasselas grape at its palest and least distinguished.

Neuchâtel

To the north, the canton of Neuchâtel produces both red and white wine, as well as a rosé. The rosé is made from the Pinot Noir grape and has the evocative name of Oeil de Perdrix — evocative, at least, to those who have come close enough to the eye of a partridge to recognize the same pink! The Pinot Noir grows well along the sheltered north side of Lake Neuchâtel, and also makes a pale red wine which may be called Cortaillod after the principal village.

Neuchâtel whites from the Chasselas grape sometimes have the distinction of being slightly fizzy because the wine is bottled while still on its yeasty sediment. If the process is taken further, an attractive fully sparkling wine results.

Ticino

To the south, in Italian-speaking Switzerland, the Ticino area has been producing wine for export for only a relatively short time. However, the Merlot, the lesser red wine grape of Bordeaux, grows well here as it does in neighbouring Italy and Yugoslavia. The Swiss Merlots are soft, full, well-rounded wines with more body than most of their national relatives to the west. The better quality reds from the Ticino areas are now called Viti — they must reach at least 12% alcohol and are quite powerful.

England

For many people England seems too far north, too cool and too wet to produce wine. But her northern position does not make wine production impossible, as the existence of 300 commercial producers with almost 430 hectares of land between them under vines shows.

Wine was introduced to England by the Romans who established a small number of vineyards. In the Middle Ages the vine became more widespread, especially at monasteries. The decline of English wine production began in the 12th century, when the English crown came into possession of large parts of south-west France, including Bordeaux, and wine began to appear in quantity across the Channel. The dissolution of the monasteries by Henry VIII finished off large-scale production, although small vineyards continued to be cultivated in the parks of country houses right up to the early 20th century.

After the Second World War, a number of experimental vineyards sprang up, including the famous Hampshire establishment of Hambledon, founded in 1952 by Sir Guy Salisbury-Jones. There was a period of great expansion in the 1970s, powered by a heady enthusiasm which waned with the poor harvests at the end of the decade. The expansion seems to have been haphazard, even reckless, and a number of concerns collapsed or were commercially unsuccessful. Poor sites were chosen and the wrong types of vine were often planted. It has to be said that, whatever the enthusiastic claims of the English wine-producers, the climate does not actively favour grapes.

Great care has to be taken for the vines to have a chance to flourish. With protected, south-facing slopes, the hardier, early-ripening varieties of grapes can do very well. On the right soil these grapes will produce a harvestable crop every year.

At its best English wine is very good and deserves to be tried and appreciated on its own merits, as a distinctive type of wine with its own special qualities. At its worst, it is thin and uninspiring.

The favoured grape type is the Müller-Thurgau, which does well on less than perfect sites in Germany. Other German vines, particularly Reichensteiner, also do well, as do the French Seyval and Madeleine Angevine.

With a few exceptions, English wines are white. The most common style is like light German wine, although English wine is usually less sweet than German. There is often a flowery bouquet and a fresh lively flavour, but rarely much body. The difficulties experienced in producing these wines mean that they are relatively expensive, and the taxman adds a high percentage.

Whatever you buy, choose carefully and make the distinction between English and British wine. The latter is made from imported grape juice and should be avoided. Some English vineyards make the error of marketing British wine as well as their home-grown product. The association can only give English wine a bad name and it negates the whole point of making real English wine in the first place. Another unfortunate practice is the addition of un-fermented grape juice to give less successful vintages body and sweetness. This is fine if the additive comes from the same vineyard, but when it is imported from Germany, the wine's Englishness is again called into question. There seems no reason to pay a high price for manufactured wine of this kind. English wines are not widely marketed, as the overall level of production is not great enough for that, nor is it likely to grow substantially. Less productive vineyards will fall by the wayside while those that succeed will grow and consolidate. Treat English wine as an occasional pleasure or experiment – interesting wine for warm summer afternoons and strawberries.

The vineyards are mostly in the south of England, but are widely scattered. Kent, Somerset, Suffolk and Norfolk seem to favour wine-production. One of the most famous sites is Adgestone on the Isle of Wight. Look out for Schönburger from Wootton Vines — the 1981 vintage won the 1982 Gore Browne Trophy for the best English wine. From Kent try wines from prize-winning Lamberhurst Priory. This vineyard produces on average 30,000 bottles a year. Among the grapes they use are Müller-Thurgau and Seyval. Other Kentish wines of particular note are Biddenden Müller-Thurgau and Penshurst, which is a blend of Müller-Thurgau, Seyval and other varieties.

A major Gloucestershire producer is Three Choirs, which produces around 20,000 bottles a year. Müller Thurgau is their major grape, but they also use the Reichensteiner grape. These two grapes are blended, with the addition of Seyval for sharpness, to make the already mentioned Adgestone wine from the Isle of Wight.

Westbury in Berkshire is an exceptionally successful producer with 30,000 bottles on average each year. Try their Reichensteiner and their red wine made from Pinot Noir.

East Anglia has a number of successful vineyards. The main ones are Bruisyard St. Peter in Suffolk and Magdalen in Norfolk. Both rely heavily on Müller-Thurgau. Elmham Park in Norfolk makes an attractive dry white, which is rather German in character.

From Sussex come several wines from the firm of Carr Taylor, including a *méthode champenoise* sparkling white. Finally from Essex comes Felstar and New Hall wines.

Vine-spraying at Wootton Vineyards, Somerset

Greece

The first of European countries to cultivate the vine, Greece has been producing wines for hundred of years. The wines vary considerably in style and include the famous and popular resinated wine, Retsina.

A mellow red wine and a white retsina – Greece's famous resinated wine.

Today a little over half of the vines which are grown in Greece are for wine production; the rest are for the provision of dessert grapes and raisins. The climate is favourable for growing vines – dry sunny heat can be relied upon in summer – but local strong winds occur and the variable nature of the terrain results in microclimates giving strongly contrasting conditions for growth within quite limited areas. Soils are generally rather poor but this is seldom a bar to the production of good wine.

There are of course many local wines produced in Greece which are never tasted outside their immediate areas. Even those which qualify for 'appellation of origin' status, under the laws which now apply throughout EEC wine-producing countries, seldom find their way to other countries – except in the baggage of returning holiday makers! These 'typical' wines are marketed under a regional place name and must be made from approved grape types, by methods traditionally associated with the area. They make up about 12% of the total Greek wine production and often reach a high standard of quality.

The bulk of the wine which Greece produces annually consists of commercial blends from various regions. These are marketed under brand names. Some of these, such as Demestica and Pendeli, are quite well known. But the most familiar of all Greek wines, certainly to those who have travelled to Greece, is Retsina.

Retsina

Hundred of years ago, when wine was stored in jars or amphoras, it was found that the wine kept better if the jars were sealed with a mixture of plaster and resin. We now know that this was because the seals kept the jars airtight, but before it was realized that air was the great enemy of stored wine, the improved quality was attributed to the resin. Hence the tradition of resinated wine. The Greeks have now acquired a taste for it and have given it the name of Retsina.

More Retsinas are consumed than any other native wines. They are entitled to their own *appellation traditionelle*. Today they are made in a similar way to other wines, but during fermentation a small quantity of resin from the native Alep pine is added to the must. This is drawn off with the lees at the first filtering or 'racking'.

The amount of resin added is only 1% of volume, but it results in a distinctive flavour usually, though perhaps unkindly, compared to turpentine. Most Retsina is made from the white Savatiano or red Rhoditis grape. The latter produces a variety of Retsina called Kokkinelli. The real home of Retsina is the region around Athens known as Attica, but wine shops and tavernas throughout the country will have a resinated wine on offer, often made on the premises. The bigger merchant houses all have their own Retsina and large quantities are exported, so commercial examples are not too difficult to find.

Main wine regions

The most important of the Greek wine producing areas, accounting for a third of the total area under vines, is the Peloponnese. Over such a large region there will of course be a great variety of wines, but worth a special mention are the red wine of Nemea, known as 'Blood of Hercules', which is made from the St George or Agiorgitiko grape, and the dry white wine of Mantinea made from the Moschofilero. The region around Patras and the neighbouring Ionian island of Cephalonia are also the sources of famous dessert wines, the white Muscat and the red Mavrodaphne.

The large island of Crete, with its particularly hot climate, produces strong full-flavoured red wines. From the regions of Sitia and Daphnes comes a fine liqueur wine in the tradition of the legendary Malvasia. This was supposed to be made in the palace of Minos from a recipe given to the Cretan King by the Delphic oracle.

The smaller Greek islands have their own distinctive wines, the most widely known outside Greece being the white wines of Samos. The vineyard is extensive and is planted exclusively with the Muscat grape.

The Northern mainland areas of Greece produce a variety of regional wines from native stocks. A fine vigorous red wine is made at Rapsani in Thessaly from three local varieties, the Xynomavro, Krassato and Stavroto. Also famous are the Naoussa and Amynteon vineyards of Macedonia.

In addition to the native grape types, some stocks from other countries are now being used in the north. An excellent red wine called Château Carras is made in the Halkidiki region from Cabernet Sauvignon, Cabernet Franc and Merlot – grapes usually associated with Bordeaux. Vinification is by traditional methods, involving a lengthy spell in oak casks. The 1975 vintage is certainly rival to a good claret. The same growers also produce a very palatable dry white from the Sauvignon Blanc and Ugni Blanc known as Domaine Port Carras, Côte de Meliton. In Epirus, a robust scented red wine is made at Metsovo from the Cabernet Sauvignon, introduced to the area after native stocks were destroyed by phylloxera.

The next few years should see a growth market for improving Greek table wines.

East and South Mediterranean

Wine has been made and drunk in the hot climates of Cyprus, the Middle East and North Africa since the earliest times. There is a strong tradition of wine-making therefore, but much of what is produced is consumed locally. However, Morocco – and until the recent unhappy troubles, Lebanon – have been slowly establishing a more cosmopolitan market.

Cyprus

Cyprus is best known for its successful 'sherry', but the island also produces table wines of all types. The ones you are most likely to come across will be the products of big modern wine firms like KEO and SODAP which have made admirable advances in the production of reliable, everyday reds and whites. Among the the reds, Othello and Afames are the best-known names, rather in the same way as the Demestica of Greece. They are not intricate wines, but they have plenty of fruit and staying power.

Domaine d'Ahera is another pleasant, fruity red wine. Arsinoe is a dry white wine, while Aphrodite is fuller and sweetish. There is a white with a slight sparkle also available under the name of Bellapais.

Perhaps the best-known Cypriot wine is Commandaria. It certainly has the longest history – legend has it that it was enjoyed by the Crusaders. It is made on the southern slopes of the Troodos mountains and, when traditional methods are followed, it is intensely sweet, pungent and concentrated. It is probably quite close in taste to the ordinary wine of ancient Greece and Rome. The modern winery product sold under the same name is a sweet dessert wine.

Turkey

Turkey grows vast amounts of grapes but only a small percentage of them are made into wine – the rest are eaten. The wine in Turkey is produced by a state-controlled monopoly and very little of it is currently exported. What is available is usually well made if not particularly exciting. Buzbag is one red wine of fairly good quality.

Lebanon

The wine makers of Lebanon are doing a very worthwhile job against the climatic odds. Quality is generally good and prices are low, considering the technical expertise involved in production here. Red wines are best, but there are some good dry whites.

Look out especially for a newly fashionable wine called Château Musar. It is not the cheapest of the Lebanese wines but both reds and whites are carefully made from traditional French grape varieties. Château Musar improves with keeping, and the mature red has been called a fascinating cross between a Burgundy and a claret.

Israel

Israel produces table wines of all colours, fruity reds and sweet whites in particular. Small quantities of wine are made from traditional grape varieties and are exported under brand names – Carmel is a reliable one. There is also a huge market within Israel for kosher wine.

North Africa

Tunisia, Algeria and Morocco are the most important wine countries of North Africa.

Algeria, the biggest producer, was once the source of huge volumes of the most basic wine, high in alcohol, which was shipped off to France for blending. Much of it was used to bring thin *vin ordinaire* up to 11%, and as such it had a useful role to play. However, changes in French wine law meant that this was no longer possible. Algerian growers were left with a huge surplus that was useless for the home market because wine is forbidden for Moslems. Other markets were found, notably the USSR, but another solution was to move the focus of wine growing from the mass production of the flat coastal plain to the less productive but higher quality slopes of the inland hills. Much better wines are now produced here, notably reds with a satisfying richness.

Algerian wine is cheap and it has to compete hard at the bottom end of the market with similar wines from France's Midi. But it is no longer invariably plonk.

Tunisia produces some drinkable reds and some pleasant sweet whites made from the ubiquitous muscat grape. Morocco is the newest producer of the three, and her wines are generally of higher quality. Holidaymakers there often enjoy the dry light rosé and meaty reds, and knowledgeably search them out on their return home. Among the reds, Sidi Larbi and Dar Bel Amri are good and are well distributed.

Berber women tending vines in Tunisia

AMERICA

With the exception of Australia, the United States – and California in particular – is the most exciting modern wine region in the world. Not only is there a great quantity and variety of good, drinkable wine, but the quality is improving all the time.

Wine growers and chemists from the older wine-producing countries of the world make constant studies of American vineyards, where some of the most far-reaching experiments in grape-growing and wine chemistry are taking place.

The extraordinary variations in soil and climate, and the incidence of so many micro-climates, combine to make wine-growing in America both a fascinating and commercially rewarding business.

Although wine is made in 29 of the American states, California is by far the largest producer. New York State's wines, which are rated as a poor second, are made 'upstate' around the Finger Lakes. These wines are made from American grape varieties or American/European hybrids. Most of them have the typical foxiness of the *labrusca* Concord grape, indigenous to America. It is a difficult taste to acquire for those brought up on European wine styles. Vineyards in other states, such as Oregon, are often small, but make good-quality wine. Oregon wines are thought to be closer in style to European wines.

California

Already one of the areas in California, the Napa Valley, is spoken of as a classic wine-producing area. This might seem odd when its relatively short history is taken into consideration. Vines were first planted in California by a Franciscan, Father Juniper Serra, at San Diego in 1796, using a Spanish grape, known as the Mission grape. This was used for sacramental wine and never intended for large-scale wine production.

Jean Louis Vignes, the son of a Bordeaux wine family, fared better with the vineyard he planted in 1831, in what is now the centre of Los Angeles. The real beginning of vine growing in California was in 1849 with the coming of the gold rush.

One of the 'forty-niners' was a Hungarian nobleman, Agaston Haraszthy. Dissatisfied with the wine from his planting of Mission grapes, he set off for Europe to buy vines. Five months later he returned to Buena Vista Estate in Sonoma, with 100,000 cuttings of some 300 varieties.

Many were sold to growers in lots of 10 and 20, but often bearing identity labels from which the names had vanished. Many of these imported vines brought with them the pest phylloxera and by 1861 Californian vineyards were all but decimated. Phylloxera was finally dealt with by the grafting of the *vinifera* vines onto the native American *labrusca* root stock, which is disease resistant.

No sooner was the wine industry under reconstruction when, from 1922-1936, Prohibition took its toll. When Prohibition was repealed there followed a period when great strides in technology and research took place, and the wine industry in America came into its own. In California many felt that after phylloxera and Prohibition, they were starting from scratch.

The most popular red wine is the Cabernet Sauvignon, made from the famous Bordeaux grape. It is usually fuller and lacks the subtlety of a good Bordeaux. Both the Cabernet Sauvignon and another famous European grape, Pinot Noir, in California have less acidity and more alcohol than their European counterparts.

The native grape, Zinfandel, found hardly anywhere else in the world, produces a dry red wine with a flavour all its own. The Gamay grape produces an attractive red wine, which is similar in style to Beaujolais.

Amongst the white wines, Californian Chardonnay is often delicious. Equally good results have been achieved with the Sauvignon grape, the wine of which is sometimes called Fumé Blanc. Johannisberg Riesling, which is the name given to the Rhine Riesling, also produces a good white wine – the late-harvest Riesling makes a very sweet, luscious wine. Light fruity wines from the Chenin Blanc and Semillon are generally well made and a number of the Gewürztraminers have matched those in Alsace.

Californians drink far more white than red because of the warm climate. This has led to the produce of a white wine, known as Blanc de Noir, which is made from black grapes without their skins.

American wines are rewarding to explore, so a good understanding of the labelling system and a greater knowledge of the main wine regions is worthwhile.

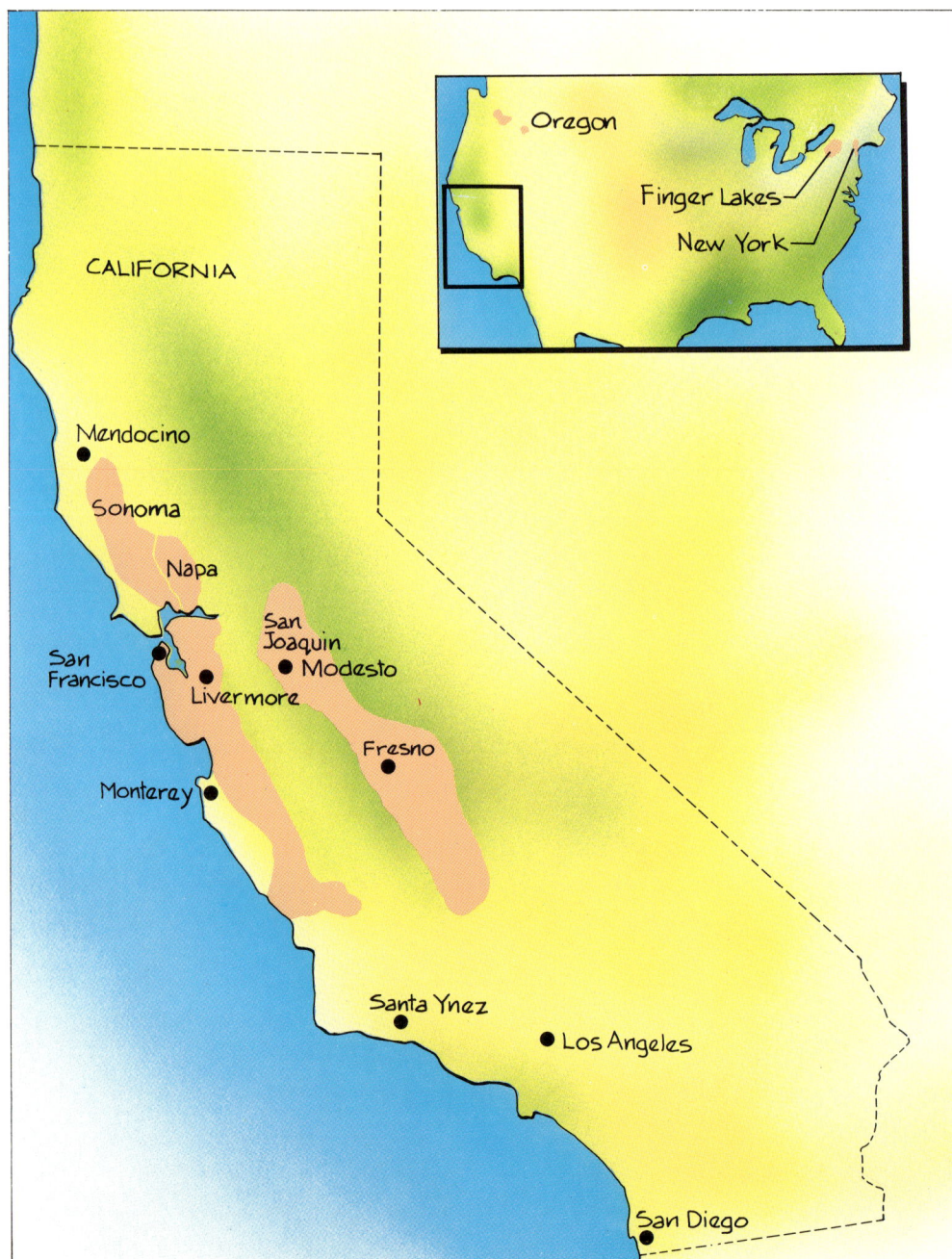

American wine labels

If you are planning to try American wines you will have to make a clear distinction between generic wines – those borrowing European wine names – and varietals – those named after individual grape varieties.

In the U.S. wine labelling is controlled by Federal law. State regulations about content and the words used to describe the wines have to be considered. Generally state regulations do not add anything to the label, except in California and Oregon, where they are stricter than Federal laws.

Generic labels

A generic or proprietary wine may be made from virtually any grape variety and is of little value to the serious wine buyer. Seventeen of these names are permitted on U.S. labels including: claret, chablis, champagne, chianti, moselle, port, rhine wine, hock, sauterne and tokay. These names offer no more than the roughest guide to the wine's characteristics, which are interpreted as the grower sees fit. Worse still, a winery may label the same wine burgundy or claret, depending on which names appeal.

Generic wines are usually cheap, mass-produced blends, or jug wines, but usually quite drinkable. It is merely the slapdash labelling which is at fault. Oregon is an exception here – no generic names are allowed on wines from this state.

Varietal labels

California more than any other wine-producing area has concentrated on the individual varieties of wine. The names of Cabernet, Pinot, Sémillon, Chardonnay and Sauvignon are strictly covered by wine laws and cannot be misused.

A varietal wine must contain 75% of that grape in the wine. Varietals are sometimes referred to as premium wines, which is the buyer's first indication of quality.

Vintage dating

If a wine is vintage-dated, 95% of it must be from the year stated on the label, though Californian State regulations insist on 100%. If there is no vintage date, the wine has been blended from several years' vintages. Some wineries give a bottling date rather than a vintage date; some add the harvest date.

The producer

In the U.S. there are no shippers as such, so the producer's name is all-important. As it is usually very prominent on the label it cannot be missed. Large wineries are allowed to market under different trademarks, but they can no longer use geographical names as brand names unless certain requirements are met.

Geographical names

The use of geographical names is tightly controlled. Wines may obtain a regional designation if at least 75% of the volume of the wine is derived from the district claimed, 85% if the district is a recognized viticultural area. California goes further still, insisting that wine claimed to be Californian, must be from 100% Californian grapes. There are regional designations on some labels. 'North Coast Counties' on a bottle of Californian wine refers to the counties of Napa, Sonoma and Mendocino. Specific vineyards are on some labels.

Bottling information

The name of the company that bottled the wine and its address must appear on the label. 'Grown, produced and bottled by' means exactly that, but 'cellared', 'blended' and 'bottled by' indicate the wine was bought, aged or bottled by a firm other than the grower.

If the wine is estate bottled it must have come entirely from grapes 'owned and controlled' by the producing winery and 'in the vicinity' of the winery. The control requirement may be met by long-term leases or contracts with independent growers.

Alcoholic content

If labelled table wine or light wine, the alcohol content will average 8–14%. Dessert wines are normally over 14% with most in the 18–20% category.

Sparkling wines produced in the U.S. and marketed under the generic name of champagne always carry a qualifying adjective, such as New York State Champagne. Those who make their sparkling wine according to the *méthode champenoise* label the product 'fermented in this bottle' rather than 'fermented in the bottle'; the latter means the wine left the bottle for disgorging and was then re-bottled.

The equivalent of *Spätlese* and *auslese* white wines is Late Harvest and Selected Late Harvest. The percentage of sugar in the grapes at harvest and the residual sugar in the finished wine must both be included on the label.

Back labels

The American passion for detail spurred the winemakers into putting back labels on bottles. Full descriptions cover the grower, the area, the vintage and the food that best accompanies the wine. Sometimes a small map of the area is added.

A selection of American wine labels

Napa Valley – South

The Napa Valley is the most famous wine-producing area of the United States. It lies north and slightly east of San Francisco Bay and is blessed by both its climate and excellent soil conditions.

Some of the Napa Valley vineyards cluster along the flat valley floor while others climb the hillsides and extend into the mountains. Those tucked into hollows often enjoy their own favourable micro-climates. The soils of the Napa Valley are mostly volcanic and well-drained, although rain is unusual during the growing season.

Many new vines have been planted during the last twenty years and and not all of them are mature yet, but fine red and white wines are available from established stocks. In California, the location of the vineyard is not so significant as the variety of grape used, which will indicate the typical style of the wine, and the name of the producer, which is usually the buyer's best guarantee of quality.

Robert Mondavi

The most famous producer in the South of the Napa Valley is Robert Mondavi. He is elder son of Cesare Mondavi, an Italian immigrant who after twenty years as a

A selection of white and red wines from Christian Brothers and Robert Mondavi

wholesaler of table grapes purchased the Charles Krug winery in 1943. Robert worked as his general manager, introducing a number of classic grape varieties and sophisticated production techniques, before leaving to start his own winery at Oakville in 1967. He was one of the first to use cool fermentation in stainless steel vats and ages his red wines – and some whites – in small oak barrels in the French style. He made his reputation with a Fumé Blanc, a dry white Sauvignon wine in the style of the French Sancerre and Pouilly Fumé, and has since made excellent Chardonnay, Cabernet Sauvignon and Pinot Noir; his Pinot Noir Reserve is an outstanding example of a wine which is rarely successful outside its native Burgundy.

In 1980 he purchased and modernised a winery at Woodbridge in the hot central valley of California where he makes large quantities of jug wines for everday drinking, but his premium wines are all from the Napa.

He recently went into collaboration with Baron Philippe de Rothschild, of Chateau Mouton – Rothschild in Bordeaux, and the result of this joint venture is a remarkable and very expensive red wine, mainly Cabernet Sauvignon, called Opus One. This is the top of the Mondavi range, but it is safe to say that any wine with his name on the label will be scrupulously made and a good example of its type.

Other producers

The Rothschilds are not the only European wine dynasty to take an interest in California; not far from Oakville is the Domaine Chandon, financed by the famous French champagne house Moet et Chandon. Though not permitted to call their product champagne, they make fine sparkling wines in the traditional style from classic Pinot Noir, Pinot Blanc and Chardonnay grapes.

Other small but reputable producers in the South are Stag's Leap, Trefethen and Mayacamas. Stag's Leap made their name with Petite Syrah and Chenin Blanc, but have gone on to make excellent Chardonnay and Cabernet.

Trefethen produce very good Chardonnay, Cabernet and Pinot Noir, and also make superior non-varietal red and white wines which are sold under the brand name Eshcol.

Mayacamas, in the mountains to the west of the Valley, are again famous for Cabernet and Chardonnay, which seem to flourish particularly well in the cooler climate; the wines are deep and long-lasting. Mayacamas also make a powerful late-harvest red from the Zinfandel grape.

Napa Valley–North

The Napa Valley, part of the young wine country of California, produces some of the best American wine. It is worth getting to know the different styles of the wineries in this area of rugged individualists.

Schramsberg vineyard in the Napa Valley

Most of the Napa Valley wineries are concentrated at the Northern end of the valley. The climate is very warm and dry, much more so than in the classic European wine-growing areas, and this affects the character of the wines which are fruitier, less acidic and higher in alcohol than their European counterparts. Some might also say less subtle, though this is in part due to the habit of producing straight varietals, with less blending than is usual elsewhere; Cabernet Sauvignon, for example, unless softened with Merlot, Cabernet Franc or Malbec as is done in Bordeaux, will be almost overpowering on the nose and palate. But the large number of small producers, all competing with one another in true American style to produce the best, ensures a wider variety of flavours than you might imagine and encourages constant experimentation and development.

Long-established Wineries

In the face of all this competition, the traditional Napa wineries have been unable to sit still and rely on past achievement. The Charles Krug winery, founded in 1861, was revolutionised after its takeover by the Mondavi family; still run by Robert's brother Peter, it retains a high reputation for its red wines, especially the Vintage Selection Cabernets, which are sold under a distinctive label bearing the signature of the late Cesare Mondavi. They are among the best produced anywhere but they should be laid down for a few years to enjoy them at their best.

Beringer is another long-established name, dating back to 1879, but the premises were much in need of modernisation when taken over by Nestlé in 1971. Since then it has put its Cabernets and Chardonnays back on the wine map and has also acquired a reputation for late-harvest Johannisberg Rieslings in the German style.

The fortunes of Freemark Abbey, founded in the 1880's, were also restored by an outstanding Johannisberg Riesling in 1973. Called Edelwein, it was a rich, full flavoured wine very like a Rhine Beerenauslese, and made the name of its creator, Jerry Luper, who has since moved on to the small but very prestigious Chateau Montelena. Though in existence since 1881, Chateau Montelena was also in decline until purchased by wealthy new proprietors in 1972;

their Chardonnay subsequently won a competition against the best French White burgundies at a blind tasting in Paris, and they also make particularly good Cabernet, though all their wines are expensive.

Another traditional producer of sound red and white wines is Christian Brothers; originally members of a religious teaching order dating back to the 17th century, they progressed from altar wine to commercial production in the 1930's and are particularly well known for a sweet white Muscat called Chateau la Salle.

Another great favourite in this style is the delicate, slightly sparkling Moscato Amabile of Louis M. Martini, a firm otherwise noteworthy for its range of reliable and reasonably priced reds.

Beaulieu Vineyard is famous for its Private Reserve Cabernets, which have been among the most consistent in Napa; This is largely thanks to the skills of Andre Tchelistcheff, known as 'The Dean of California Winemakers', who was at Beaulieu for 35 years until leaving to set up his own consultancy in 1973.

Newer producers

A number of the most successful Napa Valley producers have started from scratch within the last twenty five years. Joe Heitz is an example. A graduate of the University of California at Davis, he was briefly Tchelistcheff's assistant at Beaulieu before teaching oenology at Fresno State College. In the 1960's, with very limited capital but a good deal of technical know-how, he bought a tiny vineyard and began making his own wine.

In the early years he purchased grapes from other growers, notably Chardonnay from the Hanzell vineyards in Sonoma County, and he is still a producer rather than a grower, but his wines are excellent. In addition to the Chardonnay, look out for his Martha's Vineyard Cabernet.

A neighbour of Heitz is Joseph Phelps, who came from bridge-building to winemaking in the 1970's. His is one of the most modern and experimental of all wineries and in addition to having great success with the richer white wines such as Gewürztraminer and late-harvest Johannisberg Riesling, he markets a fine blended red, made from Cabernet Sauvignon, Cabernet Franc and Merlot, under the brand name Insignia.

Two other Napa names to remember are Stony Hill and Schramsberg. Stony Hill specialises in white wines and has a reputation for producing the finest of all the region's Chardonnays. The mountain location, with its appropriately stony soil, gives the wine great resonance and potential for ageing. The vineyard also produces good well-balanced Gewürztraminer which is halfway between the austere and the fruity, with a fine, crisp flavour. A dry, distinctive white Riesling is also produced, clean and refreshing to the taste.

Schramsberg is equally distinguished for its sparkling wines, made by the traditional Champagne method; the two main styles are Blanc de Pinot, made principally from Pinot Noir grapes, and Blanc de Blancs based on Chardonnay.

Sonoma and Mendocino

Sonoma county, north of San Francisco, is where winemaking began in northern California; it is now recognised as one of the three top wine-producing areas.

Sonoma is second only to the Napa Valley in terms of the amount of wine produced. Most of the vineyards are to be found in the three principal valleys, Alexander, Sonoma and Dry Creek.

The old-established Sonoma wineries, like others in California, have had a chequered history. No sooner had they recovered from the depredations of phylloxera at the end of the last century than Prohibition put a stop to production. Most were forced to close down or – if they owned their own land – to turn it over to table grapes or some other crop until the notorious Eighteenth Amendment was repealed. Even then there was a long wait until the wine boom of the 1960's brought their product back into favour.

Sonoma's first vineyard and winery was Buena Vista, founded by the father of Californian viticulture, Agaston Haraszthy, in 1857. After fluctuating fortunes, including a period of closure, it is now under German ownership and enjoying a real renaissance. Their white wines are particularly noteworthy and include a unique blend of Riesling and Gewürztraminer called Spiceling.

One company which has maintained continuous production since its foundation in 1904 is Sebastiani; it survived the prohibition by making sacramental wine. Now under the control of the founder's grandson, Sebastiani are best known for big gutsy reds like Barbara and Zinfandel.

Another winery famous for strong Zinfandel is J. Pedroncelli. Originally producers of generic jug wines, they have recently concentrated on varietals with the emphasis on the more robust reds, which are given plenty of wood ageing.

Some producers offer a wide range of varietal wines from small individual plots; the variety of soils and microclimates in the area make this possible, and the approach is encouraged by the general mood of experiment in Californian winemaking. The company called simply Sonoma Vineyards is one of the largest – owning 1200 acres – and offers an excellent selection of these single vineyard wines; outstanding are their Chalk Hill Chardonnay and Alexander's Crown Cabernet Sauvignon. The French Champagne house Piper Heidsieck has recently taken an interest in the property and is part-financing the production of sparkling wines under the label Piper-Sonoma.

Chateau St. Jean is another winery specialising in single vineyards wines, with the emphasis on whites. They have been remarkably successful with rich late-harvest wines in the German style, made from Johannisberg Riesling and Gewürztraminer. They are also making sparkling wines.

Another highly individual company is Hanzell. It was started in 1952 by James Zellerbach, a former U.S. ambassador to Italy, who was passionately fond of Burgundy; he planted 19 acres with the classic Burgundy grapes, Pinot Noir and Chardonnay, waiting until the vines were mature before constructing an ultra-modern winery. The wines were superb, but after his death in 1963 winemaking temporarily ceased and the grapes were sold off to other producers. Production is now under way again and the new owner, being an enthusiast for Bordeaux wines, has added a few acres of Cabernet Sauvignon.

Three other names worth remembering in Sonoma are Korbel, famous for sparkling wines, Dry Creek, who make excellent Chardonnay, Fume Blanc and Chenin Blanc in a clean style, and Jordan Winery, who concentrate on Chardonnay and Cabernet.

Mendocino County

In the neighbouring county of Mendocino, winemaking is only a recent event. The oldest and best-known winery is Parducci, and they are very experimental in their approach. John Parducci has controversial ideas about maturing wine, believing that the use of wood masks the distinctive varietal flavours, and preferring stainless steel, even for his reds. These ideas have not been fully tested yet, but most people seem to prefer his whites, especially the Chardonnay, Chenin Blanc and French Colombard.

Fetzer offer three good jug wines and a limited range of varietals; they have gained particular recognition for their Zinfandel, which combines a full blackberry flavour with depth from wood ageing. Cresta Blanca have a reliable selection of table wines at reasonable prices.

Wooden barrels in the Sebastiani cellars

Central Coast

Change and growth are the watchwords in the Central Coast wine-producing region. The growers are improving their technical knowledge and at the same time the quality of the wine, making this one of the most exciting new wine regions in the United States.

For the past twenty years sales of table wines in California have increased at a rate of between 10 and 25% annually, and the number of wineries has more than doubled.

Demand has been for quality as well as quantity, and the Californian wine industry is now the most technologically advanced in the world. At the same time, California has seen great population growth, with cities such as San Francisco sprawling outwards into what was once agricultural land, so there is a constant search for new vineyard territory, much of which has been concentrated on the Central Coast region.

Livermore Valley

Some of the oldest established wine producers are to be found in the Livermore Valley.

At Concannon, founded in 1883, there is a long tradition of altar wine – but they also produce a good range of varietal table wines. Their red Petite Syrah and white Sauvignon have won particular attention.

Just across the road from Concannon is Wente Brothers, founded in the same year by a German immigrant who learned his winemaking from Charles Krug in the Napa Valley. Wente were producing good white varietals long before it became the fashion. Their soft and fruity Grey Riesling has always been a great favourite, and so now are Pinot Blanc, Sauvignon and Chardonnay, made in a light and restrained style with little wood ageing. There is also a fine sweet Semillon with the character of French Sauternes.

Another well-known Livermore Valley operation is Weibel Champagne Vineyards which, under the direction of the Swiss Rudolf Weibel, produces a wide selection of sparkling wines, some with remarkable names such as Sparkling Green Hungarian, Crackling Rosé and Crackling Duck.

Santa Cruz Mountains

In the nearby Santa Cruz mountains is the Ridge Vineyards Company which, during its twenty year existence, has made a great reputation for itself with big, rich reds, mainly Zinfandel and Cabernet Sauvignon. Their grapes come from a wide area, but the house style is distinctive, as is their tradition of precise labelling. On their bottles you will find the exact percentage of each grape variety, as well as the vineyard name, alcohol content and date of bottling.

Santa Clara County

The headquarters of Central Coast wine production has always been Santa Clara County. Almaden, Masson and Mirassou, three of the largest and most famous Californian companies, all have their roots here, though all have been forced to expand outside the area.

Almaden owns 4500 acres of vineyards, but few remain on the original site, which is now hemmed in by San Francisco suburbs. Although they have a range of high quality varietals sold under the name of their founder, Charles le Franc, Almaden are best known for sound and reasonably priced jug wines. They are also credited with the introduction to California of the 5 gallon bag-in-a-box dispenser.

Monterey

Both Masson and Mirassou have established vineyards in neighbouring Monterey. The expansion in this county has been astonishing, from 35 acres under vines in the 1960's to 35,000 today.

Of these, 5000 are owned by Paul Masson; their best wines come from the Pinnacles region and are marketed as varietals with the additional description Pinnacles Estate. But the company is more familiar to wine drinkers as the maker of good commercial blends, especially the California Carafes. Mirassou, the oldest wine-making family in the United States, operate on a similar basis. The oldest and most distinguished winery in Monterey is the much smaller Chalone Vineyard. Occupying 125 acres of a limestone ridge, with soils similar to Burgundy, they are said to produce California's finest Chardonnays, as well as excellent Pinot Blanc and Pinot Noir; some of their wines are sold under the secondary label Chapparal.

Other regions

The area around San Luis Obispo, an old mission town, includes scattered vineyards towards the hills of Paso Rables. It is early days yet, but some of the first results are promising. The Firestone Vineyards, near Santa Barbara, are fast building a reputation for themselves.

Paul Masson Winery in Monterey

South America

Although Chilean wines are considered to be the best wines of South America, wine is produced in the neighbouring countries of Argentina, Uruguay and Brazil, where wine-making is a growth industry.

Vines were first introduced to most South American countries in the 16th century by the Spanish. The industry was given a boost in the 19th century by the arrival of European immigrants with new varieties of vines and up-to-date techniques. Also the arrival of the railway systems gave access to wider markets.

Argentina

Vines do best in the Andean foothills, some 1000 kilometres from Buenos Aires in the provinces of Mendoza and San Juan. Both provinces have Mediterranean climates with dry clear air, prolonged sunshine and a low rainfall. Irrigation is necessary but the Andean rivers prove a good water supply, which is supplemented by water from wells.

In Mendoza, red and rosé wines are made from a variety of grapes. San Juan, which has a hotter climate, concentrates more on white wines with high sugar content and low acidity. These wines form the base for vermouths, sherries and brandies. Up to half of the crop is set aside for the production of raisins. In both provinces some wines are made from the classic French white wine grapes and from the Rhine Riesling. Sparkling wines are made by both méthode champenoise and cuvé clos. Vines are also cultivated in the neighbouring provinces of Neuguen and Rio Negro to the south and La Rioja, Catamarca, Salta and Jujuy to the north, but to a lesser degree.

In the 1980s Argentina is the largest producer of wine in the southern hemisphere and fifth in the world. Wine drinking is very much a part of everyday life in Argentina – around 75 litres per head of population are drunk every year. The wine industry has concentrated on producing blended table wines of good quality to meet the demands of this substantial home market. Exports are made to Russia, the United Kingdom and the United States, as well as to other South American countries. Look out for Franchette and Parral.

Fine wines from classic individual growths are also appearing abroad. Cabernet Sauvignon and Chardonnay from the Andean Range of Bodegas Penaflor are two examples. Look out for the ten-year old Chäteau Montchenot from Bodegas Lopez; the Cabernet and Pinot Blanc from José Orfila; the Pinot Blanc 'Oro del Rhin' from Greco Hermanos and Cabernet Sauvignon 'Eminencia' from Bodegas Gargantini. They are good quality wines and are relatively inexpensive.

Brazil

The province of Rio Grande do Sul in the far south of Brazil has become the centre of wine-production in this country. In the early plantings European varieties were tried but were not as successful as an American grape, the Isabella, which accounted for 90% of production. However in the 1980s many leading wine companies are re-introducing the classic European vines, mainly on an experimental basis.

There is no reason why Brazil should not assume more and more importance as a wine producer in the future as it has an enormous, largely untapped home market. Wine consumption is a mere 2½ litres per head of population annually, and international companies like Moët and Chandon and Martini and Rossi are investing here.

Moët, together with Cinzano and the Brazilian Monteiro Aranho Group, have set up the Brazilian company, Provifin, and are now producing 30,000 cases of 'champagne' and 80,000 cases of table wine annually. Martini and Rossi produce a 'Champagne de Greville', an Italian-style spumante and a range of table wines, Baron de Lantier.

Although the emphasis is mainly on good blended wines for domestic consumption, some quality Brazilian wines are finding their way abroad. One of these, the Granja União Cabernet of Rio Grandense, beat Chilean and Argentinian wines at a blind tasting in New York.

Other producers

Uruguay also possesses a flourishing wine industry, mainly around Montevideo, but no wine is exported. The equatorial climate of the rest of South America is not suited to vine cultivation. However it does occur on a small scale in Paraguay, Peru and Venezuela; production in these countries is not sufficient to satisfy home demand, and is therefore not exported.

Vines in the Argentine province of Mendoza

Chile

The wines of Chile are not very well known outside South America, but the country is among the world's major wine producers and has a history of wine-making stretching back over 400 years.

Vines were introduced to Chile by the Spanish conquerors in the 16th century, and cultivation was encouraged by the Catholic Church, initially to produce wine for the Mass. The vines flourished so well that the main problem was soon over-production.

Easy access to the coast meant that Chilean wines were being exported to other parts of South America over 200 years ago, and more and more emphasis is now being placed on the export of wine overseas.

The climate of Chile varies enormously from one region to another. In the north, there is arid desert where it sometimes does not rain for years, while in the south, there are heavy rains and violent gales. Lowland areas are restricted because Chile is hemmed in between the Andes Mountains to the east and the Pacific Ocean to the west. This may sound an unpromising location for the growing of grapes, but there is a small area in the centre of the country, around Santiago, where conditions are almost ideal.

In Chile's colonial days, most wine was made from a grape called the *pais*, which is similar to the *criolla* of the Argentine and the Mission of California. Some sweet dessert wines and fortified wines were also made from the *moscatel*. However, in the middle of the 19th century, at the instigation of Silvestre Ochagavia – the father of Chilean viticulture – a whole new range of classic European vines was introduced, and European wine experts were contracted to supply up-to-date knowledge. This was shortly before the phylloxera plague which devastated European vineyards in the late 1800s and which has attacked European vines in other parts of the world. So far, Chile has remained immune and would appear to have the only vines in existence still grown from ungrafted stocks.

Modern wine-making

The modern Chilean wine industry is based upon these classic grape types and many wines are named after them, like Riesling, Chardonnay, Sauvignon, and so on. The reds made from the Cabernet Sauvignon grape are particularly outstanding. This is the classic Bordeaux grape and Chilean cabernets have won prizes at blind tastings when set against venerable clarets selling at several times the price.

Although there are over 30,000 vineyards in Chile, most of the production is in the hands of a few major bodegas – literally meaning cellars – but now used to mean wine merchants or houses. Wine labels will carry their names rather than the name of a particular vineyard or district. Some of them are now becoming more familiar in Europe as their wines have retail outlets in certain of the main wine shops.

The biggest wine company, Concha y Toro, has more than 1,000 hectares of vines in the favoured Maipo valley. The climate here is more reliable than in most European vineyards and the standard of the wine is therefore less variable from vintage to vintage. Their 1976 Santa Emiliane red (Cabernet Sauvignon) won a double gold award at the 1980 International Wine and Spirits Competition. Other Cabernet Sauvignon wines from Concha y Toro include Casillera del Diablo and Marques de Casa Concha, Gran Vino (gran vino being the general designation for a wine six years old or more). All these wines are matured in oak for at least 2 years and, like all good Cabernets, needs several more years in bottle before they reach their best. Concha y Toro also produce a lighter red Reservado made from a blend of Cabernet Sauvignon and Merlot, and a medium-dry white Reservado made entirely from Riesling. Other major bodegas include Cousino Macul near Santiago, which markets reds under the names Don Luis and Don Matias; Undurrago, which has a variety of old-style and modern white wines; San Pedro at Lontue in Talca district and José Canega at Valparaiso, which handle wines from many areas.

An important new addition to Chile's producers in Miguel Torres, who has opened a winery in the Maule valley, Talca district. As in Spain, he has introduced a range of fresh-tasting, modern-style white wines (such as Santa Digna Sauvignon), probably the best currently available. He has also produced distinguished reds.

In addition to table wines, Chile continues to produce some fortified wines made mainly from the muscat grape, and a native brandy called *pisco*. By law, this can only be made from grapes grown in a limited area of the north where there is a hot, semi-desert like climate: the resulting wine is high in alcohol and low in acidity. Although 20 million litres of pisco is produced annually, almost all of it is consumed at home.

All in all, however, the present almost unique combination of high quality and low price seems unlikely to last for long, and wine drinkers would be well advised to search out and sample Chilean wines while conditions are so much in their favour.

A selection of Chilean red wines

AUSTRALIA

Australian wine-making is as old as her European settlement. Today Australia makes both red and white high-quality wines, as well as some rich dessert wines, fortified wines and brandies.

Australia is a vast continent, but large areas of it are quite unsuitable for vine cultivation. The best vineyards lie between the 34th and 38th parallels of latitude, in the states of New South Wales, Victoria, South Australia and Western Australia.

These areas are roughly the same distance from the Equator as North Africa in the Northern hemisphere, and the climate is much hotter and drier than in most European vineyards. Because of this, Australia's early wines were stronger, alcoholic, full of sugar, lacking acidity and quick to mature. Much of the country's produce went for distilling or for making rich dessert and fortified wines. Australia's restricted licensing laws encouraged the drinking of these strong wines, sherries and ports.

Australia's wine revolution
Today the situation is quite different. Production of table wines has grown more than tenfold in the last 25 years and now accounts for over three quarters of the total; many of these are of the higher quality. How has this happened? The trigger was the new mobility brought about by air travel. Australians found it easier to get to other parts of the world, and especially Europe, where they discovered other styles of wine. At the same time, Europeans were emigrating to Australia, where many of them set themselves up in the catering or wine trades, and some introduced new or improved vine stocks.

The new interest in wine was encouraged by informed wine journalism and the promotional efforts of the Australian Wine Board. In the industry itself, new techniques of wine-making such as temperature-controlled fermentation in stainless steel vats, the use of small oak barrels for maturing, and vacuum bottling to minimise the risk of oxidation, have all greatly improved the quality of the product. The money from increased sales has made these methods widespread and has also led to extensive irrigation schemes, which in turn have increased the acreage under vines. And so the bandwagon keeps on rolling.

The style of wine
What are these new Australian wines like? Well, no amount of sophisticated equipment can alter their basic character, and both reds and whites are still bigger, fruitier and more alcoholic than European wines made from the same grapes.

They are made from five main varieties, Cabernet Sauvignon and Shiraz for red, Semillion (also called Hunter Riesling), Rhine Riesling and Chardonnay for white. Other strains are increasingly used to modify their varietal character – Pinot Noir, Merlot and Malbec for red, Sauvignon, Chenin Blanc and Colombard for white.

The whites do best in cooler summers, or in high-altitude locations, and, with the exception of some Semillons and special late-harvest sweet wines, should be drunk within two or three years of the vintage. The reds mature sooner than they would in Europe and are full of fruity flavour even when young, but they still benefit from ageing, the best for ten years or more.

Labelling
Along with the new wines has come a new system of labelling. Traditionally, Australian wines were called by generic names such as claret, burgundy, hock and chablis, which could mean widely different things to different producers. Sometimes they were even less specific and called for local knowledge – what would a European make of Yarra Yarra or Mudgee Mud? Now that the business is being taken more seriously, and the wines exported to countries with strict legislation, changes have had to be made.

As in California, wines are now usually identified by the grape type. A single varietal, for example Chardonnay, must contain at least 80% of wine from that grape; if more than one variety is named, for example Cabernet Shiraz, the first must be dominant.

Except in two small areas, Mudgee and Margaret River, there is no geographical system of quality control similar to the French Appellation Controlée; indeed, grapes are still often carried long distances, sometimes across state boundaries, for blending by producers. In these circumstances, the reputation of producers is important and it is useful to know their names; these will feature later when we come to look in more detail at the main red and white wines.

If a region of origin is named on the label, 80% of the wine in the bottle must come from that region. Vintages will be shown, but where the climate is so reliable, and wines from different areas so frequently blended, they are not very significant, except to let you know simply how young or old the wine is.

Finally, many Australian bottles also have a back label; this may do no more than tell you the last time the Prince of Wales came to dinner, but it can be a source of more relevant information about grapes, vineyards or producer, fermenting periods, soil and serving temperature. Statistics like bin numbers and prizes in shows are also there, not merely to impress. Bin numbers should be noted for future orders and/or comparison; as for the accolades, with new-world wine production becoming as competitive as it is, makers – and Australian buyers – take them very seriously.

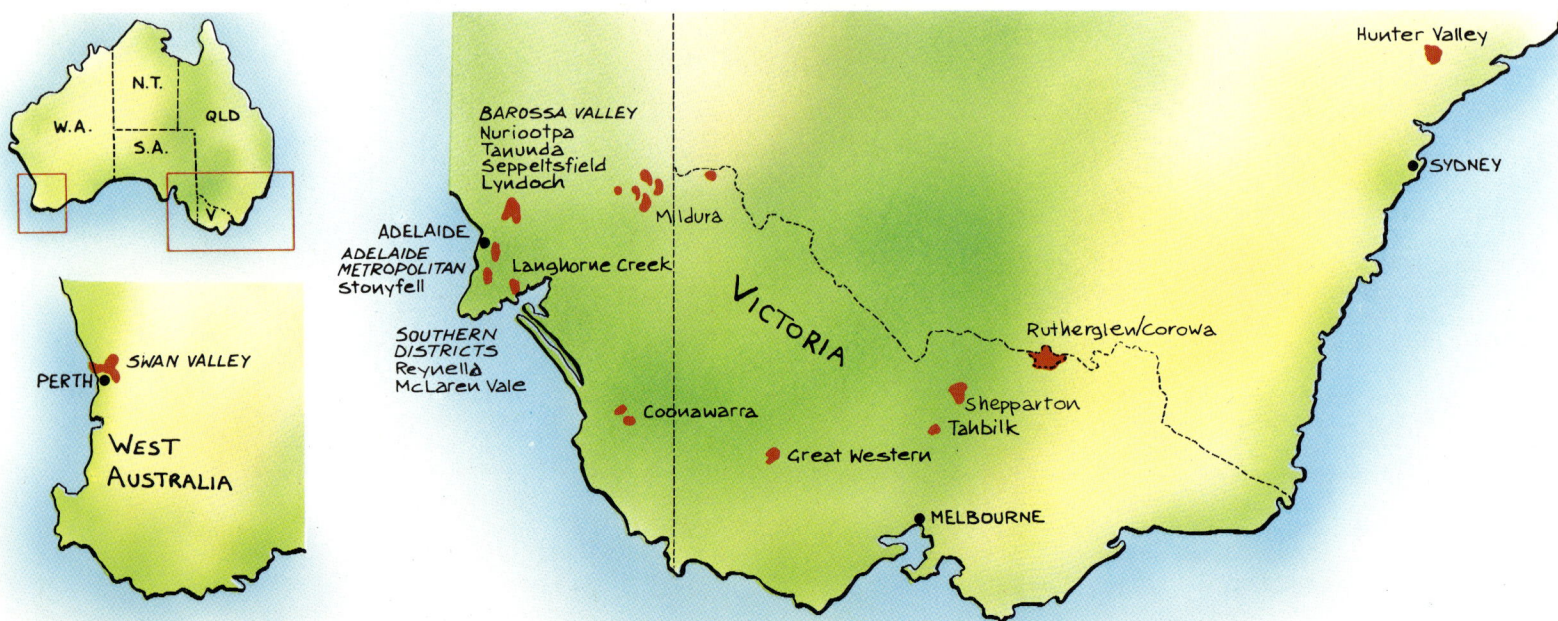

N.T.
W.A.
QLD
S.A.
V

SWAN VALLEY
PERTH
WEST AUSTRALIA

BAROSSA VALLEY
Nuriootpa
Tanunda
Seppeltsfield
Lyndoch
Mildura
ADELAIDE
ADELAIDE METROPOLITAN
Stonyfell
Langhorne Creek
SOUTHERN DISTRICTS
Reynella
McLaren Vale
VICTORIA
Coonawarra
Great Western
Rutherglew/Corowa
Shepparton
Tahbilk
MELBOURNE
Hunter Valley
SYDNEY

Red wines of Australia

Australian red wines have come a long way since the days of 'bloody kangaroo' and 'sweaty saddle'; Australians now produce many fine red wines which are exported all over the world.

Most Australian red wines come from two French classic varieties, but because of the different climate and soils, the wines made from them will not taste the same as they do in France. Their names are Cabernet Sauvignon and Shiraz.

Australian Cabernets are different again; they vary quite a lot in style according to region and producer, but lean more towards Californian fruitiness, though less heavy and with a shorter, drier finish. Shiraz is the same as Syrah, grown in the Rhône Valley to make the big, warm-hearted wines of Côte Rôtie and Hermitage; another name for the grape in Australia is Hermitage. Australia Shiraz can be an even more deep and concentrated wine, and for this reason it is often blended with Cabernet Sauvignon. Cabernet Shiraz is a great invention and an excellent introduction to Australian red wine.

Other red varieties, Pinot Noir, Merlot and Malbec, are used mainly in blending – though an Australian Pinot Noir defeated all comers at the 1979 Paris Wine Olympiad.

Traditionally, Australian wines have been producer's blends from a number of areas, and plenty of these are still made and sold either under brand names or a bin or vat number. McWilliams Inheritance Dry Red is an example, and so is Australia's most expensive red, Penfolds Grange Hermitage. But winemakers are now giving greater attention to the characteristics of individual regions and so, in addition to grape variety, vintage and producer's name, Australian wine labels often include the place where the grapes were grown. A typical wine description might be Yalumba (the name of the producer) Cabernet Shiraz (the grape blend), 1982 (the vintage), Barossa (the vineyard area).

Hunter Valley

One of Australia's oldest and most famous red wine regions is the Hunter Valley of New South Wales. The fortunes of the valley have followed a boom-bust pattern; thriving in the last century, they went into a long, slow decline until by 1960 only 7 companies were in operation, working less than 800 acres of land. Now there are over 40, and the acreage has increased to 20,000.

Two of Australia's biggest companies have vineyards here, Lindeman's Ben Ean and McWilliams Mount Pleasant, both producing good quality wines. A great favourite is McWilliams Mount Pleasant Philip Hermitage, a long-lasting wine with a distinctive smokey bouquet. A more recent company, founded in 1968, is Rothbury Estate, whose Chairman is one of the great authorities on Australian wine, Len Evans. All the wines sold under the Rothbury label must come from vineyards owned by the company, and at the top of their range they have Individual Paddock and Individual Vineyard wines with particularly outstanding qualities.

Another modern, highly efficient and well-advertised operation is Rosemount Estate; they are keen exporters, and both single varietals and blends are widely available. Other names to remember from this area are Wyndhams, Australia's oldest operating winery, Allandale and Tyrrells.

Victoria

Victoria has a number of red wine regions. In the North-East, near the border with New South Wales, the best known company is the family firm of Brown Bros., run by father and four sons, each of whom specialises in one aspect of the business. They are enthusiasts for single varietal wines, including the more unusual Pinot Noir and Merlot, which are made in an elegant, restrained style. Other respected wineries in the region include Bailey's, Campbell's of Rutherglen and Seppelt, which has other vineyards in Victoria.

In the Goulburn Valley, is the old-established winery of Château Tahbilk, run by the same family for over 50 years; their reds, especially the Shiraz, are substantial, long-lived wines. Further south, in the Bendigo – Ballarat, Yarra Valley and Geelong areas, Balgownie, Virgin Hills, Idyll Vineyard and Taltarni all make red wines of great character and refinement, especially from the Cabernet Sauvignon grape.

South Australia

South Australia produces more wine than any other state and is the home of a number of large companies. Thomas Hardy & Sons in McLaren Vale are famous for a wide range of blended wines as well as vintage ports made from Shiraz. They also have vineyards at Keppoch, further to the south, which produce good regional Cabernet Sauvignon and Cabernet Shiraz.

Yalumba, founded in the last century by the Dorset brewer Samuel Smith, is one of the most reliable names of all. Their traditional style reds, matured in small oak barrels, are full, smooth and reasonably priced. Their best wines are to be found under the Signature Series label.

The Barossa Valley, near to Adelaide, boasts several of Australia's finest growers. Penfolds were started at Magill in 1844 by an immigrant doctor from Sussex. In addition to the Grange Hermitage, named after the founder's cottage, they offer other excellent red wines at rather lower prices, notably the Bin 389 and St. Henri, both Cabernet Shiraz. Penfolds also have a holding in what is perhaps the most extraordinary and isolated of all Australian vineyard sites, Coonawarra. Only a restricted strip of soil, known as Terra Rossa, is suitable for cultivation, but yields and quality are outstanding for both Cabernet Sauvignon and for Shiraz. Other companies with an interest here are Brand's Laira, Lindemans, Petaluma, Wynn's and Mildara.

Tilling a vineyard, South Australia

White wines of Australia

In the early days of Australian wine-making, white wines were rich and fat; later with new refrigeration techniques and a more sophisticated drinking public to satisfy, Australian wine companies began producing lighter and drier white wines. These are now well-established with reputations as good as the best of European and American table wines.

A selection of Australian white, sweet and sparkling wines

The hot climate of the Australian vineyards suits red wine production better than white. But that same climate makes Australians thirsty for cool, refreshing drinks, and white wines are always much in demand; sales are currently six times those of red. Fortunately the Australian wine boom has been able to cope. New vineyards have been planted, many of them in cooler locations enjoyed by white grapes, and production has grown by leaps and bounds.

Grape types
Traditionally most Australian white wine comes from two European varieties, Rhine Riesling and Semillon. Rhine Riesling produces a light, medium dry, fruity wine, which has improved greatly in the last twenty years with the introduction of new fermentation techniques. Semillon gives an altogether bigger, longer lasting wine with a distinctive flavour all its own. Some sweet wines are made from both these grapes, by waiting until late in the vintage before picking. So that the fruit contains plenty of natural sugar. A rich, sweet wine which had long been an Australian speciality is the

fortified liqueur Muscat, made from the Frontignan grape.

The range of Australian whites has been greatly extended in recent years by the introduction of other European varieties, notably Chardonnay, which at its best gives a fine full dry wine, though the heat can make it overblown. And it lacks the backbone and austerity which gives the best French Chardonnays their unique distinction. Other varieties you are likely to find are Chenin Blanc, Sauvignon (also called Fumé Blanc), Traminer, Gewurtztraminer, Crouchen and Colombard. Many Australian white wines, like the reds, are varietals, so these grape names will appear on the label, but producers are also quite specific about the contents of their commercial blends, as Australians like to know what they are drinking and have no qualms about blending, which is rightly seen as evidence of the winemaker's skill. As in California, these new growers are using methods which can teach European 'experts' a thing or two.

South Australia to Hunter Valley
A lot of Australia's white wines come from the state of South Australia, and especially the Barossa Valley, which was settled by Silesian immigrants in the middle of the last century. Some of the state's most famous wineries were founded by these immigrants; Buring, now under the control of Lindemans, with a fine reputation for Rhine Rieslings; Seppelt, who are chiefly known for the sparkling wines produced at Great Western in Victoria; and Orlando, the first of all the Barossa companies, founded in 1850 by Joseph Gramp, and still a leader for standard and late-picked Rieslings and Traminers, many coming from individual vineyards.

The Barossa Co-operative Winery, which produces something of almost everything, sells under the label Kaiser Stuhl. Other South Australian wineries with a particular reputation for whites are Petaluma, who make very good Chardonnay; Quelltaler, for fine full-flavoured Rieslings; Lindemans, for Padthaway Chardonnay; De Bortoli, who specialise in rich botrytis affected wines made from Semillon, Rhine Riesling and Traminer; and Wolf Blass, who have excellent blended whites sold under Yellow, Grey, or Black labels.

The finest Semillon wines have traditionally come from the Hunter Valley, where for years the grape had confusingly been called the Hunter Riesling. Fine examples are made by McWilliams, Tyrrells, Rosemount and Rothbury, though the younger companies seem more interested in new arrivals such as Chardonnay and Fumé Blanc. McWilliams make a very reliable range of white varietals at their Riverina wineries in the Murrumbidgee Irrigation Area of New South Wales; the Riesling-Traminer blend is especially popular.

The hot climate of north east Victoria is not ideally suited to white wines, but this is the centre of production for the fine liqueur Muscats, similar to the vins doux of Southern France, also made from the Frontignan grape.

Fine examples come from Morris Wines of Rutherglen and Brown Bros. of Milawa. Brown Bros. also have higher altitude vineyards at Koombahla and Whitlands, and with a reputation as varietal specialists make a range of good white wines, especially Sauvignon, Semillon and Chardonnay. Look out too for the remarkable Mt. Helen Chardonnay from Tisdall, a small new company who have also been successful with late-picked Rhine Rieslings.

Western Australia
Some of the best white wines of Western Australia come from the old-established firm of Houghton, which has now been taken over by Hardys. They make an outstanding blend of Chenin and Muscadelle, which won fame for its creator Jack Mann and sold for years under the label Houghton's White Burgundy.

Further South, in the Margaret River region, Moss Wood are making a name with their Semillon, and Leeuwin Estate offer two styles of Rhine Riesling as well as fine Sauvignon and Chardonnay.

NEW ZEALAND

New Zealand is a latecomer to the ranks of large scale wine-producing nations, but is making up for this fast with high-quality wines. It is only in recent times that New Zealand producers have found a market for the light, elegant, fruity wines to which their climate and soil conditions are best suited.

Vines were introduced to New Zealand by a missionary, Rev. Samuel Marsden, who brought a selection with him from Australia and planted them at Keri Keri and Waimate on the North Island in 1819. Not long afterwards James Busby, who had made a success of wine-growing in the Hunter Valley of New South Wales, came to New Zealand as the first Official Queen's Representative. He planted cuttings of French and Spanish vines in the Bay of Islands, and by 1840 had a commercial crop.

During the course of the next century the industry developed spasmodically in the hands of European immigrants. They had to fight against phylloxera and a vigorous temperance movement, and by 1960 there were still only 1000 acres under cultivation. There are now 14,000, many of them given over to classic grape varieties, and the wineries are among the most pioneering in the world.

The revolution which has taken place over the past 25 years is largely due to the greatly increased interest in table wines world-wide which began in the 1960's. Not only were more people drinking more wine, they demanded quality and variety. New Zealand growers sought advice from experts overseas, such as the German Wine Institute at Geisenheim, who were enthusiastic about the potential of European White Grapes, and especially Müller Thurgau. Often called Riesling Sylvaner, this is the dominant grape in large areas of the Rhineland, and for a while it looked as if New Zealand would be known chiefly as the producer of Down Under Liebfraumilch.

A lot of light, fruity wines in this style are still made, but it is French varieties such as Sauvignon, Chardonnay and Pinot Blanc which have lately won most acclaim, and good red wines are now also being produced from Cabernet Sauvignon, Pinot Noir and a South African grape called Pinotage.

The cooler, wetter climate of New Zealand is more reminiscent of the North European vineyards than other Southern Hemisphere countries, and the wines have a more European character. Compare, for example, an Australian and New Zealand Chardonnay; the New Zealand wine is likely to be less full of obvious fruit and lower in alcohol, but refined and subtle, with refreshing acidity.

There are as yet no laws in New Zealand corresponding to the French Appellation Contrôlée so, as with Californian and Australian wines, the name and reputation of the producer are all-important. Most New Zealand wines are made by a handful of large companies.

Montana

Montana wines were started in 1943 by a Yugoslav immigrant, Ivan Yukich, whose family had been making wine in Europe for 300 years. They began with a modest plot near Auckland, but soon expanded into the Gisborne area – the estate is now called Ormond. In 1973 became the first commercial growers on the South Island, where they purchased some 4000 acres in Marlborough with financial backing from the giant American company, Seagram.

Montana now make almost half of New Zealand's table wines; their Sauvignon Blanc and Cabernet Sauvignon are outstanding, but look out too for their Rhine Riesling, Gewurztztraminer and Chardonnay, which are good.

Cooks

The other big name in New Zealand winemaking is Cooks. Vines have been grown at Te Kauwhata, south of Auckland, since the last century, but it was not until the 1960's that Cooks began serious planting of classic varieties, following advice from the Californian expert Professor Petrucci. They also built a modern winery, which is among the most technologically advanced anywhere.

By 1974 the gold medals were coming in, and they subsequently bought estates at Riverhead and Gisborne. Most of their wines are marketed as varietals, and they have won particular attention with their Chardonnay, rich and full by New Zealand standards, and Cabernet Sauvignon, which has plenty of blackcurranty fruit. There is also a good blend of Cabernet Sauvignon and Pinot Noir which sells under the name Cooks New Zealand Dry Red.

McWilliams

The Australian company McWilliams have had an interest in New Zealand since the 1940's and now have a number of vineyards and wineries in the Hawkes Bay area. They produce good Cabernet Sauvignon and Chardonnay in addition to fortified wines and a range of commercial blends – the red Bakano, white Cresta Dore and sparkling Marque Vue.

Corbans, founded over eighty years ago and now largely under the control of Rothmans, have all the latest equipment and offer good varietal wines, generic blends and flor sherries.

Of the small private companies, for future reference, Villa Maria, Matua Valley, Babich and Delegats are names to bear in mind.

A selection of Montana wines

THE CAPE

South African table wines have improved dramatically over the last few years. In the early 1970s the whites were dull and the reds, though better, were lacking in character. Now, so many advances have been made it is hard to believe the fine Cape wines of today had such predecessors.

Thanks to new wine laws and modern vinification methods, coupled with the enthusiasm of the growers, the wines are now consistently well made. Weather and soil may not provide for the production of the equivalent of a Château Latour, but you can be confident that almost any bottle of South African wine will be eminently drinkable and not over-priced.

The vineyards were started by the early Dutch settlers, who planted the first vines in 1655. The Huguenots followed in 1688 and then the British in 1806. Exports boomed when the British occupied the Cape, but problems followed with the abolition of preferential tariffs and a massive wine glut. For a time the wine industry faced ruin.

It was rescued in 1918 with the formation of the Co-operative Wine Growers' Association (KWV). The KWV pioneered the development of the whole industry, offering technical expertise and assistance throughout the Cape. KWV is now the central controlling body of the wine industry at producer level. All wine farmers are members and their surplus is held by KWV and then exported.

In 1972 the Wines of Origin Laws were passed and quality control came in. Every one of the thousands of wine farms within a demarcated area are now registered. Bottles of wine carry a guarantee stating not only the wines' place of origin and vintage year, but also its cultivar, or grape variety. Gradings are for Wine of Origin, Wine of Origin Superior and Estate Wine of Origin.

Wine regions

The wines come from two distinct regions. From the coastal belt between the sea and the first towering range of mountains come delicate white table wines and some of the best reds, as well as some of the lighter sherries. From the Little Karoo, beyond the Drakenstein mountains, come the sweet dessert wines, the carafe wines, South African sherries and the best muscatels.

The wine estates, whose wines are labelled Estate Wine of Origin, are to South Africa what the classified growths are to Bordeaux. There are approximately 43 classified estates. Estate wines of origin are made only from grapes grown on the estate, and are produced and bottled on the estate.

Many non-estate wine farms do have their own cellars and bottle their own wine, but most send their wines to the many co-operative wineries. Once a wine, even one from a well-known estate, has reached maturity, it is usually bought by one of the large wine companies, such as Nederburg. In general white wines tend to go to the big companies almost as soon as the grapes are harvested.

The reds are often kept in wood by the growers for two or three years before they are blended and bottled by the large companies. The system works because the grower is left free to make an individual wine that is backed by the big groups, who relieve him of all marketing worries.

Grape varieties

Of the white grapes, which account for over three-quarters of South African wines, the Steen is the most popular and is the Cape version of the Chenin Blanc. Most Steen wines are medium-dry, fruity and wonderfully refreshing. They make delicious summer aperitifs. There are also dry Steens and late-picked Steens, which are sweet enough to accompany desserts.

The Riesling grape from the Rhine, once rare in South Africa, is now planted in many of the best vineyards. Notable Riesling vineyards are at Paarl, Stellenbosch and Tulbagh. A Cape Riesling is always clean and flowery and goes well with both fish and white meat.

The red Pinotage, like Steen, is a grape variety first bred in the Cape. It is a cross between the elegant Pinot Noir and the hearty Hermitage or Cinsaut. The result is a smooth, substantial red wine with a fragrant bouquet and a fine finish.

Like Australian Cabernets, red South African Cabernets tend to be dark and full of flavour. They could well replace a French Rhône wine for fireside drinking in the depths of winter.

To these wines add a red wine of great flavour, KWV Roodeberg, a range of slightly sparkling rosés, a variety of South African sherries and brandies, and a tangerine liqueur, Van der Hum, and you will have the taste of one of the great wine countries.

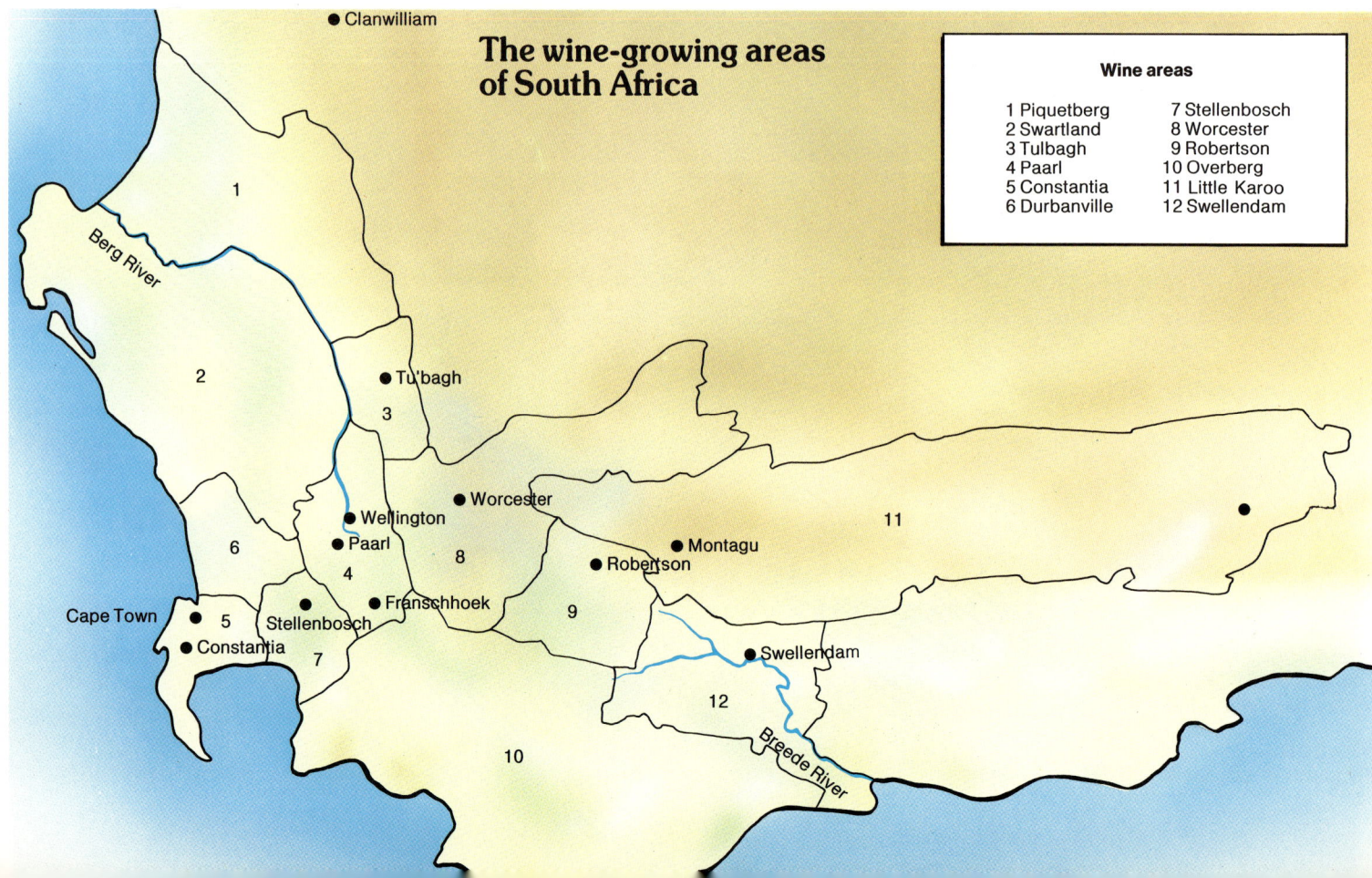

The wine-growing areas of South Africa

Wine areas

1 Piquetberg	7 Stellenbosch
2 Swartland	8 Worcester
3 Tulbagh	9 Robertson
4 Paarl	10 Overberg
5 Constantia	11 Little Karoo
6 Durbanville	12 Swellendam

White wines of the Cape

The best South African wines come from the coastal region of the Cape Province, which has a climate ideal for vines. And like Portugal, with its exposure to the west and the influence of the sea, the Cape is best known for its white wines—all reasonably priced and very drinkable.

On the sandy plains with low rainfall, the stunted vines make a poor wine, much of which goes for distillation. But in the green foothills, in the shadow of the mountains, the soil is deeper, the rainfall more generous and the wines of high quality, made by the descendants of Dutch and Hugenot settlers.

The best white wines are to be found on the individual estates along the Stellenbosch Wine Route. This takes in 15 estate wineries and four co-operatives producing the cream of Cape white wines, particularly worth buying for inexpensive summer drinking.

Delheim and Simonsig

The Delheim estate near Koelenhof is perched on the slopes of the Simonsberg mountains. These mountains give the Delheim vineyards an average of 90 cm of rain per year, while Paarl, 15 km away, gets no more than 20 cm.

Look out for the dry Delheim Riesling which has the crisp flavour of a newly pickled apple and a slight sparkle. The same estate produces a dry Steen, a uniquely South African wine, with a flowery, delicate flavour, so refreshing in warm weather.

In the modern cellars of the nearby Simonsig Wine Estate there is a full range of table wines, red, white and rosé. The Simonsig Rhine Riesling has often been mistaken for its German counterpart – it is not only equally dry and silky, with a nice long finish, but it also undercuts German Riesling in price in much of Europe. Simonsig also makes a sparkling wine by the méthode champenoise.

The soft Gewürztraminer wine from Simonsig is nearly as fruity and spicy as an Alsace Gewürztraminer, and considerably cheaper. If you have never tasted a white Cape Colombard, one of the best varietals comes from Simonsig. It is a big wine, which will go well with shellfish and creamy pasta dishes. It has ample flavour and travels well.

Overgaauw

Overgaauw, one of the oldest Cape estates, has been completely modernized. Its white wines are cold-fermented to bring out freshness and flavour. Try the crisp, concentrated Sylvaner for summer drinking. The Steen from Overgaauw is dry enough to go well with almost any variety of fish.

Blaauwklippen

Blaauwklippen is a beautiful Cape property which dates back to 1692. It produces a bone dry Chenin Blanc and a number of white varietals of good repute such as Chardonnay and Sauvignon. Its Rhine Riesling (called Weisser Riesling in South Africa) is light, with a sweet edge.

Backsberg and Tulbagh

A very versatile winegrower is Sydney Back of the Backsberg Estate. The winery here is as modern as any in the Southern Hemisphere. Backsberg is among the few private estates to bottle and age their own wines. Sauvignon Blanc, Rhine Riesling and Chardonnay predominate, with the Blacksberg Cabernet Sauvignon, a treat for lovers of red wine.

Twee Jongegezellen produces many award-winning white wines, such as the Grand Prix TJ 39, which is a blend of this estates' very best dry wines. It has a distinctive golden colour and is fragrant with plenty of fullness and depth.

Chenin Blanc from Tulbagh is lighter, with more finesse, than those from anywhere else, except Stellenbosch. The Clairette Blanche from this area is recommended.

Theuniskraal

Here there are plantations of both Rhine and South African Riesling, Gewürztraminer, Sémillon, Sauvignon and Pinot Noir. These can be outstanding.

Nederburg

Gunter Brözel, winemaker at Nederburg, thanks to his German expertise, has produced some of the Cape's finest wines. For the lightness and cheerfulness of the muscatel grape do not miss a Nederburg Fonternel. Nederburg Riesling is fresh and buoyant, while the Steen is rich and fruity. Try also the famous Paarl Edelkuer, a golden, sweet dessert wine. Made from the Chenin Blanc grape infected by noble rot, it is luscious and every bit as good as a top-quality Sauternes.

Cape vineyards near Franschhoek

Red wines of the Cape

Cape red wines represent less than a quarter of the total production of wine in South Africa. They are less popular in their home country than white wine because of the consistently warm climate, but are better appreciated in Europe where they cost less than almost any other comparable red wine.

Many of the finest examples of Cape reds come from the vineyards on the slopes of the mountains on the coastal belt. The best area is around Stellenbosch which has 24 different estates and six co-operatives making outstanding red wines.

The Pinotage and Cabernet Sauvignon are two outstanding examples of these wines. Pinotage results from the cross of the Pinot Noir and Hermitage vines. This made a grape variety unique to South Africa, but in 1922 its inventor was unimpressed with the result. Thirty years later the Pinotage was planted in a vineyard and was an immediate success. It ripens earlier than other reds and produces a full, rich wine with a noticeable flowery aroma. Deep red in colour, it is soft and round on the palate.

In inland areas like Malmesbury, the wine is fuller-bodied. In South Africa wine is generally drunk young, but most of them will improve after a few years in the bottle. Cape red wines are perfect with grills, stews, or steak and kidney pudding.

Cabernet Sauvignon, the famous grape of Bordeaux, is the other great grape of South Africa. The best Stellenbosch cabernet wines are full and elegant and need several years in cask and a few more in bottle to attain their peak. The Alto Estate makes a stylish and robust cabernet, which has been shipped to London for 40 years.

From the stunningly beautiful Constantia area, on the coast to the south of Cape Town, come quality cabernets, lighter and fruitier than those from other areas.

Another French red grape which thrives in the Cape climate is the Shiraz of the Rhône Valley. In the drier areas of Constantia, Faure and Durbanville, it yields a dry, smoky-flavoured wine of middle weight. Serve Shiraz wines with veal and lamb and remember they will be better if kept a few years after purchasing.

The only Cape wine to avoid is Cinsaut or Hermitage. As a prolific producer it accounts for 75% of local South African red wine, but it has little individual character. It comes into its own only when blended to make Pinotage.

Dotted further inland are the privately-owned wine estates producing mostly whites with a few red wines, often of surprising character and finesse. Uitkyk produces a quality cabernet and Blaauwklippen, known for its white wines, boasts one of the two Cape plantings of Californian Zinfandel. The Kanonkop Cabernet Sauvignon and Pinotage wines have a well-earned reputation for consistent quality. Meerendal produces nearly every variety of red, with Pinotage singled out for a number of awards in recent years. Meerendal Shiraz can be a huge, deeply-flavoured red which will make good winter drinking.

Another red wine to note is the Meerlust Cabernet Sauvignon. It is one of the few Cape cabernets to which, Bordeaux-style, Merlot is added, to make a more balanced wine. It is velvety and full of character after maturation in oak.

South African red wines tend to be spicier and more robustly flavoured than their French or Italian counterparts. They are delicious with some of the peppery Cape dishes, Irish stews, casseroles and game.

Cape sherry

South African sherry is produced by methods similar to those used for Spanish sherry. In the 1930s research showed that flor, the yeast that is the basis of sherry, is also present in South Africa.

There are few very dry and delicate Cape sherries and there are none of the old, nutty varieties for which Spain is celebrated. Mymering is a pale, extra dry Cape sherry of some renown and KWV Paarlsack have a trio of extra dry, medium dry and cream, with the medium dry the most acceptable. The excellent medium dry Onzerust and the richer Golden Acre are well made and good value for money. Those who prefer a delicate sherry should buy those made in Paarl, Stellenbosch or Tulbagh. Heavier ones come from the Robertson, Montagu and Worcester districts. Other sherry ranges offering sound value are Ravendrost, Marievale, Cape House and RSL. The nearest to the delicate Spanish dry fino is probably Cape Cavendish Extra dry. This goes well with soup or a fish course.

Port and brandy

South African tawny ports are lighter in colour and a little raisiny in flavour, compared to the Portuguese ports. One of the best is made on the Allesverloren Estate.

South Africans are generally fonder of their brandies than their wines. By law, young brandies must mature in oak casks for a minimum of three years to achieve mellowness and the desired amber colour. They may seem a bit rough to an American or European palate and rarely enter the same class as a French cognac or armagnac.

However, the mandarin-flavoured liqueur, Van der Hum, is a splendid alternative to Cointreau or Grand Marnier. This liqueur was first made by Dutch settlers at the Cape of Good Hope.

South African port, red wines and sherry.

Dishes for wine

The earlier pages of this book have provided a thorough mini-course in the appreciation of wine. But experience is inarguably the best teacher. Drinking wine on its own, at a professionally conducted tasting or in the relaxed company of friends, is one way to learn more and allows real freedom to choose and experiment. But nothing is more enjoyable than sharing the pleasure of wine with a good meal. A fine claret is truly set up by a good cut of beef, and what is more fun than eating outside on a warm summer's day, washing down olives, fresh, crisp salads, and perhaps a marinated, barbecued chicken, with a clear, clean rosé – wishing you were in the south of France or the Algarve? But with that to enjoy, why wish you are anyplace else?

Wine and food go together – but certain wines complement particular foods. It is a form of matchmaking and, while many wines adapt adequately to a number of foods, when you make that perfect marriage, the 'rightness' of the two together is immediately apparent. Light crisp white wines with spicy dishes, a luxuriant white burgundy with rich fish such as lobster or salmon, Chianti with spaghetti Bolognese, young red burgundy with casseroled chicken, a fine elegant sauternes with a fruit flan or crème brûlée – these combinations are matchless. At the same time, such partnerships are not rigid. Personal taste, the time of year, the importance of the occasion, family finances – all can influence your choice. On the following pages are a selection of delicious recipes with suggested wines to go with them. Try the suggestions or introduce your own – eat, drink and be merry!

Starters

Contents

Turnip soup

This is a simple recipe ideal for baby turnips which are full of flavour and have no coarse fibres. It could also be made equally well with tender young carrots. A dry white Loire would make a good partner to the soup.

Serves 4
500 g /18 oz baby turnips, peeled
850 ml /1½ pt chicken stock
fat removed
50 g /2 oz butter
2 garlic cloves, crushed

salt
freshly ground black pepper
100 g /4 oz Gruyère cheese, grated
For the croûtons
4 slices of bread
50 g /2 oz butter for frying

1 Cut the turnips into small sticks, slightly larger than matchsticks. Blanch them in boiling salted water for 2 minutes. Drain well. Put the stock on to heat through.
2 Heat the butter in a heavy-bottomed saucepan over medium-low heat until it foams. Fry the garlic in the butter for 1 minute. Add the turnip sticks and cook for about 4 minutes, turning them occasionally until golden and tender.
3 To make the croûtons, remove the crusts from the bread and cut the bread into cubes. Melt the butter in a frying-pan over medium-low heat and sauté the cubes until brown on all sides, about 2 minutes. Drain the cubes thoroughly on absorbent paper.
4 Divide the croûtons between the 4 bowls. Season the hot stock with salt and pepper and pour into the bowls. Spoon the turnip sticks into the bowls and sprinkle with the cheese. Serve the soup immediately.

making chicken stock, then 15 minutes

Leek and asparagus soup

This is a light and delicious soup, simple to make and equally good hot or cold. The asparagus gives a subtle and unusual taste. Serve with a chilled blended Moselle.

Serves 4

500 g /1 lb leeks
50 g /2 oz butter
300 ml /10 fl oz milk
1 bay leaf
850 ml /1½ pt chicken stock
250 g /8 oz canned asparagus tips
salt
freshly ground black pepper
5 ml /1 tsp dried chervil

1 Wash and finely chop the leeks, including the tenderest parts of the green tops. Melt the butter in a large saucepan over moderate heat and sauté the leeks for 10 minutes or until soft.

2 Meanwhile in a small saucepan bring the milk with the bay leaf almost to boiling point over low heat.

3 Add the chicken stock to the pan of leeks. Remove the bay leaf from the infused milk and add the milk and asparagus tips to the leeks. Stir well, remove from heat and leave to cool.

4 Pour the cooled soup into a blender and blend thoroughly. Return to the large pan and heat through. Check for seasoning, adding salt and freshly ground black pepper if necessary, and transfer to individual warmed soup bowls or a warmed soup tureen. Garnish with the chervil and serve immediately.

30 minutes

Terrine of pork and veal

A light pâté makes the perfect lunch, served with green salad, crusty French bread, and inviting Anjou rosé wine.

Serves 8

500 g /1 lb lean pork, minced
500 g /1 lb pie veal, minced
250 g /8 oz pork fat, minced
1 medium-sized onion, finely chopped
1 garlic clove, crushed
25 g /1 oz butter
150 ml /5 fl oz brandy or dry white wine
1 medium-sized egg, beaten
10 ml /2 tsp salt
1.5 ml /¼ tsp freshly ground pepper
pinch of allspice
2.5 ml /½ tsp dried thyme
500 g /1 lb streaky bacon slices
lettuce, tomato and gherkins to garnish

1 Combine the minced pork, veal and pork fat in a large mixing bowl. Heat the oven to 180C /350F /gas 4.
2 In a frying-pan, sauté the onion and garlic in the butter until soft. Remove the onion and add to the bowl of minced meat. Rinse the pan with brandy or wine and pour on to the meat and onion.
3 Mix in the egg. Season the meat mixture with salt, pepper, allspice and thyme and beat well.
4 Remove the rinds from the bacon slices. Use two-thirds of the slices to line a 1.5 L /2½ pt mould or rectangular ovenproof container. Press the meat mixture into the bowl or tin and cover with the remaining bacon slices.

5 Cover the terrine tightly with foil and a lid. Stand the bowl in a baking tin of water and bake in the oven for 2 hours. It is ready when a skewer stuck into the terrine comes out clean.
6 Remove the lid and place a weight on top of the foil. Leave to cool overnight, then chill for at least 8 hours.
7 Run a knife around the dish to loosen the bacon lining from the sides, if the pâté has not shrunk. Turn the terrine out on to a plate. Surround with small lettuce leaves; garnish the top as shown.

⚄ 2½ hours,
plus 8 hours chilling

Terrine of hare

This is an ideal way of cooking an older hare, especially if you do not plan to eat it immediately, as the terrine keeps for up to a month if refrigerated. Try serving it with a German red wine.

Serves 8

450 g /1 lb cooked hare meat, finely minced
5 ml /1 tsp freshly grated nutmeg
5 ml /1 tsp ground ginger
salt and ground black pepper
275 ml /10 fl oz strong stock
225 g /8 oz sausage-meat
10 ml /2 tsp freshly chopped parsley
5 ml /1 tsp dried thyme

5 ml /1 tsp dried sage
1 garlic clove, cut in half
25 g /1 oz butter
30 ml /2 tbls brandy
8 streaky bacon slices, 6 of them chopped
175 g /6 oz canned chestnuts, drained and
    chopped
175 g /6 oz clarified butter
hot buttered toast to serve

1   Mix the hare with the nutmeg and ginger in a bowl. Season highly with salt and black pepper, then moisten with the stock: add enough to make the mixture wet without being slushy.
2   In another bowl, mix the sausage-meat with the parsley, thyme and sage. Season with salt and black pepper. Heat oven to 180C /350F /gas 4.
3   Rub a 2 L /3½ pt mould all over inside with the cut sides of the garlic and then grease well with the butter. Spread half the minced hare mixture on the bottom, pressing it well down, and sprinkle with 10 ml /2 tsp brandy. Cover with half the chopped bacon, then half the chestnuts. Put all the sausage-meat and herb mixture over the chestnuts, again pressing well down, and sprinkle with 10 ml /2 tsp

brandy. Cover with the remaining chestnuts, then the bacon, finishing with a layer of hare. Sprinkle with the rest of the brandy. Lay 2 whole bacon slices on top and cover tin with buttered foil.
4   Place the mould in a roasting tin half filled with boiling water and bake for 1¾ hours or until the mixture has shrunk away from the sides of the tin. Remove from the oven and cool.
5   When the terrine is cool, remove the bacon slices from the top and pour the clarified butter over. Refrigerate and serve well chilled with hot buttered toast.

🍴🍴 2¾ hours

Gin pâté

Gin and its flavouring, juniper berries, give a lift to this smooth chicken liver pâté. Serve with an Alsace Gewürztraminer.

Serves 4–6

250 g /8 oz chicken livers, trimmed
15 g /1/2 oz butter
1 garlic clove, finely chopped
30 ml /2 tbls gin

4–6 juniper berries, crushed
salt and freshly ground black pepper
50 g /2 oz curd cheese
juniper berries and parsley to garnish

1 Pat the chicken livers dry with absorbent paper. Melt the butter in a frying-pan over moderate heat. When the foaming subsides, add the chopped garlic and cook for 1 minute. Then add the livers and fry for 2–3 minutes, stirring, until cooked but still pink inside.

2 Transfer the livers with a slotted spoon to the goblet of a blender. Blend to a smooth purée.

3 Add the gin and crushed juniper berries to the frying-pan and heat through, stirring to incorporate all the crusty bits from the pan. Add the liquid in the frying-pan to the liver purée in the blender and blend once more. Season with salt and pepper.

4 Add the curd cheese and blend again. Transfer the pâté to a 250 ml /10 fl oz earthenware terrine and smooth the top of it with a round-bladed knife. Chill in the refrigerator for 2 days to let the flavour mature.

5 Before serving, decorate the chilled pâté with both juniper berries and parsley. It can be served, cut into thin slices, accompanied with hot toast and butter curls.

🕐 ⏲ 30 minutes
plus 48 hours maturing

Tuna mousse

This is a deliciously light and creamy mousse which would be perfect for lunch on a hot summer's day, or, set in a fish mould, would make a simple but spectacular appetizer for a grand dinner party. Serve with a dry Australian white wine.

Serves 4–6
350 g /12 oz canned tuna fish
15 ml /1 tbls gelatine powder
30 ml /2 tbls lemon juice
5 ml /1 tsp cayenne pepper
5 ml /1 tsp horseradish sauce
90 ml /6 tbls thick cream
2 large egg whites

For the garnish
1 medium-sized cucumber
10 ml /2 tsp grated onion
1 small chilli, finely chopped
10 ml /2 tsp fresh chervil, finely chopped
15 ml /1 tbls lemon juice
salt and ground black pepper
celery leaves and flat-leafed parsley

1   In a small bowl sprinkle the gelatine powder over 30 ml /2 tbls cold water. Place the bowl in a small pan of simmering water and stir to dissolve the gelatine.
2   Drain the tuna and in a large bowl mash it thoroughly. Add the lemon juice, cayenne pepper and horseradish sauce. Season to taste with salt and freshly ground black pepper. Mix in the cream. Add the dissolved gelatine, stirring well.
3   In another bowl, whisk the egg whites until stiff peaks form. With a large metal spoon, carefully fold the whites into the fish mixture. Turn the mousse into a 575 ml /1 pt soufflé dish or a fish-shaped mould and leave to set in the refrigerator.
4   Ten minutes before serving make the garnish. Cut the cucumber, unpeeled, into fine julienne strips. Place in a bowl and mix with grated onion, green chilli, chervil and lemon juice. Season with salt and pepper. Take the mousse out of the refrigerator, turn out onto a plate if using a mould, and garnish with cumber, celery leaves and parsley. Serve immediately.

40 minutes, plus setting time

92

Creamed aubergine salad

Finely chopped aubergine in a mayonnaise and yoghurt dressing makes an interesting and delicious salad to go with a plain grilled meat dish. Alternatively it makes an unusual vegetable appetizer – serve with a Retsina to set off the richness of the aubergines.

Serves 4

1 large aubergine
45 ml /3 tbls olive oil
700 ml /7 fl oz Mayonnaise
700 ml /7 fl oz yoghurt
1 small onion, finely chopped
7.5 ml /1½ tsp dried marjoram

5 ml /1 tsp honey
5 ml /1 tsp horseradish sauce
5 ml /1 tsp lemon juice
salt
freshly ground black pepper
pinch of cayenne pepper
pitta bread to serve

1 Wipe the aubergine with a damp cloth but do not peel. Cut it in half and chop each half into very fine strips. Put on a plate, sprinkle liberally with salt and leave to drain for 30 minutes.

2 Put the aubergine strips into a colander and thoroughly rinse under running cold water. Shake well to drain.

3 Put 45 ml /3 tbls olive oil in a large frying-pan over medium heat and, when nearly smoking, add the aubergine. Cook for 10 minutes stirring occasionally. Remove from pan and drain on absorbent paper. Leave to cool.

4 Mix the mayonnaise with the yoghurt in a large bowl. Add the onion, marjoram, honey, horseradish and lemon juice and mix thoroughly. Add the cold aubergine, season to taste with salt and freshly ground black pepper, mix well and put in the refrigerator to chill for 30 minutes.

5 Pile on to a serving dish, sprinkle a pinch of cayenne pepper over the top and serve immediately with crisp, piping hot rounds of pitta bread.

draining aubergines then 30 minutes plus chilling

Creamy vegetable casserole

Serve this luxurious-looking yet economical starter with a well-chilled Californian wine, such as Gallo's Chablis Blanc, at an informal party.

Serves 6

900 g /2 lb small courgettes
150 ml /5 fl oz Chicken stock
450 g /1 lb carrots, cut lengthways into 10 mm /⅓ in batons
90 ml /6 tbls aspic powder
425 ml /15 fl oz boiling water
105 ml /7 tbls thick cream
105 ml /7 tbls mayonnaise

15 ml /1 tbls white wine vinegar
5 ml /1 tsp lemon juice
30 ml /2 tbls finely chopped fresh parsley
salt
freshly ground black pepper
2 canned pimentos, drained and thinly sliced
fresh herbs, to garnish
sliced tomatoes, to garnish

1 Steam the courgettes, whole, for 10 minutes. Cool them quickly and slice them lengthways into 10 mm /⅓ in thick batons.
2 Bring the chicken stock to the boil in a saucepan, add the carrots and simmer for 5–6 minutes or until they are just tender. Drain, discarding the stock, and cool the carrots quickly.
3 Put the aspic into a bowl, pour on the boiling water and stir to dissolve. Let stand for 10 minutes.
4 Stir in the cream, mayonnaise, vinegar, lemon juice and parsley. Season with salt and pepper. Beat the mixture until all the ingredients are well-blended. Chill in the refrigerator for about 20–25 minutes, until it has the consistency of unbeaten egg white.
5 Rinse a 1.5 L /3 pt loaf tin with cold water. Arrange a layer of courgette strips on the base, along the length of the tin. Then place a layer of carrot strips across the tin. Add four layers of courgettes and three of carrots, in the same way. Then add all the pimentoes in one layer. Finish with one more layer each of courgettes and carrots.
6 Pour the aspic cream over the vegetables and rap the sides of the tin so that the cream penetrates all the layers and there are no air bubbles trapped inside. Cover the tin and refrigerate for at least 2 hours, so the aspic cream firms up.
7 To turn out, run a knife around the edges of the terrine. Invert a serving platter over the top, turn over the tin and platter together and give a sharp shake. Garnish and serve sliced.

making stock,
then 1 hour, plus chilling

Avocado mousse

This luxurious mousse makes a light starter to a summer dinner party, if served with a fresh white wine, such as a Vinho Verde.

Serves 6

2 large ripe avocados
30 ml /2 tbls lemon juice
10 ml /2 tsp onion, finely chopped
2.5 ml /½ tsp Tabasco sauce
250 ml /10 fl oz chicken stock
15 g /½ oz gelatine powder
150 ml /5 fl oz thick cream
2 medium-sized egg whites

150 ml /5 fl oz thick mayonnaise
salt
freshly ground black pepper

For the garnish
lemon slices, halved
cucumber slices
150 ml /5 fl oz vinaigrette

1   Peel, stone and chop the avocados. Blend them with the lemon juice, onion, Tabasco sauce and chicken stock until smooth.
2   Place the gelatine in a small pan with a little water and heat until the gelatine has dissolved. Pour the gelatine into the avocado mixture in a thin stream, stirring constantly. Chill for about 15 minutes, until the mixture is just setting.
3   Meanwhile, whip the cream so that it just holds its shape but is not stiff. Whisk the egg whites until they form stiff peaks.
4   Carefully fold the cream into the avocado mixture, followed by the mayonnaise and the egg whites. Season with salt and pepper.
5   Rinse out a 1 L /2 pt charlotte mould. Turn the avocado mixture into the mould. Cover and refrigerate to set for about 2 hours.
6   Turn out onto a plate 30 minutes before serving. Garnish the top with halved lemon slices and cucumber slices. Surround with cucumber twists; dribble the vinaigrette over the garnishes.

1 hour, plus chilling time

Stuffed courgettes

Courgettes, filled with a tasty stuffing and served with a smooth cheese sauce, make an interesting vegetable starter. Accompany the dish with a light white wine, such as a Swiss Fendant or a Muscadet de Sevre et Maine, that can happily be served through the rest of the meal.

Serves 4

8 large courgettes
salt
45 ml /3 tbls oil
1 small onion, finely chopped
100 g /4 oz ham, finely chopped
100 g /4 oz fresh white breadcrumbs
30 ml /2 tbls freshly chopped parsley
5 ml /1 tsp dried thyme
15 ml /1 tbls lemon juice
freshly ground black pepper

1 medium-sized egg, beaten
butter for greasing
parsley sprigs to garnish
For the cheese sauce
25 g /1 oz butter
25 g /1 oz flour
275 ml /10 fl oz milk
100 g /4 oz Cheddar cheese, grated
a pinch of grated nutmeg
salt and freshly ground pepper

1 Hollow out the centres of the courgettes by pushing an apple corer into each end. Heat the oven to 190C /375F /gas 5.

2 Boil the hollowed-out courgettes in salted water for 10 minutes, to blanch them. Drain thoroughly and pat dry with absorbent paper.

3 Heat the oil in a frying-pan, add the onion and fry for 5 minutes until soft. Remove from the heat and stir in the ham, breadcrumbs, parsley, thyme, and lemon juice. Season to taste with salt and freshly ground black pepper, then bind all the ingredients together with the beaten egg.

4 Carefully stuff the hollowed-out courgettes with the filling. Arrange the courgettes in a lightly buttered dish, cover with foil and bake for 30 minutes.

5 Meanwhile, make the cheese sauce. Melt the butter in a saucepan and, using a wooden spoon, stir in the flour. Cook over moderate heat for 2 minutes, then remove from the heat. Add the milk gradually, stirring until thick and smooth. Add the cheese, a pinch of nutmeg and salt and pepper to taste. Heat until the cheese has melted into the sauce.

6 Remove the courgettes from the oven and divide them between 4 small plates. Pour a little of the sauce over each serving and garnish with parsley sprigs. Serve immediately.

1 hour

Montpellier appetizer

Montpellier, in the Languedoc, is famous for its green, herby butter mixed with mustard and anchovies. The butter gives a deliciously piquant flavour to the mushrooms and tomatoes in this appetizer. Serve with crusty French bread and a light and fruity Côteaux de Languedoc red.

Serves 6
3 large tomatoes
450 g /1 lb large button mushrooms
30 ml /6 tsp fresh white breadcrumbs
salt
freshly ground black pepper
crusty French bread, to serve (optional)

For the butter
225 g /8 oz butter, softened
45 ml /3 tbls finely chopped parsley
30 ml /2 tbls finely chopped fennel
45 ml /3 tbls finely chopped tarragon
2 garlic cloves, crushed
6 canned anchovy fillets, pounded
15 ml /1 tbls mustard

1 Cut the tomatoes across in half, scoop out the seeds, being careful not to break the flesh, turn the tomato halves upside down and let them drain.
2 Peel the mushrooms and cut off the stalks. Finely chop these and reserve.
3 Put the herbs in a mortar and pound them well with the pestle. Add the crushed garlic, anchovy fillets, mustard and mix well. Whisk the herb mixture into the softened butter in a large bowl, making sure that it is thoroughly and evenly distributed.
4 Divide the butter mixture into 2 and mix the chopped mushroom stalks into one half of the mixture.
5 Heat the oven to 190C /375F /gas 5.
6 Grease a large roasting pan with some of pounded butter mixture (the half without the mushrooms) and lay the tomatoes in the pan.

7 Fill the tomatoes with the mushroom stalk and butter mixture and sprinkle 5 ml /1 tsp breadcrumbs over the top of each one. Put in the oven and bake for 25 minutes.
8 Remove the pan from the oven and add the mushroom caps. Spread the plain butter mixture over the mushrooms, sprinkle them and the tomatoes with salt and freshly ground pepper and return to the oven for a further 10 minutes.
9 To serve, carefully transfer a tomato half to each of 6 individual plates. Place 6 button mushrooms on each plate and pour over some of the juice. Serve immediately, accompanied by crusty French bread, if wished.

♧♧ 1¼ hours

Baked scallops

Serve these delicate shellfish as the starter for an outdoor evening meal. A Moselle from the Saar region, lightly chilled, would make a perfect accompaniment.

Serves 4

8 large scallops
2 garlic cloves, finely chopped
25 g /1 oz parsley, finely chopped
2 medium-sized onions, finely chopped
1 pinch of ground cloves

1.5 ml /¹⁄₄ tsp freshly grated nutmeg
salt
freshly ground black pepper
50 g /2 oz fresh white breadcrumbs
olive oil
sprigs of watercress, to garnish
lemon wedges, to garnish

1 Heat the oven to 200C /400F /gas 6. Prepare the scallops: clean away the beard, which appears in a black translucent line behind the coral. Ease the scallop away from its shell and wash and dry the scallops and 4 rounded shells.
2 Chop the scallop meat and corals and place them in a mixing bowl. Add the garlic, parsley and onions. Add cloves and nutmeg, season with salt and freshly ground pepper and mix the ingredients until they are well blended.

3 Divide the mixture into portions and pile it into each of the shells. Cover with the breadcrumbs and sprinkle over a little olive oil.
4 Place the shells on a baking sheet and bake for 20 minutes or until lightly browned on top. Garnish, then serve.

🕐 30 minutes

Cheese and ham soufflé

This soufflé makes a showy starter for 6 people or a main course for 4, accompanied by a green salad and crusty French bread. Serve it with a clean, refreshing Nahe wine.

Serves 4-6

50 g /2 oz butter
50 g /2 oz flour
425 ml /15 fl oz milk
6 medium-sized eggs
1 extra egg white

5 ml /1 tsp mustard
100 g /4 oz ham, cubed
150 g /5 oz Cheddar, grated
25 g /1 oz Parmesan, grated
salt and freshly ground black pepper
butter for greasing

1 Heat the oven to 180C /350F /gas 4. Melt the butter in a medium pan. Off the heat stir in the flour until smooth. Very slowly add the milk, stirring constantly. Return to the heat and cook slowly until the sauce is thick and smooth. Remove the pan from the heat.

2 Separate the eggs and add the extra white to the other 6. Lightly mix the egg yolks together then stir them quickly into the sauce with a wooden spoon.

3 Add the mustard, cubed ham and the grated cheeses, and salt and pepper to taste. Mix everything in well. Lightly butter a 2 L /3½ pt soufflé dish.

4 Whisk the egg whites until they are very stiff, then gently fold them into the cheese mixture with a metal spoon.

5 Turn the soufflé mixture into the prepared dish. With a knife mark a circle round the top of the soufflé about 25 mm /1 in from the edge. (The centre of the soufflé inside this line will rise higher than the edge.) Bake for 40 minutes.

6 Test the soufflé with a clean knife inserted into the centre to see if it is ready. If the mixture is still runny, cook for 5 minutes more. Serve at once.

1 hour

Smoked salmon cones

Serve this beautiful luxury canapé with champagne or a sparkling
Saumur wine. Everyone will remember it.

Makes about 30 canapés

125 ml /4 fl oz thick mayonnaise
15 ml /1 tbls yoghurt
1.5 ml /¼ tsp horseradish relish
100 g /4 oz boiled, peeled prawns, chopped
pinch of salt

several drops of lemon juice
freshly ground black pepper
about 600 g /1¼ lb smoked salmon cut in 8 long slices
parsley sprigs, to garnish (optional)
lemon slices, to garnish

1 The day before the party, mix the mayonnaise, yoghurt, horseradish relish and chopped prawns together and season the mixture with salt, lemon juice to taste and a generous amount of freshly ground black pepper.

2 Cut the salmon slices into triangles, measuring approximately 7.5 × 6.5 × 6.5 cm /3 × 2½ × 2½ in. Fold the 2 shorter sides around your index finger, pressing the edges together to make a cone shape. It is easy to 'patch' any cones and make up any other cones with unused bits of salmon.

3 Use a teaspoon to fill the salmon cones with the mayonnaise mixture, then arrange the cones carefully on the serving dish, overlapping them slightly.

4 Cover the dish with cling film and refrigerate overnight.

5 Remove the cling film just before serving, garnish with the parsley sprigs and thin slices of lemon, if wished, and serve.

40 minutes
plus overnight chilling

Californian avocado

This simple-to-prepare starter combines some of the best of Californian produce. Large ripe avocados, sliced thinly, are delicious in combination with egg and succulent fresh prawns. Serve it with a chilled Californian Chardonnay.

Serves 4-6

2 large ripe avocados
juice of 3 lemons
6 hard-boiled eggs
225 g /8 oz boiled, peeled prawns

salt
freshly ground white pepper
150 ml /5 fl oz mayonnaise
8-12 large prawns, tail shells
  intact, to garnish

1 Halve, stone and peel the avocados. Slice each half into 3 lengthways. Sprinkle the slices with lemon juice, using 2 lemons, to prevent discoloration. Arrange 2 slices on individual plates in a slightly overlapping shape.

2 Reserve 2 of the hard-boiled egg yolks. Slice the remaining eggs and the egg whites lengthways and place them on the plates.

3 Season the prawns with salt and freshly ground white pepper and pile onto the plates, on the egg.

4 Add the remaining lemon juice to the mayonnaise and blend well. Fit a piping bag with a star nozzle and fill with mayonnaise. Pipe the mayonnaise on top of the prawns.

5 Sieve the reserved egg yolks through a nylon sieve over the mayonnaise. Garnish each plate with 2 prawns.

boiling the eggs,
then 20 minutes

Prawn bouchées

Savouries to serve before dinner not only stimulate the appetite but also help solve the problem of drinking on an empty stomach. Choose types that are not too heavy – these prawn bouchées fit the bill perfectly and marry well with a dry white Mâcon.

Makes 36

500 g /1 lb frozen puff pastry, defrosted
1 beaten egg, for glazing
40 g /1½ oz butter
30 ml /2 tbls finely chopped onion
30 ml /2 tbls flour
425 ml /15 fl oz hot milk
½ bay leaf
6 black peppercorns
good pinch of freshly grated nutmeg
2 shallots, finely chopped
150 ml /5 fl oz dry white wine
15 ml /1 tbls finely chopped parsley
30 ml /2 tbls thick cream
15 ml /1 tbls cognac
Tabasco sauce
175 g /6 oz peeled prawns
salt
freshly ground black pepper

To serve
lettuce leaves, shredded
a few whole prawns, to garnish

1   Using a lightly floured rolling pin, roll the pastry with light, even strokes in one direction to an even thickness of 5 mm /¼ in. Use a sharp 4 cm /1½ in fluted metal cutter, lightly coated in flour, to cut circles of pastry.

2   Using a palette knife, transfer the circles to a damp baking sheet. Mark 20 mm /¾ in rounds in the centre of each circle but do not cut right through. Brush with beaten egg and leave to rest in a cool place for 15 minutes. Heat the oven to 200C /400F /gas 6.

3   Bake the bouchées in the centre of the oven for 20 minutes until risen and golden. With the point of a sharp knife, gently ease away the centre circle. Reserve the caps. With a teaspoon carefully scrape away any soft pastry and return the cases to the oven for 2–3 minutes to dry out. Transfer to a cooling tray.

4   Melt the butter in a small saucepan over a moderate heat. Add the onion and sauté gently, until soft and transparent.

5   Add the flour and cook gently, stirring constantly, for 2–3 minutes. Remove from the heat and gradually stir in a quarter of the hot milk. Return to the heat and gradually bring to the boil, stirring constantly. Still stirring, gradually add the remaining milk and bring to the boil.

6   Add the bay leaf, peppercorns and nutmeg. Pour the sauce into the top of a double boiler or a heatproof jug in a saucepan of gently bubbling water and cook, stirring occasionally, for about 30 minutes until reduced to 275 ml/10 fl oz. Sieve and return to the boiler.

7   Place the chopped shallots, in a small saucepan with the wine and reduce to 15 ml /1 tbls. Add to the sauce with the parsley, cream, cognac and a dash of Tabasco.

8   Roughly chop the prawns and add to the sauce. Add salt and freshly ground black pepper.

9   Ten minutes before serving, heat through the bouchée cases and caps in a 180C /350F /gas 4 oven. Then fill with the hot sauce and replace the caps. Arrange the lettuce around the bouchées and dot with the whole prawns. Serve immediately.

1½ hours

Avocado with crab

A light, fruity Moselle would make an excellent accompaniment to this colourful avocado starter.

Serves 4

2 ripe avocados
juice of ½ lemon
75 g /3 oz canned crabmeat,
    drained
½ red pepper, seeded and finely
    chopped
salt
freshly ground black pepper
lettuce heart leaves to garnish

For the dressing

15 ml /1 tbls lemon juice
45 ml /3 tbls olive oil
2.5 ml /½ tsp French mustard
½ garlic clove, crushed
30 ml /2 tbls tomato chutney
15 ml /1 tbls finely chopped parsley
salt
freshly ground black pepper

1   Divide the lettuce leaves among 4 individual plates. Cut the avocados in half, remove the stones and sprinkle each half with the lemon juice. Arrange each half on a plate of lettuce.
2   Flake the crabmeat with a fork in a bowl and add the red pepper. Mix gently with the fork.
3   To make the dressing, mix together the lemon juice, olive oil,

French mustard, garlic, chutney and parsley and season.
4   Gently stir the dressing into the crabmeat and pepper mixture, then spoon into the avocado halves. Serve immediately.

15 minutes

Cocktail cheese puffs

Champagne makes the perfect aperitif, but it calls for something really stylish in cocktail party food. Serve these little cheese choux puffs, freshly baked, with a choice of two special fillings, one made with cream cheese and the other with smoked salmon.

Makes 40 puffs
75 g /3 oz butter
5 ml /1 tsp salt
pinch of white pepper
pinch of nutmeg
100 g /4 oz flour, sifted
4 medium-sized eggs, beaten
100 g /4 oz Gruyère cheese, grated
1 medium-sized egg, beaten for glazing

For the fillings
225 g /8 oz full fat cream cheese
60 ml /4 tbls thick cream
60 ml /4 tbls chives, finely chopped
freshly ground black pepper
225 g /8 oz smoked salmon trimmings
125 ml /4 fl oz soured cream
10 ml /2 tsp lemon juice
sprigs of parsley

1 Heat the oven to 200C /400G /gas 6. Butter 2 baking sheets. Sift the flour ready to use.

2 Bring 275 ml /10 fl oz water to the boil. Add the butter and seasonings and boil until the butter has melted. Quickly remove from the heat and immediately stir in all the flour at one go. Beat with a wooden spoon or hand-held mixer until smooth.

3 Return pan to a low heat and beat vigorously for 1–2 minutes until a smooth ball is formed which leaves the sides of the pan without sticking.

4 Remove the pan from the heat and make a well in the centre. Pour a little of the eggs into the well and beat to incorporate. Continue to beat in the rest of the eggs a little at a time, until the mixture is smooth.

5 Beat the cheese into the choux pastry and season to taste. Fit a piping bag with a medium-sized plain nozzle and fill the bag with the cheese choux pastry. Holding the bag vertically, pipe out small bun shapes, about 1 tablespoonful in size, onto the buttered sheets, 2.5 cm/1 in apart. Brush the puffs with the beaten egg to glaze.

6 Bake the choux puffs for 15 minutes, then reduce the heat to 190C /375F /gas 5 and cook for a further 10 minutes. Remove from the oven and make very small slits in the puffs to allow the steam to escape, and cool completely on racks.

7 Meanwhile, make the two fillings. Beat the cream cheese until it is light and fluffy, then beat in the thick cream. Add the chives and season to taste with black pepper. Set aside.

8 Pound the salmon trimmings to a smooth paste and stir in the soured cream. Add the lemon juice and season to taste with black pepper.

9 Not long before serving, split open the cold puffs and fill half of them with the cream cheese filling and half with the smoked salmon filling. Garnish the dish of puffs with sprigs of parsley.

1 hour

Savoury mille-feuille

Served with a medium red wine such as Costières du Gard, this melt-in-the-mouth pastry makes a delightful savoury to serve at the end of a dinner party. It can be made a couple of hours in advance and reheated at the last moment. The name, mille-feuille, means thousand leaves in French, and refers to the way the pastry separates into many paper-thin layers, one on top of the other, when cooked.

Serves 8

200 g /7 oz ready-made puff pastry	1 egg yolk
100 g /4 oz blue cheese	30 ml /2 tbls thin cream
50 g /2 oz butter, softened	freshly ground black pepper
15 ml /1 tbls freshly chopped parsley	beaten egg mixed with milk to glaze

1 Divide the pastry into 3 and roll each piece into a rectangle 10 × 20 cm /4 × 8 in. Carefully roll each piece of pastry over the rolling pin and unroll on to a dampened pastry sheet. Prick 2 of them with a fork. Place in the refrigerator for 30 minutes.

2 Meanwhile, heat the oven to 200C /400F /gas 6 and make the filling: beat the cheese until soft and then beat in the softened butter and parsley. Beat the egg yolk with the thin cream and mix into the cheese mixture. Season with the pepper.

3 Remove the pastry rectangles from the refrigerator and brush the unpricked rectangle with the beaten egg and milk glaze. Bake the pastry for 20 minutes or until lightly golden and puffy. Cool the rectangles on a wire rack until cold.

4 Heat the oven to 190C /375F /gas 5. Spread 1 unglazed rectangle with half the blue cheese mixture. Cover with the other unglazed rectangle and spread that with the remaing cheese mixture. Finally top with the egg-glazed rectangle. Return to the oven for 5–10 minutes, until heated through.

1 hour, plus cooling time and 5–10 minutes reheating

Main dishes
with red wine

Contents

Beef bordelaise

Pot-roasted fillet of beef, in a sauce enriched with marrow-bone jelly, makes a succulent dinner party dish. Order your marrowbones well in advance from the butcher as they are not always available, and they make all the difference. Serve with a full-bodied claret, or a Cabernet Sauvignon from South Africa or California.

Serves 8-10

1.5 - 1.7 kg /3 lb 5 oz – 3lb 12 oz
  fillet of beef in one piece
2 large marrowbones, chopped
50 g /2 oz butter
2 large onions, finely chopped
15 ml /1 tbls brandy
575 ml /1 pt claret

15 ml /1 tbls thyme
5 ml /1 tsp freshly grated nutmeg
15 ml /1 tbls tomato purée
1 garlic clove
salt and freshly ground black pepper
7.5 ml /1½ tbls beurre manié
7.5 ml /1½ tbls Dijon mustard
watercress, to garnish

1 Heat the oven to 100C /200F /gas low. Put the marrowbones, standing them upright if possible, in a large ovenproof casserole. Cover, using foil, if necessary, as some of the bones may protrude above the dish. Place in the oven for 3-3½ hours until the marrow is soft.
2 Remove from the oven, and with a marrow spoon, or long thin flat knife, extract all the marrow jelly from the bones. Strain through a fine sieve to remove the excess fat and reserve the jelly.
3 Turn up the oven to 220C /425F /gas 7. Melt the butter in a flameproof casserole and sauté the onions for 15 minutes until soft and golden. Remove from the pan and reserve, keeping warm.
4 Add the beef and brown it all over, quickly.
5 Flambé the beef with brandy, then add the marrowbone jelly,

wine, thyme, nutmeg, tomato purée, garlic, salt and freshly ground black pepper. Cover the casserole and put it in the oven for 45-55 minutes. Baste it once, half way through the cooking. If you prefer beef to be well done, add a further 20-25 minutes to the cooking time.
6 Remove the beef from the casserole, place on a warmed serving platter and carve it into thick slices. Keep warm.
7 Stir the beurre manié into the sauce, whisking it well to thicken it, then add the mustard, stirring it in well. Pour the sauce over the beef, garnish with watercress and serve immediately.

preparing the marrowbone jelly,
then 1 hour 10 minutes

Roast wing rib of beef

This cut of beef, cooked on the bone, is generally reckoned to be one of the tastiest joints you can buy. Serve it with roast potatoes and Yorkshire puddings, and a full-bodied Pomerol.

Serves 6–8
2.3 kg /5 lb wing rib of beef
  on the bone
freshly ground black pepper
45 ml /3 tbls Dijon mustard
15 ml /1 tbls dried oregano

30 ml /2 tbls flour
300 ml /10 fl oz beef or other stock
salt
To serve
roast potatoes
Yorkshire puddings

1 Remove the beef from the refrigerator at least 2 hours before cooking and leave to come to room temperature.
2 Heat the oven to 200C /400F /gas 6. Sprinkle the beef with freshly ground black pepper. In a small bowl, mix together the Dijon mustard and dried oregano.
3 Place the joint in the oven and cook, basting and turning as necessary. Allow 33 minutes per kg /15 minutes per lb plus an extra 15 minutes, if you like your beef rare. If you prefer your meat well done allow up to 55 minutes per kg /25 minutes per lb plus 20 minutes extra. About 30 minutes before the meat is done, spread the mustard mixture over the fat.
4 Remove the beef from the oven, transfer to a carving board and leave to stand in a warm place for 15–20 minutes.
5 Meanwhile, strain any excess fat from the roasting tin, leaving about 30 ml /2 tbls of the juices. Add the flour and stir well over a low heat for 3–4 minutes to form a roux. Gradually add the stock, stirring, and bring to the boil. Season with salt and freshly ground black pepper and simmer.
6 To carve the beef, rest the joint on its rib bones. Run a sharp knife down the backbone and then along the ribs to free the meat from the bones. Remove the meat from the bones and place it, fat side up, on the carving board. Carve downwards into thin slices and arrange the slices on a heated serving dish. Pour the gravy into a heated sauceboat and hand it round separately. Serve the beef with roast potatoes and Yorkshire puddings.

2 hours standing,
then 1½–2½ hours

French beef casserole

The French Mediterranean feel of this delicious dish is enhanced if you serve it with a rich St Emilion wine.

Serves 6

1.2 kg /2½ lb braising or stewing
   steak cut into 5 cm /2 in cubes
30 ml /2 tbls olive oil
salt
freshly ground black pepper
2 medium-sized onions, sliced
2 garlic cloves, crushed
600 ml /1 pt red wine
2 large strips orange zest

1 bouquet garni
1 bay leaf
175 g /6 oz black olives, stoned
100 g /4 oz mushrooms, quartered
15 ml /1 tbls flour
25 g /1 oz butter
15 ml /1 tbls freshly chopped
   parsley
croûtons

1 Heat the oven to 170C /325F /gas 3. Heat the olive oil in a frying-pan and fry the meat in the oil in batches until browned on all sides. With a slotted spoon, transfer the meat to an ovenproof casserole and season with salt and pepper to taste.

2 Sauté the onions in the remaining oil in the frying-pan until golden. Add the garlic and cook for a further minute. Transfer the contents of the pan to the casserole, then add the red wine, orange zest, bouquet garni and bay leaf.

3 Cover the casserole and cook in the oven for 2½ hours. Remove the orange zest bouquet garni and bay leaf from the casserole, then stir in the olives and mushrooms. Blend the flour and butter together to make a beurre manié paste and stir into the casserole. Return the casserole to the oven for 15 minutes. Meanwhile, make the croûtons.

4 Serve sprinkled with chopped parsley and garnished with croûtons.

3¼ hours

Tournedos with artichoke hearts

A fine claret from the Médoc would be a fitting accompaniment to this extremely elegant dinner party dish.

Serves 4

4 tournedos steaks, about 3 cm /1¼ in thick, with a thin band of fat tied round each
150 g /5 oz butter, plus extra for greasing
8 canned artichoke hearts, drained
4 slices white bread, cut into rounds slightly larger than the tournedos

salt and ground black pepper
125 g /4 oz frozen petit pois
30 ml /2 tbls vegetable oil
5 ml /1 tsp arrowroot
75 ml /3 fl oz Madeira
15 ml /1 tbls freshly chopped parsley
15 ml /1 tbls freshly chopped tarragon
sprigs of parsley to garnish

1 Heat the oven to 170C /325F /gas 3. Melt 50 g /2 oz butter in a flameproof casserole over medium heat. When frothing, remove from the heat and add the artichokes, upside down. Baste with the butter, cover with buttered greaseproof paper and place in the oven for 20 minutes. When cooked, keep warm.

2 In a frying-pan, sauté the bread rounds in the remaining butter over medium heat, until golden and crisp on both sides. Remove with a slotted spoon, drain on absorbent paper and place on an ovenproof serving dish. Keep warm in the bottom of the oven.

3 Bring a pan of salted water to the boil, add the peas and simmer for 3 minutes. Drain and keep covered.

4 Meanwhile, add the oil to the frying-pan. Put over medium heat and when hot, add the tournedos. Fry for 3–4 minutes per side.

Discard the strings and strips of fat from the cooked tournedos. Season the tournedos with salt and pepper, then place each one on a fried-bread round and keep warm in the oven.

5 Pour the excess fat from the frying-pan. Bring the remaining juices to the boil, mix the arrowroot with the Madeira and add to the pan. Boil rapidly, stirring, for 1 minute, to thicken the sauce. Adjust the seasoning and pour over the tournedos. Sprinkle with the chopped parsley and tarragon. Divide the peas between the hollows of the artichoke hearts and arrange around the tournedos. Garnish with parsley sprigs and serve immediately.

⌁ 1¼ hours

Rump steak special

Accompany this rich dish with a Rioja, a full-bodied wine.

Serves 6
2 rump steaks, one just over
  700 g /1½ lb and one just under
freshly ground black pepper
Meaux mustard
6 thick bacon slices, rindless
25 ml /1 fl oz vegetable oil
60 ml /4 tbls red wine
1 onion, finely chopped
For the filling
175 g /6 oz full-fat soft cheese,
  flavoured with garlic and herbs

75 g /3 oz full-fat soft cheese
5 ml /1 tsp dried tarragon
1 onion, finely chopped
1 large egg, beaten
45 ml /3 tbls dried breadcrumbs
salt and ground black pepper
For the garnish
1 ham slice, cut into strips
stuffed olives, sliced
2 tomatoes, skinned and chopped
18 large mushroom caps, sautéed
parsley sprigs

1 Heat the oven to 190C /375F /gas 5. Thoroughly mix together the filling ingredients. Trim the steaks and season with pepper.

2 Spread a thin layer of mustard on one side of each steak and cover the larger piece with half the bacon. Spread the filling over the bacon and cover with the remaining bacon.

3 Place the smaller piece of steak, mustard side down, on the bacon and tie securely at 25 mm /1 in intervals along the length, then tie longitudinally. Brown the meat in the oil in a frying pan.

4 Place a piece of foil large enough to enclose the meat on a baking sheet. Place the meat on the foil and fold up the sides like a bowl.

5 Pour the wine into the frying-pan and stir to dislodge the sediment. Pour the wine over the meat. Sprinkle on the onion.

6 Fold over the foil to make a parcel. Cook in the centre of the oven for about 1 hour until the juices nearly run clear when a skewer is inserted in the centre (the time will depend on the thickness of the meat). Open the foil and continue to cook for 15 minutes.

7 Remove the meat from the oven and let it stand for 2–3 minutes. Place on a serving dish; remove the string. Pour over the juice.

8 Arrange the ham strips in a criss-cross pattern on the meat and dot with sliced olives. Fill the mushroom tops with chopped tomatoes and arrange around the meat. Garnish with parsley.

1½ hours

Steak pastry parcels

Fillet steak wrapped in pastry not only looks impressive but is, in fact, a most economical way to serve meat. The smoothness of a claret would combine perfectly with the succulence of the beef.

Serves 4

4 fillet steaks, each weighing 125 g
  /4 oz
25 g /1 oz butter, melted
freshly ground black pepper
10 ml /2 tsp freshly chopped mixed
  herbs
250 g /8 oz made-weight frozen
  puff pastry, defrosted
4 large tomatoes, blanched, peeled,
  seeded and chopped
1 medium-sized egg, beaten
lettuce and tomato wedges

For the sauce

2 shallots, finely chopped
2.5 ml /1/2 tsp freshly chopped
  thyme
2.5 ml /1/2 tsp freshly chopped
  tarragon
1 bay leaf
175 ml /6 fl oz red Bordeaux wine
275 ml /10 fl oz beef stock
salt
freshly ground black pepper
15 ml /1 tbls tomato purée

1 Put all the ingredients for the sauce in a saucepan and boil until reduced by a third. Leave to cool.

2 Brush the steaks with the melted butter. Heat the grill and when it is very hot, sear the steaks for 1 minute on each side. Season well with black pepper, and sprinkle with the chopped mixed herbs. Leave until cold.

3 Divide the pastry into 4 and roll each piece to about 4 cm /1½ in larger than each steak. Divide the chopped tomatoes between the pieces of pastry and place a steak in the centre of steach. Dampen the edges of the pastry and fold over to encase the meat completely. Trim the edges and press firmly together. Using a fish slice, transfer to a damp baking tray with the seam underneath.

4 Re-roll the trimmings and cut into flowers and leaves. Mark the veins with the point of a sharp knife, place on the pastry parcels and brush the surfaces with beaten egg. Refrigerate for 30 minutes. Meanwhile, heat the oven to 200C /400F /gas 6.

5 Remove the pastry parcels from the refrigerator and brush again with beaten egg. Cook in the oven for 15–20 minutes until the pastry is golden.

6 Serve the parcels on a bed of lettuce, garnished with tomatoes. Reheat the sauce, strain into a sauceboat and pass separately.

defrosting pastry, then
1½ hours

Pepper and anchovy beef

The anchovy-stuffed olives add a distinct flavour to this delicious casserole. Cook it a day ahead if you wish, adding the peppers, mushrooms and olives about 30 minutes before the meal. Serve with a sunny red Côtes du Rhône.

Serves 4–6

1 kg /2¼ lb braising steak, trimmed and cut into 4 cm / 1½ in cubes
30 ml /2 tbls olive oil
1 large Spanish onion, finely chopped
25 ml /1½ tbls flour
200 ml /7 fl oz dry red wine
400 g /14 oz canned tomatoes
2 large cloves garlic, crushed
5 ml /1 tsp dried thyme
1 bay leaf
salt
freshly ground black pepper
1 small red pepper, cut into thin rings
1 small green pepper, cut into thin rings
100 g /4 oz finely chopped mushrooms
65 g /2½ oz anchovy-stuffed green olives, halved

1 Heat the olive oil in a large flameproof casserole. Sauté half the cubes of beef until evenly browned. Transfer to a plate with a slotted spoon and repeat with the remaining cubes.

2 Add the chopped onion to the fat in the pan and cook over a low heat for about 10 minutes, or until soft.

3 Return the brown beef to the pan. Sprinkle in the flour, stirring well to coat. Add the wine, canned tomatoes and their liquid, crushed garlic, dried thyme and bay leaf. Season to taste with salt and freshly ground pepper. Stir well and bring to simmering point.

Cook, covered, over a low heat for 1¾ hours, stirring occasionally.

4 Add the pepper rings, finely chopped mushrooms and halved anchovy-stuffed olives and cook for a further 30 minutes, or until the pepper rings are tender.

5 Remove the bay leaf from the beef, check the seasoning and correct if necessary. Serve hot.

⁇ 2½ hours

Crown roast of lamb

A good claret is an excellent accompaniment for this elegant lamb dish. The stuffing combines a slightly sweet fruitiness with a hint of sharpness, to complement both the wine and lamb.

Serves 6–8

2 best end joints, each with 6–8
    cutlets
salt and ground black pepper
30 ml /2 tbls rosemary crushed
25 g /1 oz butter
watercress and 1 segmented orange
For the stuffing
425 g /15 oz canned apricot halves,
    drained

grated zest and juice of 1 orange
2 oranges, peeled and segmented
grated zest and juice of 1 lemon
225 g /8 oz cooked rice
100 g /4 oz white breadcrumbs
1 medium-sized onion, finely
    chopped
2.5 ml /1/2 tsp ground cinnamon
salt and freshly ground pepper

1   Cut off the skin from the best ends, then trim the meat from the tops of the bones. Weigh the joints and calculate the cooking time at 44 minutes per kg /20 minutes per lb.

2   Sew one end of each joint together, sewing around the last bone of each joint. Stand the tied joints upright and bend them round until the other ends meet. Stitch these together to form a crown. Then tie around the base to hold the crown in shape. Season the lamb inside and out with salt and pepper and sprinkle a little of the rosemary inside. Heat the oven to 190C /375F /gas 5.

3   Reserve 12 apricot halves. Chop the rest and mix with the rest of the stuffing ingredients; season with salt and pepper.

4   In a roasting tin, melt the butter with rest of the rosemary, then place the lamb in the tin. Spoon the stuffing loosely into centre of the crown. Cover bone ends with foil and roast for the calculated time basting occasionally and covering stuffing with foil if it becomes too brown.

5   Place the lamb on a warmed serving dish. Remove string and foil and place cutlet frills on the bones. Garnish with reserved apricot halves, watercress and orange segments.

45 minutes
plus roasting time

Amaretto roast lamb

Amaretto liqueur and apricots flavour the stuffing for this succulent lamb dish. Serve the dish with new potatoes, sprinkled with freshly chopped parsley, and a fine Barolo.

Serves 6-8

$1^1/_2$–2 kg /$3^1/_2$–4 lb shoulder of
  lamb, boned
150 ml /5 fl oz Amaretto di Saronno
100 g /4 oz dried apricots, chopped
1 small onion, chopped
15 g /$^1/_2$ oz butter
75 g /3 oz fresh breadcrumbs
15 ml /1 tbls freshly chopped parsley

50 g /2 oz walnuts, chopped
2.5 ml /$^1/_2$ tsp ground cinnamon
salt
freshly ground black pepper
30 ml /2 tbls lemon juice
juice of 2 oranges
300 ml /10 fl oz stock
15 ml /1 tbls cornflour
sprigs of watercress to garnish

1 Pour 50 ml /2 fl oz Amaretto over the chopped apricots, stir well and leave to soak for 2 hours.
2 Lightly sauté the onions in the butter, then mix with the apricots, breadcrumbs, parsley, walnuts and cinnamon. Season to taste with salt and pepper and heat the oven to 200C /400F /gas 6.
3 Lay the boned shoulder, skin side down, on a board and season well. Spread the stuffing over the meat. Roll up and tie securely with string at about 5 cm /2 in intervals. Place in a roasting pan.
4 Mix the lemon and orange juice with a further 50 ml /2 fl oz Amaretto and pour this over the lamb. Roast, uncovered, for 30 minutes, basting occasionally.
5 Reduce the heat to 180C /350F /gas 4 and continue cooking for

$1^1/_2$ hours, basting every 15 minutes.
6 Lift the lamb on to a warmed serving dish and remove the string. Pour off the fat from the pan juices, add the stock and the remaining Amaretto. Blend the cornflour with a little water and stir this into the liquid in the pan. Adjust the seasoning to taste and bring to the boil over medium heat. Boil the sauce, stirring, until clear, then pour into a sauceboat.
7 Garnish the lamb with watercress and serve accompanied by the sauce.

2 hours soaking,
then $2^3/_4$ hours

Hearty hot pot

Sweet-tasting neck of lamb is the basic ingredient of traditional Lancashire hot-pot. This version has a flavouring of kidney and mushrooms and is topped with a layer of potato slices. Serve it with an equally hearty wine, such as Bull's Blood.

Serves 4

*1 kg /2¼ lb middle neck of lamb,
 chopped
30 ml /2 tbls flour
salt
freshly ground black pepper
25 g /1 oz dripping or lard*

*3–4 lamb's kidneys, trimmed and
 thickly sliced
 quartered if large
100 g /4 oz mushrooms, quartered
450 ml /15 fl oz beef stock
750 g /1½ lb potatoes, sliced*

1 Heat the oven to 170C /325F /gas 3 and wipe the meat with absorbent paper. Season the flour with salt and pepper, then coat the meat in the seasoned flour. Reserve the left-over flour.
2 Heat the fat in a large saucepan and fry the meat, in batches, until lightly browned and sealed. Transfer the meat to a hotpot or deep casserole. Scatter the kidney and mushrooms over the meat.
3 Fry the sliced onion gently in the fat left in the saucepan for a few minutes, then transfer to the hotpot with a slotted spoon. Add the remaining seasoned flour to the pan and stir until lightly browned.

Stir in the stock and bring to the boil. Check the seasoning and simmer for a few minutes, until slightly thickened.
4 Cover the meat with overlapping potato slices. Pour the sauce over the potatoes, cover the hotpot and cook in the oven for 1½ hours. Uncover the pot and cook or a further 30 minutes to brown the potatoes. Serve from the pot.

🍴 2½ hours

116

Barbecued riblets

Divide breasts of lamb into riblets and cook them in tangy sauce to serve as finger food for an informal summer lunch or dinner party. A medium New Zealand wine like Nobilos Pinotage would bring out their fruity flavour.

Serves 4

2 breasts of lamb
30 ml /2 tbls vinegar
boiling water, to cover
For the sauce
30 ml /2 tbls tomato ketchup

30 ml /2 tbls clear honey
30 ml /2 tbls soy sauce
30 ml /2 tbls plum jam
15 ml /1 tbls dry mustard
10 ml /2 tsp Worcestershire sauce

1 Remove and discard the skin and excess fat, then put the breasts into a saucepan large enough to hold them both. Cover with boiling water and add the vinegar. Cover the saucepan and simmer for 15 minutes.

2 Mix all the sauce ingredients together in a saucepan and heat gently, stirring until all the ingredients are combined.

3 Heat the oven to 180C /350F /gas 4. Drain the breasts, then cut between the ribs into 25 mm /1 in wide strips.

4 Arrange the riblets close together in a roasting tin, pour the sauce over to coat them and cook for 30 minutes. Turn the riblets over once during the cooking time.

5 Baste thoroughly, then increase the heat to 200C /400F /gas 6 and cook for a further 15–20 minutes until the riblets are crisp.

6 Serve the riblets with any remaining sauce as a main course, allowing about 3–4 riblets per portion. Or serve as finger food for an informal party, where sticky fingers are acceptable. Remember to provide finger bowls.

1½ hours

Pork noisettes with prunes

A delicious prune and onion sauce goes well with this prime cut of pork. Serve Pork noisettes with prunes with a dark, full-flavoured, fruity red wine from Cahors.

Serves 4–6

1.4 kg /3 lb loin of pork, skinned, boned and rolled
500 g /1 lb prunes, stoned
425 ml /15 fl oz red wine
salt

freshly ground black pepper
50 g /2 oz butter
30 ml /2 tbls olive oil
2 small onions, finely chopped
watercress, to garnish

1   Soak the prunes, preferably overnight, in 300 ml /10 fl oz of the red wine.

2   Heat the oven to 170C /325F /gas 3. Cook the prunes, covered, in the oven for 1 hour. Remove and reserve.

3   Meanwhile, cut the loin of pork into noisettes, approximately 25 mm /1 in thick. Season them well with salt and freshly ground black pepper. In a frying-pan heat 25 g /1 oz of the butter and the olive oil and sauté the noisettes for 2–3 minutes on each side or until golden brown. Transfer the noisettes to a flameproof casserole.

4   Pour off any excess fat from the frying-pan and use 30 ml /2 tbls red wine to deglaze it. Pour these juices over the pork, cover the casserole tightly and cook in the oven for 1 hour.

5   Meanwhile, melt the remaining butter in a saucepan and cook the finely chopped onions, stirring occasionally, for 3–4 minutes or

until transparent. Blend the onions to a purée with 6 of the cooked prunes and 60–90 ml /4–6 tbls of the red wine.

6   Add the cooking liquid from the prunes to the casserole and cook for a further 15 minutes. Warm the prunes in the oven.

7   When the pork is cooked transfer it to a heated serving dish with the prunes. Put the casserole over a high heat and bring the liquid to the boil and boil for about 6–8 minutes, or until the liquid is reduced to about one-third of its original quantity. Add the onion and prune purée and cook, stirring, for 1–2 minutes more.

8   Pour the sauce over the pork noisettes, garnish with watercress and serve immediately.

Overnight soaking, then 2½ hours

Pork with pepper

This pork dish with its spicy marinade is unusual in being cooked under a low grill instead of in the oven. It can be prepared well in advance. Serve with saffron rice and accompanied by a Cabernet Sauvignon.

Serves 4–6

900 g /2 lb boneless pork steaks
3 garlic cloves
2.5 ml /1/2 tsp cumin seeds
2.5 ml /1/2 tsp coriander seeds
2.5 ml /1/2 tsp turmeric
2.5 ml /1/2 tsp chilli powder
1.5 ml /1/4 tsp salt

75 ml /5 tbls olive oil
1 1/2 Spanish onions
1 large green pepper
1 large red pepper
4 large tomatoes, blanched and skinned
freshly ground black pepper
flat-leaved parsley to garnish

1 Cut the pork into 2 cm /3/4 in cubes and put in a large shallow flameproof dish.

2 Using a mortar and pestle, pound the garlic with the cumin and coriander seeds. Add the turmeric, chilli powder and salt. Stir in 45 ml /3 tbls oil. Pour this mixture over the pork and mix well so that all the pieces are well coated. Marinate for at least 1 hour.

3 Heat the grill to low. Coarsely chop onions, peppers and tomatoes. Add the onion and peppers to the pork. Pour in the remaining oil, season with salt and freshly ground black pepper and stir well to distribute the seasonings. Grill for 30 minutes on a low heat, basting and turning the meat and vegetables every 10 minutes and turning the dish as well to cook evenly.

4 Add the tomatoes to the dish and grill for another 20–30 minutes or until the meat is cooked through. Garnish with parsley and serve immediately with saffron rice.

marinating for 1 hour, then 1 1/4 hours

Pork and chick-pea stew

This hearty stew is perfect for a cold winter meal. Cook and serve it with a full-bodied Argentine Cabernet Sauvignon.

Serves 4

800 g /1¾ lb shoulder of pork,
    cut into 25 mm /1 in cubes
30-45 ml /2-3 tbls olive oil
100 g /4 oz dried chick-peas,
    cooked and drained
2 medium-sized onions, halved
    and thinly sliced
100 ml /3½ fl oz red wine
3 medium-sized tomatoes,
    blanched, skinned, seeded
    and chopped

1 bay leaf
1 large red pepper, sliced
sautéed aubergine slices, to
    serve
freshly chopped parsley, to
    garnish

For the marinade
7.5 ml /1½ tsp salt
freshly ground black pepper
large pinch ground allspice
1.5 ml /¼ tsp dried marjoram
2 large garlic cloves, crushed

1 Place the cubed pork in a bowl with the marinade ingredients and mix well with your hands, making sure the marinade is evenly distributed. Cover and refrigerate overnight, stirring once or twice, if convenient. Soak and cook the chick-peas.

2 Dry the meat on absorbent paper, reserving any juices. Heat 15 ml /1 tbls oil in a large frying-pan over moderate heat. Add half the pork and fry, stirring, until it changes colour. Transfer the meat to a flameproof casserole, using a slotted spoon. Fry the second batch of pork, adding more oil as needed.

3 Add more oil to the pan, if necessary, then add the onions and cook for a few minutes, until they are softened. Transfer them to the casserole. Deglaze the pan with the wine, stirring in the crusty bits.

4 Pour the wine into the casserole and add the tomatoes, bay leaf and reserved meat juices. Bring to simmering point, then lower the heat, cover and simmer gently for 30 minutes, stirring occasionally.

5 Add the sliced pepper and chick-peas. Continue to cook, stirring occasionally, for a further 1-1½ hours until the meat is very tender.

6 Transfer the meat and vegetables to a heated serving platter with a slotted spoon. Boil the remaining juices quickly until they thicken slightly. Taste and adjust the seasoning, then pour over the pork. Surround with aubergine, sprinkle with parsley and serve.

overnight marinating, cooking
chick-peas, then 2–2¼ hours

Chicken with tarragon

Tarragon is a wonderfully delicate herb which goes particularly well with chicken. If you cannot find fresh tarragon, try frozen, which is excellent. Serve with a colourful vegetable such as carrots. The fresh, bold flavour of a Beaujolais Villages should match this dish admirably.

Serves 4–6

1.8 kg /4 lb chicken
50 g /2 oz butter
30 ml /2 tbls chopped fresh (or frozen) tarragon leaves or 30 ml /1 tbls dried tarragon
1 garlic clove, crushed
salt and freshly ground black pepper
15 ml /1 tbls oil
50 ml /2 fl oz brandy
75 ml /3 fl oz thick cream

1　Heat the oven to 190C /375F /gas 5. Mash together the butter, tarragon, garlic, salt and pepper. Divide the mixture into three.

2　Gently push your fingers between the skin and the breast of the chicken and insert one third of the butter mixture on each side of the breast, under the skin. Flatten the butter slightly by patting the skin. Put the remaining piece of butter into the cavity of the bird.

3　Rub a little oil on the outside of the bird. Arrange the chicken so it rests on one breast on a rack in a roasting tin and roast for 35 minutes. Turn it onto the other side and roast for a further 35 minutes.

4　Remove the tin from the oven, lift off the bird, take out the rack and return the bird to the tin.

5　Put the brandy into a soup ladle and warm it gently. Set a match to it and pour it over the chicken. When the flames subside, carefully remove the chicken, tipping the juices from the cavity into the tin. Place the bird on a serving dish and keep warm.

6　Add the cream to the pan and warm it through gently, stirring well to incorporate all the juices. Pour the sauce over the chicken and serve immediately. There will not be a great deal of sauce, but it is very rich. If you prefer more sauce, add some chicken stock to the pan before the cream.

1½ hours

Roast duck with peaches

A Mercurey or Givry from the Chalonnais will complement this succulent dish perfectly.

Serves 4

2.25 kg /5 lb oven-ready duck
800 g /1 lb 13 oz canned peach slices, drained
salt and freshly ground pepper
30 ml /2 tbls lemon juice
225 ml /8 fl oz port
45 ml /3 tbls brandy (optional)

45 ml /3 tbls sugar
75 ml /5 tbls red wine vinegar
425 ml /15 fl oz duck stock, made from the
* giblets*
15 ml /1 tbls arrowroot
sprigs of watercress

1 Heat the oven to 220C /425F /gas 7. Prick the duck skin all over and rub it with salt and pepper. Place the duck, breast-side up, in a roasting tin and roast for 15 minutes, to brown slightly. Reduce the heat to 180C /350F /gas 4 and continue to roast for 1 hour 10 minutes. Turn the duck over, breast-side down, and roast for a further 15 minutes, then turn it breast-side up again for a final 5 minutes' roasting.

2 Place the peach slices in a pan and pour over the lemon juice and 45 ml /3 tbls port, or brandy if you prefer. Set aside until needed, but baste occasionally.

3 Meanwhile, dissolve the sugar in the vinegar, then boil it for 5 minutes until a caramel syrup is formed. As soon as it is dark brown, remove from the heat, pour in 150 ml /5 fl oz stock and stir over low heat to dissolve the caramel. Add the rest of the stock. Mix the arrowroot with 30 ml /2 tbls port and add to the pan. Simmer for 3 minutes and set aside.

4 Remove the duck from the oven. Remove the trussing, place on a dish and keep warm.

5 Tip off the fat from the roasting tin. Add the remaining port, then boil to reduce to 45 ml/3 tbls. Strain into the reserved sauce and simmer for 1 minute.

6 Pour the sauce over the peaches. Heat for 3 minutes, then remove the peaches with a slotted spoon and arrange around the duck.

7 Boil the sauce to reduce it slightly. Adjust the seasoning. Pour into a warmed sauceboat and spoon some over the duck. Garnish. with sprigs of watercress.

1¾ hours

Duck with olives

The olives enhance the flavour of the duck in this dish, which is delicious with plain brown rice and an inviting red Graves.

Serves 4
2 kg /4¹/₂ lb oven-ready duckling
salt
30 ml /2 tbls oil
25 g /1 oz butter
1 medium-sized onion, chopped
15 ml /1 tbls tomato purée

2.5 ml /¹/₂ tsp dried thyme
2.5 ml /¹/₂ tsp dried rosemary
1 bay leaf
freshly ground black pepper
275 ml /10 fl oz dry white wine
250 g /9 oz green olives, stoned
200 g /7 oz mushrooms, halved

1 Prick the skin of the duck all over and sprinkle with salt.
2 Heat the oil and butter in a flameproof casserole. Brown the duck evenly on all sides for about 20 minutes until the skin is coloured and crisp.
3 Remove the duck from the casserole, put it on a heated plate and keep it hot. Drain off the excess fat from the casserole, keeping only 15 ml /1 tbls.
4 Fry the onion in the reserved duck fat until soft. Then add the tomato purée, thyme, rosemary, bay leaf, pepper and 225 ml /8 fl oz of the white wine. Cook until the mixture reduces and thickens.

5 Return the duck to the casserole, cover and simmer for about 1¹/₄ hours, turning and basting it occasionally. Add the olives and mushrooms and cook for a further 30 minutes, adding a little water if necessary.
6 Joint the duck and arrange on a serving dish with the olives and mushrooms. Add the rest of the wine to the casserole, stir and bring to the boil. Reduce the heat, strain the sauce and serve it separately.

2¹/₄ hours

Glazed bacon

Serve this delicately-flavoured joint with a light red wine such as Beaujolais.

Serves 8

1.8 kg /4 lb middle gammon or bacon joint,
   rolled and tied
5 whole black peppercorns
100 g /4 oz brown sugar

20 cloves
15 ml /1 tbls flour
275 ml /10 fl oz cider
salt and freshly ground black pepper
12 apple rings, fried in butter

1 Place the joint in a large pan and add enough water to cover. Add the peppercorns and bring to the boil. Then reduce the heat, cover and simmer for 30 minutes.

2 Heat the oven to 180C /350F /gas 4. Wrap the joint in foil and place on a rack in a roasting pan. Add enough water to the pan to cover the bottom and place in the oven.

3 Roast for 1 hour, then remove from the oven and open the foil. Discard the water in the pan. Increase the oven heat ot 200C /400F /gas 6. Remove the string and rind from the joint and, using a sharp knife, lightly score the fat in a criss-cross pattern.

4 Cover the fatty surface with brown sugar, pressing it down on to the fat. Stud the sugared surface with the cloves, following the

criss-cross pattern cut into the fat.

5 Leaving the foil open and only loosely covering the lean meat surface, return the joint to the oven for a further 30 minutes. Remove from the oven and transfer to a serving dish. Keep warm.

6 Pour the juices left in the foil into the roasting pan. Stir in 15 ml /1 tbls flour and cook over a moderate heat for 2 minutes. Remove the pan from the heat and stir in the cider. Bring to the boil, stirring.

7 Season to taste, then pour into a sauceboat. Garnish the dish with the fried apple rings and parsley sprigs.

2¼ hours

124

Gammon with Madeira sauce

Madeira and gammon marry here to produce this melt-in-the-mouth dish. Serve with a Rosé from the Loire or Ventoux.

Serves 4

*4 gammon steaks, 15 mm /½ in
  thick, with the fat slashed
25 g /1 oz butter
15 ml /1 tbls oil
1 small onion, finely chopped
100 g /4 oz button mushrooms,
  sliced
25 g /1 oz flour
175 ml /6 fl oz ham or brown stock
150 ml /5 fl oz dry Madeira
15 ml /1 tbls tomato purée
salt
freshly ground black pepper
150 ml /5 fl oz thick cream
braised spinach to serve*

1 Heat the butter and oil in a heavy-based frying-pan over moderate heat. Add the gammon and fry each side for 4 minutes, until golden brown. Transfer with a slotted spoon to a plate and keep warm.

2 Add the chopped onion and mushrooms to the pan and cook until softened. Stir in the flour with a wooden spoon and cook for 2 minutes stirring continuously.

3 Remove the pan from the heat and stir in the stock and Madeira. Stir in the tomato purée and season to taste with salt and pepper.

4 Return the pan to the heat and bring the sauce to simmering point, stirring continuously. Then add the cream. Simmer for 5 minutes, until the sauce has reduced slightly.

5 Return the gammon to the pan and simmer for 10 minutes until tender. Arrange the gammon on a bed of braised spinach and pour the sauce over the steaks.

40 minutes

Burgundy ham

This is a traditional Eastertide dish in Burgundy. Its pretty green and pink marbled appearance makes it a spectacular centrepiece for a buffet party or cold luncheon. Serve it with a chilled Pinot Noir rosé, such as Bourgogne-Marsannay-la-Côte.

Serves 6-8

1.4 kg /3 lb piece of gammon
  or ham
veal knuckle or beef marrow
  bone, chopped in 2–3 pieces
2 calf's feet or 4 pig's trotters
5 ml /1 tsp dried chervil
5 ml /1 tsp dried tarragon
2.5 ml /¹/₂ tsp dried marjoram

2 bay leaves
5 ml /1 tsp dried thyme
4 sprigs fresh parsley
12 black peppercorns
75 cl bottle dry white wine
15 ml /1 tbls finely chopped parsley
green salad, to serve
garlic bread, to serve

1 Place the gammon or ham in a large saucepan, cover with cold water and bring to the boil over a medium heat. Taste the water and if it is very salty, pour it away and cover the gammon with fresh cold water.

2 Bring to the boil again and then simmer very gently for 45 minutes. Remove the gammon or ham from the pan and discard the cooking liquid.

3 Chop the meat into sizeable chunks, removing and discarding any rind or very fatty pieces. Return the chopped meat to the rinsed-out pan and add the veal knuckle or beef marrow bone, the calf's feet or pig's trotters, the herbs and the peppercorns. Pour in the wine and top up with cold water, if necessary, so that everything is covered with liquid. Bring to the boil over a low heat, skimming off any fat as it rises. Simmer for 2½-3 hours.

4 Remove the bone and feet or trotters and discard them. Transfer the ham with a slotted spoon to a large bowl and let it cool slightly.

5 Strain the cooking liquid through a fine sieve and pour it into a jug. Plunge the jug into a bowl of iced water to cool it quickly. Any fat that forms can then be easily removed from the top with absorbent paper. Put the stock aside for the jelly to set slightly.

6 With 2 forks flake the ham but do not mash it too much.

7 Add the finely chopped parsley to the jelly, stirring it well in, then pour over the ham and mix everything well together.

8 Put the mixture into a wetted 1 L /1¾ pt mould, and leave overnight in the refrigerator to set.

9 To turn out the mould, put a tea-towel soaked in hot water round the bottom of the mould for about 1 minute. Put a plate over the mould, invert the two and the ham should fall out onto the plate. Serve with a green salad and garlic bread.

4½ hours plus cooling, then overnight setting

Mullet provençale

Serve this cold mullet dish for an outdoor luncheon. A Provence rosé would be a delicious wine to accompany it.

Serves 4–6

1.6 kg /3½ lb grey mullet, cleaned
15–30 ml /1–2 tbls dry white wine
juice of ½ lemon
15–30 ml /1–2 tbls olive oil
sprigs of thyme
salt and ground black pepper
25 g /1 oz butter
30 ml /2 tbls olive oil

2 medium-sized onions, sliced
2 green peppers, cut into
    25 mm /1 in squares
500 g /1 lb tomatoes, quartered
125 g /4 oz black olives, stoned
150 ml / 5 fl oz French dressing
For the garnish
lemon slices
sprigs of thyme

1 Heat the oven to 170C /325F /gas 3. Cut a piece of foil large enough to enclose the fish completely. Place the fish on the foil and sprinkle with the white wine, lemon juice and olive oil. Add the sprigs of thyme and season. Wrap the foil around the fish, sealing it tightly. Cook in the oven for 1 hour.

2 Remove the fish from the oven and leave to cool a little. Remove the skin carefully leaving the head and tail in place. Leave to cool.

3 Meanwhile, heat the butter and olive oil in a frying-pan and cook the onions for 3–4 minutes or until transparent. Remove with a slotted spoon and leave to cool.

4 Cook the peppers in the remaining fat for 5 minutes, stirring occasionally. Remove and cool.

5 Mix the onions, pepper, tomatoes and black olives together carefully. Season with salt and freshly ground black pepper to taste and toss with the vinaigrette. Spoon onto a serving dish.

6 Arrange the mullet on top of the vegetables, garnish with the lemon slices and sprigs of thyme and serve.

1¾ hours including cooling

Main dishes with white wine

Contents

Turkey escalopes chasseur

Sautéed mushrooms and shallots are the classic ingredients of a dish cooked *au chasseur.* Here they are combined with light-textured turkey escalopes – delicious served with a dry white Graves.

Serves 4

4 × 125 g /4 oz fillets of turkey breast
40 g /1½ oz butter
15 ml /1 tbls olive oil
3 shallots or 1 medium-sized onion, chopped
350 g /12 oz tomatoes, blanched, skinned, seeds and juice removed
½ garlic clove, finely chopped
salt and freshly ground black pepper
10 ml /2 tsp arrowroot
50 ml /2 fl oz meat juice from beef or good beef consommé
125 ml /4 fl oz dry white vermouth
2.5 ml /½ tsp chopped fresh basil or tarragon (optional)
350 g /12 oz button mushrooms, sliced
chopped parsley to garnish

1 Flatten the turkey breasts slightly with a rolling pin. Dry the surfaces with absorbent paper. Heat 15 g /½ oz butter with the oil in a frying-pan over moderate heat until the butter foams. Put in the escalopes. Fry for 4–5 minutes on each side to seal and brown. Remove from the pan and keep warm.

2 Fry the shallots or onion in the pan for 1 minute, scraping up the sediment from the bottom of the pan. Chop the tomato flesh and stir it into the pan with garlic and seasoning. Cover and simmer for 5 minutes.

3 Mix the arrowroot with a little of the beef juice or consommé. Add the vermouth, arrowroot mixture and remaining beef juice or consommé to the pan and boil rapidly until it is reduced by half.

4 Season the escalopes and return them to the pan. Sprinkle with the herbs if available. Cover with a lid and simmer very gently for 4–5 minutes.

5 Meanwhile, melt 25 g /1 oz butter in a separate pan and sauté the mushrooms for 4 minutes over moderate heat, tossing them until they are brown. Season with salt and pepper.

6 Transfer the escalopes and sauce to a heated serving dish. Spoon over the sautéed mushrooms and serve garnished with parsley.

◊ 30 minutes

Honeyed chicken

The stuffing for this bird is a delicious combination of sweet and savoury. Onion, bacon and rice blend perfectly with cooked banana, and all the flavours are sealed inside the crisp, golden, honey-coated skin of the chicken. Serve with a Riesling d'Alsace.

Serves 4–6

1.8 kg /4 lb chicken, dressed
    weight
25 g /1 oz butter
1 small onion, finely chopped
125 g /4 oz bacon, in one piece
30 ml /2 tbls oil

2 firm bananas
50 g /2 oz rice, cooked and cooled
salt
freshly ground black pepper
pinch of cinnamon
30–45 ml /2–3 tbls honey
sprigs of watercress, to garnish

1   Heat the oven to 190C /375F /gas 5.
2   Melt the butter in a small saucepan, add the finely chopped onion and cook over a medium heat until soft and translucent, about 5 minutes. Remove from the pan with a slotted spoon. Dice the bacon and add it to the pan and cook for 5–10 minutes, stirring occasionally. Remove from the pan and leave to cool.
3   Meanwhile, in a frying-pan, heat the oil until very hot. Split the bananas lengthways and fry them in the hot oil, turning them once with the spatula, until golden brown. (The oil must be very hot so it seals the outside of the bananas, otherwise they will absorb the oil and be soggy.) Remove from the pan.
4   Mix the onion and bacon with the cooked rice, chop the bananas and add them to the rice mixture. Season with salt and freshly ground black pepper and a pinch of cinnamon. Leave to cool.
5   Wipe the chicken inside and out with a damp cloth. Spoon the cold rice mixture into the cavity; do not pack it too tightly. Truss the chicken. Spoon the honey over the chicken, using the back of the spoon to spread it evenly.
6   Cook the chicken for about 1 hour 20 minutes or until the juices run clear when the thickest part of the thigh is pierced with a skewer. Cover the chicken with foil if it browns too quickly.
7   Remove the chicken from the oven, transfer to a heated serving dish and serve, garnished with sprigs of watercress.

⚔ 2 hours

Chicken breasts Leoni

The chicken in this recipe is kept beautifully succulent by the simple device of coating it with egg before frying. A small amount of grated cheese is included to bring out the flavour of both the chicken and the garnish of asparagus spears. A delicately flavoured Moselle would be the perfect partner to this dish.

Serves 4

4 chicken breasts, boned and
   skinned
½ lemon
25 g /1 oz flour
salt
freshly ground black pepper
2 small eggs

50 g /2 oz Parmesan cheese or dry
   mature Cheddar cheese, finely
   grated
30 ml /2 tbls oil
25 g /1 oz butter
12–16 cooked asparagus spears
   (fresh, frozen or canned) to garnish
lemon slices and parsley to garnish

1 Lay the chicken breasts between damp greaseproof paper and flatten gently with a rolling pin until about 10 mm /½ in thick. Rub the chicken lightly with the cut side of the lemon, squeezing the lemon gently to extract a little juice.

2 Season the flour liberally with salt and pepper and coat the chicken with the seasoned flour on each side. In a deep plate beat the eggs lightly with 30 ml /2 tbls of the finely grated Parmesan or Cheddar cheese.

3 Heat the oil and butter in a shallow frying-pan. When it is hot dip the chicken breasts one at a time in the beaten egg, coating each side, and immediately lower into the hot fat.

4 Fry over moderate heat, turning once, 5–6 minutes each side until golden and just cooked through. Meanwhile heat the grill.

5 With a fish slice transfer the cooked chicken breasts to the grill rack, lay 3–4 drained asparagus spears on each and sprinkle with the remaining grated cheese. Grill gently for 2–3 minutes until the cheese melts.

6 Arrange the chicken breasts on a hot serving dish. Garnish with lemon slices and parsley.

35 minutes

Almond chicken puffs

These 'pillows' of puff pastry, encasing chicken breasts poached in white wine and served with a delicate almond and orange sauce, make an impressive main course. Serve with an Australian dry white wine, well chilled.

Serves 4

4 chicken breasts, boned and
   skin removed
225 g /8 oz frozen puff pastry,
   defrosted
150 ml /5 fl oz dry white wine
10 white peppercorns
1 small onion, coarsely chopped
4 sprigs of parsley
1 garlic clove

4 large oranges
175 g /6 oz butter
50 g /2 oz fresh breadcrumbs
100 g /4 oz ground almonds
1 egg yolk, beaten
50 g /2 oz blanched whole almonds
salt
100 g /4 oz thick cream
butter for greasing
flour

1 Put the wine, white peppercorns, onion, parsley and whole garlic clove into a large saucepan and add 1.1 L /2 pt cold water. Bring to the boil. Add the chicken breasts and simmer gently for 15–20 minutes until the breasts are almost cooked through.

2 Remove the chicken and cool.

3 Add the grated zest of one orange to the stock in the pan. Boil the stock hard until reduced to 275 ml /10 fl oz, then strain.

4 Melt 125 g /4 oz butter in a large frying-pan and add the breadcrumbs, stirring so that all the crumbs are coated with butter and evenly browned. Put into a blender together with the ground almonds and the stock and blend thoroughly.

5 Squeeze the juice from 3 oranges and add to the sauce, which should be quite thick. Heat the oven to 220C /425F /gas 7.

6 Divide the pastry into 4 and, using a lightly-floured rolling pin and board, roll out each portion into a 15 cm /6 in square. Place a chicken breast in the centre of each portion and spoon 10 ml /2 tsp of the sauce over each breast. Fold over the pastry to form an envelope and firmly seal the edges. Brush the edges with beaten egg yolk and place the chicken envelopes on a lightly greased baking sheet. Bake for 20–25 minutes until golden and risen.

7 Melt the remaining butter in the frying-pan and sauté the blanched almonds until evenly browned. Drain on absorbent paper and sprinkle with salt.

8 Peel the remaining orange, removing all the pith, and cut into 8 thin slices. If there is any orange juice on the plate add it to the sauce and stir to blend thoroughly.

9 Put the chicken puffs on a serving platter and keep warm while finishing the sauce.

10 Add the cream to the remaining sauce, stir well and then pour immediately over the chicken. Put 2 orange slices on each envelope, sprinkle with the whole almonds and serve at once.

🍴🍴 1½ hours

Chicken with port

Port and brandy give this casseroled chicken a luscious flavour.
Serve with a dry white Portuguese Dão.

Serves 4

1.4 kg /3 lb oven-ready chicken
salt
freshly ground black pepper
40 g /1½ oz softened butter
15 ml /1 tbls chopped mixed herbs
25 g /1 oz butter
2.5 ml /½ tsp lemon juice

500 g /1 lb button mushrooms,
    cleaned and halved
10 ml /2 tsp cornflour
275 ml /10 fl oz thick cream
1 shallot, finely chopped
75 ml /3 fl oz port
50 ml /2 fl oz brandy

1 Heat the oven to 180C /350F /gas 4. Rub the chicken with salt and pepper. Blend together the butter and herbs and smear this over the chicken. Roast the chicken in the oven for 1¼–1½ hours, basting frequently.

2 Meanwhile, put 50 ml /2 fl oz water in a saucepan. Bring to the boil, then add 15 g /½ oz butter, lemon juice and salt to taste. Add the mushrooms and cook gently for 10 minutes.

3 Pour the cooking liquid out of the saucepan and reserve. Blend the cornflour with 15 ml /1 tbls of the cream, then stir this cornflour mixture and the rest of the cream into the mushrooms. Simmer for 2 minutes then set aside.

4 Transfer the cooked chicken to a wooden board and pour off most of the fat from the roasting tin. Divide the chicken into serving portions and set aside.

5 Add the shallot to the fat remaining in the roasting pan and cook over gentle heat for 5 minutes. Add the port and reserved mushroom juice and boil down rapidly, until reduced to about 75 ml /3 fl oz.

6 Add the mushroom mixture to the pan and simmer for 3 minutes, until the liquid is slightly thickened. Season to taste.

7 Smear the inside of a flameproof casserole with the remaining butter and arrange the chicken pieces in the casserole. Place over moderate heat and when the chicken begins to sizzle, pour the brandy over it. Ignite and shake the casserole slowly until the flames have subsided. Then pour in the mushroom mixture, cover and heat through without boiling for 5 minutes.

2½ hours

Pork paprika

The piquancy of paprika blends superbly with the full grapey flavour of a fine Rheinhessen wine.

Serves 4–6

1 kg /2 lb stewing pork
15 ml /1 tbls oil
15 g /½ oz butter
1 large onion, sliced
15 ml /1 tbls caraway seeds
30 ml /2 tbls mild paprika

400 g /14 oz canned peeled
    tomatoes
salt
freshly ground black pepper
450 g /1 lb tagliatelle verdi
150 ml /5 fl oz soured cream

1   Cut the pork into 4 cm /1½ in cubes and set aside. Heat the oil and butter in a large frying-pan over moderate heat. Add the sliced onion and soften for 5 minutes.
2   Add the caraway seeds and paprika to the pan and cook for 3 minutes, stirring well with a wooden spoon. Add the pork cubes to the pan, a few pieces at a time, allowing the meat to colour lightly.
3   Pour in the tomatoes and season with salt and freshly ground black pepper. Stir well, cover and cook over a low heat for 1 hour.
4   Fifteen minutes before the pork is cooked, prepare the tagliatelle. Bring a pan of salted water to the boil, add the tagliatelle and boil for 10 minutes or until *al dente* – firm to the bite. Drain and transfer to a large platter, keep warm.
5   Stir the soured cream with a fork, then add to the cooked pork mixture. Stir the soured cream to distribute it, and allow to warm through but do not boil.
6   Spoon the pork on to the centre of the tagliatelle and serve immediately.

⚴ 1½ hours

134

Pork with soured cream

This exotic-tasting dish is very simple to make. Accompanied by steamed carrot sticks sprinkled with chopped dill, and a brightly coloured mixed salad, it makes an appetizing and attractive supper dish. A dry white wine, such as Mâcon-Villages, would make an excellent partner to this meal.

Serves 4

4 loin pork chops
60 ml /4 tbls Moutarde de Meaux
   or any other coarse grain mustard
2.5 ml /1/2 tsp ground ginger
1.5 ml /1/4 tsp freshly ground black pepper
1.5 ml /1/4 tsp salt
30 ml /2 tbls olive oil
150 ml /5 fl oz soured cream

1 Place the mustard, ginger, pepper, salt and 1.5 ml /1/4 tsp of the oil in a bowl and mix together.
2 Spread one third of the mustard mixture over the chops on one side only. Heat the remaining oil in a large frying-pan over moderate heat and place the chops in the pan, *uncoated* side downwards. Cook for 7–10 minutes.
3 Turn the chops over and cook for another 7–10 minutes. While cooking, spread the upturned cooked sides of the chops with another third of the mustard mixture.
4 Once cooked, remove the chops from the pan and keep warm on a serving dish. Stir the soured cream into the juices left in the pan. Mix in the remaining mustard mixture and heat through for one minute, stirring well, then pour over the chops. Serve immediately.

25 minutes

Juniper pork

Delicately flavoured with juniper berries and sweetened with pimentos, this is a light dish which would complement a wine from the Middle Moselle.

Serves 4
12 thin slices of pork fillet
10 ml /2 tsp juniper berries, crushed
salt and ground black pepper
100 g /4 oz butter

60 ml /4 tbls white wine
275 g /10 oz fresh green beans,
*   topped and tailed*
350 g /12 oz canned pimentos
10 ml /2 tsp sugar

1   Put the slices of pork fillet between two sheets of greaseproof paper and beat with a meat bat or rolling pin until they are really thin. Season with the crushed juniper berries and salt and pepper.
2   Melt the butter in a large frying-pan over a low heat and add the white wine, letting it bubble for 1–2 minutes. Place 3–4 slices of pork in the pan, in one layer. Sauté for 3–4 minutes each side, remove and keep warm. Repeat until all the slices are cooked.

3   Add the beans and cook for 5 minutes over medium-low heat.
4   Stir in the pimentos and the sugar and cook for a further 4–5 minutes. Season the vegetables and arrange on a serving platter.
5   Lay the slices of pork on top of the beans and pimentos, pour over the remaining pan juices and serve immediately.

45 minutes

Watercress veal

This *nouvelle cuisine*-style dish is best served on individual plates. Serve it with a medium white wine such as Orvieto.

Serves 4

50 g /2 oz shelled, halved walnuts
1 bunch of watercress, washed
50 g /2 oz butter
1 small onion, finely chopped
150 ml /5 fl oz thick cream

salt and freshly ground pepper
lemon juice
milk (optional)
4 veal escalopes, thinly beaten out
cooked new potatoes, to serve
cooked broccoli florets, to serve

1 Put the halved walnuts in a small bowl and pour over enough boiling water to cover. Leave to stand for 10 minutes.
2 Discard the stalks from the watercress; chop the leaves.
3 Remove the walnuts from the water with a slotted spoon. Remove the thin brown skin that covers the nuts. Chop them finely.
4 In a heavy-based frying-pan, melt half the butter. When the foaming subsides, add the finely chopped onion and sauté, stirring occasionally, for about 5 minutes or until soft. Add the chopped watercress leaves, thick cream and chopped walnuts. Season with salt, freshly ground black pepper and lemon juice to taste. Cover the pan tightly and simmer gently over a very low heat for 7–10 minutes.

(Add a little milk if the sauce reduces and thickens too rapidly.)
5 Remove the sauce from the heat and purée in a blender until smooth. Return the sauce to a pan and keep warm over a low heat.
6 Meanwhile, melt the remaining butter in a frying-pan. Cut each beaten escalope into 2 evenly-shaped, smaller escalopes. Sauté over a medium heat until cooked through, 3–4 minutes.
7 To serve, arrange the veal on invidual heated plates and spoon the sauce over. Serve with tiny new potatoes and florets of broccoli.

1¼ hours

Normandy veal escalopes

Flavoured with calvados and cream, the classic ingredients of Normandy cooking, this delicious dish would be suitable for a dinner party. Serve with a full-bodied white Sancerre.

Serves 4

4 escalopes of veal, slightly beaten
2 medium-sized red dessert apples
50 g /2 oz butter
salt
freshly ground pepper
30 ml /2 tbls lemon juice
60 ml /4 tbls calvados
200 ml /7 fl oz thick cream

To garnish
sprigs of parsley
triangular croûtons

1 Peel the apples and cut into small cubes. Melt the butter in a heavy-based frying-pan over medium heat. When it starts to foam, add the apple and cook for 2 minutes. Remove with a slotted spoon and set aside.

2 Sprinkle the veal with salt and pepper and the lemon juice. Then add to the frying-pan, over medium heat. Brown the veal quickly on both sides.

3 Heat the calvados in a small pan. Set it alight, then pour it, while still flaming, over the meat, turning the heat up under the frying-pan. Rotate the pan until the flames die down. Then lower the heat and pour in the thick cream.

4 Add the apple cubes to the meat and cook gently for about 2 minutes. Stir continuously; do not allow the sauce to boil.

5 When the sauce has thickened, transfer the veal to a warmed serving dish. Arrange the apple cubes on top of the veal and pour the sauce over the apple. Garnish with parsley sprigs and croûtons and serve.

15 minutes

Stir-fried beef with corn

This Chinese-style dish can be served as part of a Chinese meal or try it on its own with soft noodles. Either way it is a good accompaniment for wines from the Northern Napa Valley, such as a Chardonnay.

Serves 4-6

15 ml /1 tbls dry sherry
15 ml /1 tbls soy sauce
7.5 ml /1½ tsp cornflour
500 g /1 lb rump steak, thinly sliced across the grain
15 ml /1 tbls oil
1 small onion, quartered

125 g /4 oz mange tout
5 ml /1 tsp salt
400 g /14 oz canned miniature corn cobs, rinsed and drained
400 g /14 oz canned straw mushrooms, drained
10 ml /2 tsp sugar
plain boiled noodles, to serve

1 In a bowl, blend the sherry and soy sauce into the cornflour. Add the beef and turn it so that it is thoroughly coated.
2 Heat the oil in a wok or frying-pan. Fry the onion for 2 minutes over a high heat. Remove the beef from the cornflour mixture with a slotted spoon, reserving the liquid. Add the beef to the frying-pan and stir fry until lightly browned. Add the mange tout and the salt and stir fry for another 30 seconds.
3 Add the baby corns and the straw mushrooms and stir fry for 1 minute. Add the sugar to the frying-pan and blend.
4 Blend the remaining cornflour liquid with 10 ml /2 tsp cold water and stir into the pan. Cook for another minute until thickened. Serve as part of a Chinese meal or pile the stir-fried beef and vegetables onto plain boiled noodles.

🔪 20 minutes

139

Cod steak in crab sauce

A delicate pink sauce with sliced, pimento-stuffed olives transforms cod steaks into a grand and pretty dinner party dish. Serve with an elegant Chablis.

Serves 4

4 large cod steaks, 25 mm /1 in
thick
For the court bouillon
600 ml /1 pt dry white wine
15 ml /1 tbls white vine vinegar
2 small onions, finely chopped
1 bouquet garni
1 sprig of fennel
16 black peppercorns

For the crab sauce
100 g /4 oz butter
45 g /1½ oz flour
50 g /2 oz crab pâté
3 medium-sized egg yolks
5–10 ml /1–2 tsp lemon juice
75–125 ml /3–4 fl oz thick cream
salt and ground black pepper
75 g /3 oz pimento-stuffed olives

1 Place the ingredients for the court bouillon in a large saucepan with 600 ml /1 pt water and bring to the boil over high heat. Lower the heat and simmer for 30 minutes.
2 Strain the court bouillon and return to the rinsed-out pan. Add the cod steaks and simmer for 15–20 minutes, or until they are just cooked. Remove them with a slotted spoon.
3 Remove the skin and the centre bone, if wished. Arrange the steaks on a serving platter and keep warm while you make the sauce.
4 Boil the court bouillon rapidly until it is reduced to 600 ml /1 pt. Strain and reserve.
5 Melt 50 g /2 oz butter in a saucepan over low heat. Stir in the flour, cook for 2 minutes, then beat in the crab pâté. Add the reduced court bouillon a little at a time. Then stir for 5 minutes over

gentle heat, or until the sauce is slightly reduced and thickened.
6 In a small bowl, beat the egg yolks with 5 ml /1 tsp lemon juice. Add 50 ml /2 fl oz cream and mix thoroughly. Add to the sauce, stirring, and cook over low heat for 2–3 minutes. Do not allow the sauce to boil. Add the remaining butter in small knobs, mixing well after each addition.
7 Adjust the seasoning, adding the remaining lemon juice, if necessary. Then add a further 25–50 ml /1–2 fl oz cream, to give the sauce a thin pouring consistency. Slice the olives and stir them into the sauce. Pour over the fish and serve at once.

🔪🔪 1 hour 40 minutes

Salmon with mousseline sauce

The harmonious blend of dill and cucumber goes perfectly with a fresh salmon trout, or salmon. As it is an expensive fish with a subtle, delicate flavour, salmon deserves to be served with a good white Burgundy wine – perhaps a Puligny Montrachet.

Serves 6

1 salmon trout, weighing about
   1.4 kg /3 lb
15 ml /1 tbls dried dill
salt and pepper
oil for greasing
1 small cucumber, peeled
watercress

For the mousseline sauce

1/2 cucumber
275 ml /10 fl oz mayonnaise
150 ml /5 fl oz thick cream,
   whipped
2.5 ml /1/2 tsp lemon juice
15 ml /1 tbls dried dill
salt and white pepper

1 Keep the fish whole and clean it well. Season it inside and out with the dill, salt and pepper. Place the fish on a large piece of lightly oiled foil and wrap it up, sealing the edges thoroughly by pinching the foil together.

2 Place the foil-wrapped fish in a fish kettle, or bend it very gently into a very large pan. Pour boiling water into the kettle or pan to come three-quarters of the way up the sides of the foil packet. Cover the kettle or pan and simmer gently for 30 minutes.

3 Remove the fish kettle or pan from the heat and leave the fish to cool just a little in the kettle or pan for up to 15 minutes.

4 Carefully lift the fish out, holding it by the foil. Place it on a large serving platter and unwrap it. There will be some liquid in the foil which you should drain off very carefully, keeping a firm hold on the fish. Ease the foil away from under the fish and discard it.

5 Carefully remove the skin of the fish, leaving the head intact. Clean the serving dish with absorbent paper and leave until completely cold.

6 Meanwhile, make the mousseline sauce. Peel and finely grate the cucumber, then mix with the mayonnaise and whipped cream. Stir in the lemon juice and dill and season to taste with salt and pepper. Chill the sauce until required.

7 Thinly slice the peeled cucumber and use to decorate the fish. Garnish with watercress and serve with the mousseline sauce.

1 hour, plus chilling time

Sardines in white wine

Fresh sardines are plentiful and cheap in Portugal and they are often baked on a layer of potatoes in a white wine and tomato sauce. Red mullet are also delicious cooked this way. Serve a dry white wine, such as a Portuguese white Dão.

Serves 4

8 fresh sardines, gutted
4 medium-sized potatoes
2 medium-sized onions
105 ml /7 tbls olive oil
salt
freshly ground black pepper
freshly grated nutmeg

15 ml /1 tbls tomato purée
125 ml /5 fl oz white wine,
   such as Dão
5 ml /1 tsp dried thyme
For the garnish
black olives
lemon slices

1 Heat the oven to 180C /350F /gas 4. Slice the potatoes and onions on a mandolin or very finely with a sharp knife.
2 Put 45 ml /3 tbls of the olive oil in a casserole dish large enough to hold the fish in one layer. Swirl the oil around so the bottom of the dish is thoroughly coated. Place the potatoes in a thin layer at the bottom of the dish and cover with the onions. Season with salt, freshly ground black pepper and nutmeg. Pour over 30 ml /2 tbls of oil. Bake for 40 minutes.
3 Rinse the sardines carefully under cold water and pat dry. Place the sardines neatly in one layer on top of the baked potatoes and

onions. Set on one side.
4 Mix the tomato purée with the white wine and pour over the fish. Season with salt and freshly ground black pepper, sprinkle over the thyme and 30 ml /2 tbls oil. Bake for 15 minutes, basting occasionally if the potatoes become too dry.
5 Garnish with the black olives and lemon slices if wished. Serve immediately.

⚔ 1¼ hours

Plaice meunière

Plaice meunière would make a delightful dinner party main course, accompanied by new potatoes and steamed asparagus or broccoli. A Sauvignon Blanc would go very well with this meal.

Serves 4

8 fillets of plaice
parsley sprigs
30 ml /2 tbls seasoned flour

100 g /4 oz butter
15 ml /1 tbls lemon juice
oil, for deep frying

1 Skin any dark-skinned fillet, then rinse all the fillets and pat dry. Remove the stalks from the parsley sprigs, then wash the sprigs and dry thoroughly. Spread the seasoned flour on greaseproof paper and press the fillets into the flour. Shake off the surplus flour.

2 Heat 50 g /2 oz butter in a large frying-pan. When the butter is foaming, add the fillets to the pan. Fry for about 3–4 minutes on each side or until both sides are golden. Arrange the fillets on a hot serving dish and keep hot.

3 Heat oil in a deep frier to 185C /360F. Wipe out the frying-pan and put in the remaining butter. Heat rapidly until the butter is golden brown. Pour the butter promptly over the plaice, then pour over the lemon juice. Keep hot.

4 Put the parsley sprigs into the deep frier basket and plunge the basket into the hot oil for 30 seconds, or until the parsley is bright green and crisp. Garnish the plaice with the fried parsley and serve.

30 minutes

Salmon with fennel

Delicious pink salmon steaks are ideal for a special summer occasion, especially with this rich but subtly flavoured fennel sauce. Serve the salmon steaks with a crisp, green, summery salad and a fine Pouilly Fumé.

Serves 4

*4 salmon steaks, about 175 g
/6 oz each
150 ml /5 fl oz dry white wine
1 small onion, chopped
1 bulb fennel, quartered
1 bay leaf*

*2-3 parsley stalks, crushed
2 egg yolks
125 g /4 oz unsalted butter
salt
freshly ground black pepper
sprigs of fennel, to garnish*

1 Heat the oven to 180C /350F /gas 4.

2 Place the salmon steaks in a shallow ovenproof dish. Pour the dry white wine over and add the chopped onion, fennel, bay leaf and parsley stalks. Cover tightly and cook in the oven for 15 minutes.

3 Remove from the oven and strain off 60–75 ml /4–5 tbls of the poaching liquid into a small saucepan. Reserve one of the quarters of fennel, chop it finely and measure out 10 ml /2 tsp. Turn the oven down to 150 C /300F /gas 2 and return the fish to the oven.

4 Over a high heat reduce the poaching liquid to 15 ml /1 tbls, about 5 minutes. Remove from the heat and leave to cool.

5 In the top pan of a double boiler, put the cooled reduced poaching liquid, egg yolks and 25 g /1 oz butter. Season with salt and freshly ground black pepper. Over gently simmering water whisk the mixture until the butter has melted. Gradually add the remaining butter, whisking between each addition until the sauce is thick. Do not let the water boil or the sauce may curdle. When the sauce is thick, add the reserved chopped fennel and allow to heat through in the sauce.

6 Remove the salmon steaks from the oven and with a slotted spoon, transfer them to a warmed serving dish. Spoon the fennel sauce over and serve garnished with sprigs of fennel.

🔪🔪 1 hour 10 minutes

Cold seafood platter

Serve this delicious mixture of seafood as a dinner party starter or as the main course for a special supper for two. The texture and taste of steamed seafood contrast well with the spicy sauce, and are perfect with a Yugoslav Fruska Gora Sauvignon.

Serves 2

500 g /1 lb or 1 pt mussels,
scrubbed
150 ml /5 fl oz dry white wine
8 raw scampi, with heads and
shells on
8 large scallops
For the sauce
25 g /1 oz butter
15 ml /1 tbls oil
1 onion, finely chopped

1 garlic clove, crushed
1 green pepper, finely diced
500 g /1 lb tomatoes, blanched,
skinned and chopped
10 ml /2 tsp lemon juice
1.5 ml /1/4 tsp ground coriander
2.5 ml /1/2 tsp paprika
2.5 ml /1/2 tsp cumin
salt
freshly ground black pepper

1 To make the sauce, in a saucepan, heat the butter and oil and sauté the finely chopped onion until soft, about 5 minutes. Add the crushed garlic and the finely diced pepper and continue cooking, stirring occasionally, for 5 minutes. Add the tomatoes, lemon juice, coriander, paprika and cumin. Stir well and season with salt and freshly ground black pepper. Simmer the sauce gently for 20 minutes, stirring occasionally.

2 Meanwhile, put the mussels in a large saucepan with 150 ml /5 fl oz water and the dry white wine. Cover the pan tightly and steam over a high heat, shaking the pan occasionally, for about 5 minutes or until the mussels have opened. Strain the mussels, reserving the liquor, discard any that have not opened and set the remainder aside to cool.

3 Bring the reserved liquor to the boil, add the scampi and turn the heat down. Simmer for 1½–2 minutes. Remove with a slotted spoon

and set aside to cool.

4 Separate the orange corals from the scallops and remove and discard the black membrane. Poach the scallops for 3–5 minutes in the liquor, adding the corals for the last minute of the cooking time. Drain and leave to cool.

5 Remove the sauce from the heat and allow to cool. Remove the cooled mussels from their shells and discard the shells.

6 To arrange, pour the sauce into individual ramekins and place one on each plate. Arrange the scampi and mussels on the plates. Slice the scallops in half horizontally and arrange them with the corals placed decoratively on top. Serve accompanied by fingerbowls and large napkins.

45 minutes, plus cooling

Monkfish salad

Monkfish (*ange de mer* in French) tastes like lobster or scampi, but is much less expensive. Monkfish salad makes a light, refreshing lunch dish or an unusual starter and is the perfect partner for the dry white wine of Spain – choose from a Penedés or Rioja.

Serves 4
350 g /12 oz tail piece of monkfish
1 medium-sized fennel bulb
For the dressing
60 ml /4 tbls olive oil
30 ml /2 tbls lemon juice
1 garlic clove, crushed
2.5 ml /1/2 tsp fresh tarragon, chopped
2.5 ml /1/2 tsp fresh chervil, chopped
2.5 ml /1/2 tsp fresh basil, chopped
salt
freshly ground black pepper

For the court bouillon
2 carrots, peeled and finely chopped
1 medium-sized onion, finely chopped
2 celery stalks, cleaned and chopped
bouquet garni of fresh herbs
30 ml /2 tbls lemon juice
300 ml /10 fl oz dry white wine
6 black peppercorns, crushed
salt
To serve
2 small or 1 large lettuce heart
stuffed olives

1 Trim the base and the fronds from the fennel. Slice the bulb finely and put in a bowl. Blend the dressing ingredients together and pour over the fennel. Leave to marinate for 2 hours.
2 Meanwhile put all the court bouillon ingredients into a saucepan with 600 ml /1 pt water. Bring to the boil then simmer for 15 minutes. Cool slightly.
3 Put the monkfish in a saucepan and strain the court bouillon over the fish. Bring slowly to the boil, cover, reduce the heat and simmer for about 10 minutes or until the flesh just flakes.

4 Carefully remove the fish with a slotted spoon and leave to cool.
5 With a sharp knife, cut the cold fish into 4 × 1.2 cm /1½ × ½ in pieces and toss with the fennel and its dressing. Chill for 30 minutes.
6 Finely shred the lettuce heart and arrange around the edge of a plate. Pile the fish in the centre and decorate with olives. Serve immediately.

2½ hours including marinating

Buttered lobster

For an intimate and rather special dinner for two, try this extravagant lobster dish. As you will have splashed out on the food, serve it with a good Chablis. Baking in the oven is easier than grilling lobster as you do not have to watch it.

Serves 2
1 fresh uncooked lobster, weighing
   700–900 g /1½–2 lb
butter for greasing
salt
freshly ground pepper
juice of ½ lemon

75 g /3 oz unsalted butter
lemon wedges for garnishing
watercress sprigs for garnish
For the butter sauce
100 g /4 oz clarified butter
juice and zest of ½ lemon
30 ml /2 tbls chopped parsley

1 Heat the oven to 180C /350F /gas 4 with a baking tray in it. Plunge the lobster into boiling water, cover and boil for 1 minute to kill it. Starting at the head end, split the lobster in half lengthways with a knife. Discard the stomach sac (which is in the head), and the dark intestinal cord (which runs along its back). Crack the claws with a blow from a hammer or with nutcrackers.
2 Grease a gratin dish with butter and, using buttered paper, lightly rub the lobster shells all over until they gleam. Place the lobster on the gratin dish. Sprinkle the flesh with a little salt, a generous sprinkle of black pepper and 5 ml /1 tsp lemon juice.
3 Cover the flesh completely with dots of the unsalted butter. Place the gratin dish on the warm baking tray and bake in the oven for 15

minutes. Remove from the oven and baste with the buttery juice, adding another 5 ml /1 tsp lemon juice. Return to the oven and cook for 15 minutes longer.
4 Meanwhile, make the butter sauce. Heat the clarified butter, lemon juice and zest in a small saucepan until very hot. Remove from the heat, stir in the parsley and pour into a warmed sauceboat.
5 Remove from the oven, baste with the juices and serve immediately, garnished with the watercress and lemon wedges and accompanied by the butter sauce.

🔪🔪 1 hour

Italian-style scampi

This delicious dish is reminiscent of hot, exotic settings – perhaps a terrace overlooking the Adriatic. Complete the scenario with a crisp, dry white wine – a Soave would be the ideal choice.

Serves 4

1 kg /2 lb frozen peeled scampi, thawed and drained
60 ml /4 tbls olive oil
2 garlic cloves, finely chopped
15–20 ml /3–4 tsp lemon juice
90 ml /6 tbls freshly chopped parsley
30 ml /2 tbls capers, drained
boiled rice to serve
lemon slices to garnish

1 Pat the scampi dry with absorbent paper. Heat the oil in a large heavy-based frying-pan and cook the scampi very gently over low heat, turning them now and then, for 7–8 minutes, until almost cooked.

2 Stir the garlic, lemon juice, parsley and capers into the frying-pan and cook, stirring, for a further 1–2 minutes.

3 Spoon the scampi and cooking juices over a bed of plainly boiled rice arranged on a large serving platter. Garnish the edge of the platter with lemon slices. Serve immediately.

15 minutes

Crawfish with asparagus

This luxurious but delicate dish is perfect for that special dinner for two or makes a delicious appetizer for 4 people for a grand dinner party. A very lightly chilled, Cape white wine would be an ideal accompaniment.

Serves 2

450 g /1 lb asparagus
salt and freshly ground black pepper
1 kg /2 lb female crawfish or rock lobster with roe, boiled

olive oil to polish (optional)
25 g /1 oz butter
30 ml /2 tbls finely chopped parsley
125 ml /4 fl oz dry white wine
150 ml /5 fl oz thick cream

1 Trim off the ends of the asparagus to make them an even length and scrape off any leaf scales on the stalks. Tie firmly into a bundle with string. Bring a large pan of salted water to the boil, place the bundle of asparagus standing upright in it, and cover the tips loosely with a cap of foil, crimping this round the top of the saucepan. Cook for 30–40 minutes or until the tips are tender but still firm.

2 Meanwhile prepare the shellfish; remove the roe from under the tail, cut the body into 2 pieces lengthways with a cleaver or sharp, heavy knife and remove the stomach bag and dark vein. (Cut the shell in half again, crossways above the tail, if serving 4.) Carefully remove the white meat from the tail, cut into chunks and put on a plate. Put the soft head meat and any leg meat with the roes. Rinse the body shells, and polish with a little olive oil if wished.

3 Melt the butter in a large frying-pan and add the tail meat. Sauté for 2–3 minutes, remove with a slotted spoon and keep warm.

4 Add the roes and remaining meat to the pan and sauté for 2 minutes. Remove, keep warm but do not mix with tail meat.

5 Add the parsley to the pan and stir-fry for 1 minute. Add the wine, bring to boiling point and boil for 2 minutes. Turn down the heat and simmer to reduce by half, about 5 minutes.

6 Pour in the cream, season with salt and freshly ground black pepper and stir for 3–4 minutes but do not allow to boil. Check the seasoning, adjusting if necessary.

7 Pile the tail meat into the shells, top with the remaining meat and the roes. Place the shells on a warmed plate, drain the asparagus and put some spears on either side of each helping. Pour some sauce over each portion and serve immediately.

⚔ 40–50 minutes

Desserts

Contents

Sherry surprise

This is a light but very rich pudding ideally accompanied by a Cape dessert wine. Do not be tempted to add more sherry to the pudding as the chilling brings out the full flavour.

Serves 4–6
275 g /10 oz sponge cake
100 ml /4 fl oz sherry
275 ml /10 fl oz custard

60 ml /4 tbls raspberry or
*   strawberry jam*
275 ml /10 fl oz thick cream
rose petals, to garnish

1 Cut the sponge into slices and put in a large bowl. Pour over the sherry and mash the sponge with a fork.

2 Add the custard and the jam and whisk everything together thoroughly so that there are no lumps of sponge or jam in the mixture.

3 In another bowl, whisk the cream until soft peaks form. Add half of the cream to the sponge mixture, mixing well in. Transfer the mixture to a glass serving dish, 18 cm /7 in in diameter.

4 Spread the remaining cream over the pudding, smoothing the top flat with a spatula. Put in the refrigerator and chill for at least 2 hours.

5 Just before serving, sprinkle the rose petals over the surface to garnish.

making the custard, then 25 minutes plus chilling

151

Old-fashioned trifle

This is trifle like your grandmother used to make. Complement it with a fine dessert Barsac.

Serves 6

6 trifle sponge cakes
100 g /4 oz raspberry jam
50 g /2 oz ratafias or small
   macaroons
150 ml /5 fl oz medium-dry or
   sweet sherry
4 medium-sized eggs

50 g /2 oz caster sugar
10 ml /2 tsp cornflour
600 ml /1 pt milk
1.5 ml /¼ tsp vanilla essence
6 large, fresh peaches
425 ml /15 fl oz thick cream
For the decoration
diamonds of angelica

1 Split the trifle sponge cakes in half, spread the cut sides thinly with the jam, then sandwich them together again. Cut each sponge cake sandwich into 3 pieces and arrange them in a glass bowl.

2 Crumble the ratafias over the sponge, then sprinkle with the sherry. Cover the bowl and leave to stand overnight.

3 Make the custard: place the eggs in a bowl with the sugar and cornflour and whisk lightly. Heat the milk to just below boiling point then pour it on to the egg mixture, stirring well. Return the mixture to the pan and cook over a very gentle heat, stirring constantly with a wooden spoon until the custard has thickened, and coats the back of the spoon.

4 Strain the custard into a bowl, stir in the vanilla essence. Cover with a piece of dampened greaseproof paper and leave to cool.

5 Skin, halve and stone the peaches. Cut each half into 3 slices and arrange them over the soaked sponge. Remove the paper from the custard and pour the cold custard over the fruit.

6 Softly whip the cream. Spread two-thirds of it over the custard then pipe the remaining cream in swirls around the edge. Decorate with diamonds of angelica and serve.

15 minutes, plus overnight soaking, then 45 minutes plus cooling

Caramelized grapes

This is a rich but refreshing dessert that would make a pleasant end to a dinner party. Serve with a chilled sparkling white wine.

Serves 6–8
450 g /1 lb large, sweet, white grapes
125 ml /4 fl oz maraschino

275 ml /10 fl oz thick cream
175 g /6 oz brown sugar

1 Skin and seed the grapes and put them into a flameproof dish 18 cm /7 in in diameter or in individual ramekins. Sprinkle over the maraschino.

2 In a bowl, beat the cream until it is thick but not buttery and spread in a thick layer over the grapes. Put in the refrigerator overnight to chill.

3 Heat the grill to high about 10 minutes before you are ready to serve the dessert. Cover the cream with an even layer of sugar and grill for 5–8 minutes until the sugar melts. Serve immediately.

overnight chilling, then 30 minutes

Striped soufflé glacé

With its flavourings of apricot, pistachio and almond, this multi-tiered dessert would complement a luscious sweet wine such as a Monbazillac.

Serves 6-8
350 g /12 oz dried apricots
100 g /4 oz shelled pistachio
   nuts, blanched and skinned
9 large egg yolks
250 g /8 oz caster sugar

750 ml /1¼ pt thick cream
3 drops each of orange and green
   food colouring
100 g /4 oz ground almonds
8-16 langues de chat biscuits or
   fan wafers

1 Simmer the apricots with enough water to cover for 25 minutes. Drain, reserving the cooking liquid. Purée the fruit with 75 ml /3 fl oz of the liquid. Measure 275 ml /10 fl oz purée into a jug and add 75 ml /3 fl oz cooking liquid. Stir, then set aside for the sauce. Reserve the remaining thick purée for one coloured layer of the dessert.
2 Reserve 9 pistachio nuts for decorating and blend the rest to a coarse paste. Halve the reserved nuts.
3 Wrap a collar of double-thickness greaseproof paper around a 12.5 cm /5 in soufflé dish, so that the collar extends 10 cm /4 in above the rim. Secure with an elastic band and paper clips.
4 In a large bowl set over a pan of simmering water, whisk the yolks and sugar, preferably with a hand-held electric whisk, until the mixture is pale and thick and doubled in bulk, about 10 minutes. Stand the bowl in a larger bowl containing crushed ice and continue to whisk until cold.
5 Whip the cream to soft peaks then fold it into the yolk and sugar mixture. Divide the mixture equally between 3 bowls. Stir the thick apricot purée and orange food colour into one of the bowls. Stir

the pistachio paste and green food colour into the second, and the ground almonds into the third.
6 Put half the apricot mixture in the soufflé dish and transfer it to the freezer; put the bowls in the refrigerator to chill. When the apricot layer has set (about 45 minutes), add a second layer using half of the almond mixture; freeze until set. Add a third layer using half of the pistachio mixture; freeze again. Continue in this way until the layers are complete. Freeze for 4 hours or until firm.
7 Transfer the soufflé glacé to the refrigerator 30 minutes before serving. Just before serving, slip a knife between the paper and the soufflé all round, then peel off the paper collar. Decorate with the reserved pistachio nuts. To serve, cut the top trio of layers into quarters, then cut horizontally across the soufflé. Cut the second trio of layers into quarters and serve, accompanied by the apricot sauce and biscuits or wafers.

🕐🔪🔪 1½ hours plus
chilling

Pansy jelly

Serve this traditional English dessert – both lovely to look at and delicious to eat – after a rich main course. A well-chilled English wine with a flowery bouquet would be a perfect accompaniment.

Serves 8
50 g /2 oz gelatine
225 g /8 oz sugar
thinly pared zest of 4 lemons
300 ml /10 fl oz lemon juice
1 stick of cinnamon

whites and finely crushed shells of 3
* eggs*
125 ml /4 fl oz medium-dry sherry
* or sweet white wine*
8 pansy flowers, washed and dried
16 small meringues, to serve

1 Sprinkle the gelatine over 45 ml /3 tbls cold water in a small bowl. Leave to soften, then dissolve by standing the bowl in hot water.
2 Pour 850 ml /1½ pt water into a large pan (do not use an aluminium one). Add the sugar, lemon zest and juice and cinnamon stick.
3 Stir over medium heat until the sugar is dissolved. Remove the cinnamon stick and leave the pan on the heat. Stir in the dissolved gelatine.
4 Beat the egg whites and crushed shells together until they are frothy. Pour them into the pan, add the sherry or wine and whisk until the mixture boils. Remove the pan from the heat and leave until the froth sinks.
5 Bring to the boil again and set aside, twice more. Leave the mixture to cool for about 15 minutes.

6 Line a sieve with a double thickness of scalded muslin or cheese-cloth and place over a bowl. Pour in the liquid jelly, leaving the frothy sediment in the bottom of the saucepan. Roll the sediment very gently into the sieve then strain the liquid again, pouring it through the sediment.
7 Reserve 275 ml /10 fl oz of the jelly mixture. Divide the rest equally between 8 old-fashioned champagne glasses. Float a pansy, face upwards on top of each jelly. Place in the refrigerator to set.
8 Melt the remaining jelly, if it has begun to set, and pour some over each pansy. Place the jellies in the refrigerator to set.
9 When ready to serve, stand each glass on a small plate with 2 small meringues.

ⵌ 30 minutes,
then 4 hours setting

Malakoff dessert

A lovely way to end a dinner party, this mouth-watering dessert would be set off well by a sweet Muscat wine such as Muscat de Beaumes de Venise.

Serves 6–8
225 g /8 oz fresh strawberries,
    washed and hulled
100 g /4 oz butter
75 g /3 oz caster sugar
75 g /3 oz ground almonds

150 ml /5 fl oz thick cream
90 ml /6 tbls orange liqueur
24 sponge fingers
For the decoration
150 ml /5 fl oz thick cream
toasted flaked almonds

1 Line an 800 ml /1½ pt loaf tin with greaseproof paper, then grease it lightly.
2 Cream the butter and sugar together until pale and fluffy. Beat in the almonds. Gradually stir the cream into the almond mixture being careful not to overstir to avoid curdling.
3 Arrange a layer of sponge fingers in the base of the tin. Sprinkle the fingers with 30 ml /2 tbls liqueur. Halve the strawberries, reserving eight whole ones for decoration, and arrange half of the strawberry halves in a layer upon the fingers. Carefully cover the layer of strawberry halves with half the almond mixture.
4 Cover with another layer of sponge fingers and sprinkle the fingers with 30 ml /2 tbls liqueur. Cover with the remaining strawberry halves and spread the remaining almond mixture on top of that. Finish with a layer of sponge fingers, sprinkled with the remaining 30 ml /2 tbls liqueur. Chill for 6 hours or until firm.
5 Remove from the refrigerator, turn out on to a serving plate and peel off the greaseproof paper. Whip the cream for decoration. Spread two-thirds of it on top of the dessert and pipe the remaining cream just inside the edge. Arrange the reserved strawberries on the piped cream and sprinkle the centre with the toasted almonds.

45 minutes,
plus chilling time

Tequila cream

Save this special cream dessert for when you are feeling extravagant. Rich in taste and texture it should satisfy anyone's wish for luxury. Serve with a chilled Californian dessert wine such as a Simi Trockenbeerenauslese Gewürztraminer.

Serves 4

425 ml /15 fl oz thick cream
2 large lemons
150 ml /5 fl oz tequila

icing sugar to taste
3 large egg whites
mint sprigs, to garnish

1 Pare the zest thinly from one of the lemons and cut it into julienne strips. Bring a saucepan of water to the boil and add the julienne strips. Boil for 2–3 minutes until soft and then drain. Refresh under cold running water and drain again.

2 Put the thick cream in a large bowl and add the grated zest of the second lemon. Whip the cream until it stands in soft peaks; be careful not to overwhip at this stage. Gently fold in the tequila and the juice from both lemons. Add icing sugar to taste.

3 In a clean dry bowl whisk the egg whites to stiff peaks, then fold them into the tequila cream. Spoon the mixture into individual glass dishes and chill in the refrigerator for at least 2–3 hours.

4 Just before serving stir each tequila cream and sprinkle the julienne of lemon on top. Garnish and serve immediately.

30 minutes,
then 2–3 hours chilling

157

Caramel bavarois

Serve a luxurious Sauternes with this creamy dessert, which is one of the French classics.

Serves 4

oil for greasing
100 g /4 oz sugar
275 ml /10 fl oz milk
3 medium-sized egg yolks
165 g /5½ oz caster sugar
15 ml /1 tbls gelatine
150 ml /5 fl oz thick cream
ice for chilling

1 Lightly oil a 600 ml /1 pt mould. Put the sugar with 75 ml /3 fl oz water in a medium-sized saucepan. Place over low heat and dissolve the sugar. Then turn up the heat and boil steadily to form a dark brown caramel.

2 Carefully pour 50 ml /2 fl oz water into the pan and stir with a wooden spoon, until the caramel has dissolved. Add the milk and bring back to boiling point. Remove from the heat.

3 In a heatproof bowl, beat the egg yolks with 40 g /1½ oz caster sugar until light-coloured, then pour the caramel milk on to this mixture. Stir and return to the saucepan. Place the pan over low heat and stir, without boiling, until the custard is thick. Strain into a bowl and cool.

4 Put the gelatine in a small saucepan and add 75 ml /5 tbls water. Allow to soak for a few minutes then dissolve over low heat. Whip the cream until thick and set aside.

5 Gradually add the dissolved gelatine, in a stream, to the custard. Place the bowl over ice and stir until the custard has thickened. Then quickly fold in 30 ml /2 tbls whipped cream.

6 Immediately pour into the prepared mould and leave to set for about 1½ hours.

7 To make the caramel chips, put rest of the caster sugar with 45 ml /3 tbls water in a small heavy-based saucepan over a low heat. Dissolve, stirring continuously. Then boil until the sugar turns a golden brown and turns to a golden-brown caramel – 170C /325F on a sugar thermometer.

8 Line a baking tray with foil and grease well. Pour the caramel into the baking tray and allow to become completely cold. Remove the foil from the tray and break the caramel in half. Remove one half, and fold the foil over the remaining caramel. Beat the foil-covered caramel with a rolling pin to break into chips. Repeat with the other piece of caramel.

9 Turn the mould out on to a serving dish and decorate with the remaining cream and caramel chips.

⏱ 45 minutes
plus cooling and setting

Grapefruit and vermouth granita

An unusual way of using vermouth, this sorbet makes a distinctive end to a meal, before or after the cheese course. Serve with a light Vinho Verde.

Serves 6
175 g /6 oz caster sugar
2 large juicy grapefruit

75 ml /5 tbls dry vermouth
orange tuiles or wafers, to serve

1 Put 300 ml /10 fl oz water and the sugar in a pan and bring to the boil. Then simmer gently for 5 minutes, remove from the heat and leave to cool.
2 Peel the grapefruit and divide up the segments, removing all pips with the point of a knife. Blend the grapefruit flesh and vermouth in an electric blender or food processor until liquid. Mix with the sugar syrup, pour into a tray and freeze overnight.

3 Remove the sorbet from the freezer and thaw for 10 minutes. Blend again in the blender until pale yellow and fluffy.
4 Refreeze. Serve straight from the freezer, scooping the sorbet into glasses, with orange tuiles or wafers.

25 minutes, plus freezing and 10 minutes thawing

Wine jelly in melon

A delectable combination of wine-flavoured jelly and sweet melon, this dessert is quite delicious served with a light fruity wine, such as Vouvray.

Serves 4
2 small sweet melons
25 g /1 oz powdered gelatine
100 g /3½ oz sugar

500 ml / 18 fl oz dry white wine
juice of 1 lemon
30 ml /2 tbls slivovitz or kirsch

1 Using a very sharp knife, cut the melons in half, across the middle, in a zig-zag pattern. Carefully remove the seeds with a spoon and refrigerate the prepared melon halves.
2 Soften the gelatine in 50 ml /2 fl oz cold water. Put the sugar, wine, lemon juice and 350 ml /12 fl oz cold water in a medium-sized pan and heat gently. Add the softened gelatine and stir over a low heat until the gelatine has dissolved completely. Set the mixture aside to cool.
3 When the mixture is just beginning to set – it should be of an almost syrupy consistency – pour all but about 225 ml /8 fl oz into the melon halves. Put the melons and remaining 225 ml /8 fl oz jelly into the refrigerator to set.
4 Just before serving, whisk the reserved 225 ml /8 fl oz jelly with the slivovitz or the kirsch, until frothy. Pile a little of this mixture on top of each melon half.

15 minutes plus chilling time

Ice cream stripe

This cool, delicious dessert is perfect for hot summer days or warm balmy evenings. Serve it with a well-chilled Californian dessert wine – it makes a memorable end to any meal.

Serves 6

700 ml /1¼ pt chocolate ice cream
700 ml /1¼ pt vanilla ice cream
700 ml /1¼ pt coffee ice cream
oil for greasing

125 g /4 oz sugar
50 g /2 oz almonds, unpeeled
whipped cream and chopped nuts, to
   decorate

1 Put the ice cream in the main part of the refrigerator to soften. Chill a 2 L /3½ pt loaf tin and grease a baking sheet.

2 To make the praline, put the sugar and nuts in a heavy-based saucepan and melt the sugar over a very low heat. Do not stir.

3 Once the sugar has dissolved, turn the heat up a little and stir the nuts in the caramel. Cook carefully until the syrup turns a deep golden colour. Turn the praline out onto the baking sheet and leave to harden.

4 Once the praline has set, remove it from the baking sheet and crush it to a fine powder, either in a blender or using a pestle and mortar.

5 Remove the chocolate ice cream from the refrigerator and spoon it into the loaf tin, level it off and sprinkle with half the praline. Put in the freezer for a few minutes to firm up a little. Repeat with the vanilla ice cream and the remaining praline. Again put in the freezer to firm up and finally add the coffee ice cream. Put in the freezer for at least 3–4 hours to harden.

6 To serve: unmould the ice cream about 15 minutes before serving and leave in the refrigerator to soften slightly. Either serve whole, decorated with whipped cream and chopped nuts, or serve in slices decorated with cream and nuts.

⚔ 1½ hours plus chilling

Summer pudding

Serve this wonderful, traditional pudding with a sweet white wine such as a Cérons. Do use good quality white bread.

Serves 4

100 g /4 oz mixed red and blackcurrants, stalks removed
225 g /8 oz raspberries, cleaned
100 g /4 oz strawberries, hulled
100 g /4 oz caster sugar
15 ml /1 tbls orange juice or water
5-7 thin slices day-old white bread, trimmed of crust
softly whipped thick cream to serve

1 Place the currants in a heavy-based saucepan and sprinkle over the sugar. Add the orange juice or water and bring to the boil. Cover the pan and cook very gently for about 5 minutes, shaking the pan occasionally, until the sugar has melted and the fruit juices flow.

2 Add the raspberries to the pan and stew gently, covered, for 2-3 minutes. Allow to cool, then gently stir in the strawberries.

3 Meanwhile use most of the bread to line the base and sides of 600 ml /1 pt pudding bowl. Cut the bread so that it fits neatly and fill any gaps with the trimmings.

4 Reserve about 75 ml /5 tbls of the fruit juices, then fill the bowl with the fruit and remaining juices. Neatly cover the surface with bread. Place a plate which fits just inside the rim of the bowl on top and weigh this down with a heavy tin or weight.

5 Place the pudding in the refrigerator and leave for at least 8 hours or overnight.

6 Just before serving, run a palette knife around the inside rim of the bowl then turn out the pudding on to a flat serving dish. Spoon the reserved fruit juices over any areas of unsoaked bread. Accompany the pudding with a bowl of softly whipped cream.

🕐 🍴 30 minutes plus minimum of 8 hours chilling

Baked oranges

Oranges are often served hot as a dessert in their native Mediterranean countries. This Turkish dish is an ideal accompaniment for the sweet Cypriot dessert wine, Commandaria.

Serves 6

6 large sweet oranges
90 ml /6 tbls Cinzano bianco
50 g /2 oz butter

100 g /4 oz soft brown sugar
15 ml /1 tbls rose-flower water
275 ml /10 fl oz thick cream

1 Peel the oranges with a sharp knife making sure all the pith is removed. Do this over a bowl or plate to catch any juice that may be squeezed out while you are peeling the oranges. Reserve the juice.

2 Place the oranges in a saucepan large enough to hold them in one layer. Cover with water and bring to the boil over moderate heat. Simmer for 20–30 minutes or until the oranges are tender when pierced with a skewer.

3 Remove from the pan with a slotted spoon and discard the water. Heat the oven to 180C /350F /gas 4.

4 Slice the oranges fairly thickly and arrange on a large, shallow, heatproof dish. Pour over the Cinzano and the reserved orange juice,

dot with the butter and sprinkle with the sugar and rose-flower water. Add about 60–90 ml /4–6 tbls water, just enough to come level with the top layer of oranges. Bake for 20–30 minutes or until the juice is bubbling. Turn off the oven and leave the oranges in the oven for 10 minutes.

5 In a large bowl, whip the cream until it forms soft peaks. Take the oranges out of the oven and decorate with the whipped cream. Serve the dessert immediately.

1½ hours

Peach shortcake

Serve this mouth-watering treat with a luscious Muscat dessert wine to make a special end to a dinner party.

Serves 4–6

100 g /4 oz flour
65 g /2½ oz butter, diced
40 g /1½ oz icing sugar
1 large egg yolk
a few drops of vanilla essence

350 g /12 oz fresh or canned peach slices
45 ml /3 tbls redcurrant jelly to glaze
150 ml /5 fl oz thick cream, whipped

1 Sift the flour on to a smooth surface. Make a well in the centre and add the butter, icing sugar, egg yolk and vanilla. Work the ingredients together with your fingers to form a smooth paste. Chill for 30 minutes.

2 Heat the oven to 180C /350F /gas 4. Roll out the pastry to a large round, 5 mm /¼ in thick. Prick all over with a fork and bake in the oven for 20 minutes. Cool on a rack.

3 Melt the redcurrant jelly in a small saucepan over gentle heat. Arrange the peach slices in a pattern to cover the shortcake, then brush with the melted redcurrant to glaze. Decorate with rosettes of whipped cream.

⚱ 45 minutes plus cooling, then decorating

Mixed melon salad

A refreshing way to end a meal, this fragrant salad should be served with a wine that is neither too overpowering nor too distractingly dry or sweet – a medium Cabernet d'Anjou would fit the bill perfectly.

Serves 6–8

1 small honeydew melon
1 cantaloupe or Charentais melon
250 g /8 oz black grapes

1 medium-sized orange
600 g /1¼ lb canned, stoned
   lichees in syrup

1 Cut the melons in half and scoop out the seeds. Use a melon ball cutter to cut the flesh into small balls, then place them in a large bowl.
2 Seed the whole grapes by cutting half way into them with a sharp knife and removing the seeds with the point of a knife. Add the seeded grapes to the melon balls.
3 Using a sharp knife, cut the peel and all the pith from the orange. Carefully cut out the segments from between the membranes and extract any pips from them with the point of the knife. Place the

segments with the other fruit in the bowl. Squeeze the orange membranes over the bowl to extract any remaining juice.
4 Pour the lychees together with their canned syrup into the bowl. Stir the fruit to mix well and transfer to individual glass bowls. Leave to chill in the refrigerator for 1–2 hours before serving.

45 minutes, plus chilling time

165

Fruit salad a la russe

This delicious fruit salad makes a colourful finale to a dinner party. A rich dessert wine from the Rheingau would be a superb accompaniment.

Serves 8

2 ripe pears, peeled and cored
4 peaches
juice of 2 oranges
1/2 pineapple
100 g /4 oz grapes or 4 kiwi fruit
225 g /8 oz raspberries or
    strawberries
225 g /8 oz red plums or red
    cherries
100 g /4 oz sugar
1/4 bottle of medium-dry
    champagne or 250 ml /9 fl oz
    sweet sparkling wine
1 kiwi fruit, sliced, to garnish

1　Cut the pears into chunks. Skin and stone the peaches, and chop the flesh into chunks. Put the fruit in a large shallow dish, pour over the orange juice and toss the fruit.
2　Peel the pineapple, slice it, then cut into chunks, removing the core. Seed the grapes, or peel the kiwi fruit, and cut into chunks. Hull the strawberries, if using.
3　Stone and halve the plums. Add half the raspberries or strawberries and the remaining fruit, plus any fruit juices, to the dish. Gently spoon the orange juice over the fruit. Sprinkle with the sugar and macerate for 1-2 hours.
4　Purée the reserved strawberries or raspberries through a sieve. Choose 8 large coupe glasses. Divide the strawberry purée between the glasses, then divide the fruit and juice between the glasses.
5　About 1 hour before serving, top up each glass with champagne or sparkling wine. Chill the fruit salad, then garnish and serve.

🍴 35 minutes, plus chilling

Index

Picture Credits

J. Allan Cash Ltd: 41.
Bryce Attwell: 96, 99, 110, 116, 146.
Tom Belshaw: 81, 101, 107.
Peter Baker: 25.
Anthony Blake: 13, 57.
Paul Bussell: 11, 45, 53, 105, 112, 119, 129, 130,
    131, 135, 137, 138, 147, 148, 160, 162.
Eric Chrichton: 16, 24.
Bruce Coleman Ltd: 10, 16, 23, 24, 67, 83.
Chris Crofton: 12.
G. Cubitt: 83.
Daily Telegraph Colour Library: 34, 47, 79.
Peter Esterhazy: 51.
Laurie Evans: 43, 84, 108, 120, 144, 153, 155.
Virginia Fass: 31.
Fotobank: 46, 60, 75.
Food and Wine from France: 15.
Michael Freeman: 10, 75.
French Government Tourist Office: 27.
Robert Golden: 95.
Edmund Goldspink: 152.
Melvin Grey: 122.
Susan Griggs Agency: 32.
W. Hasenberg: 76.
Tony Hogarth: 73.
Alan Huchison Library: 18.
Denis Hughes-Gilbey: 60.
Image Bank: 55, 56.
James Jackson: 72, 77, 90, 92, 94, 133, 136, 149,
    151, 157, 161, 164.
K. Kerth: 22, 30.
Chris Knaggs: 9, 35, 64, 68, 71, 91, 102, 103, 109,

111, 114, 123, 134, 156, 163.
Coriat/Explorer/Vision International: 61.
David Levin: 89.
William MacQuitty: 74.
Colin Maher: 21, 37, 38, 46, 59.
Peter Myers: 87, 93, 97, 98, 100, 113, 118, 126,
    127, 132, 139, 141, 145, 154, 166.
Ian O'Leary: 125.
Roger Philips: 54, 63, 142.
Peter Reilly: 28, 29, 39, 48, 49, 59, 62.
H. Schumacher: 69.
Spectrum Colour Library: 66.
John Topham: 67.
Paul Webster: 88, 115, 158.
Hed Weisner: 42.
Paul Williams: 8, 80, 104, 121, 143.
Peter Williams: 40, 140.
Adam Woolfitt: 32.
ZEFA: 14, 22, 30, 37, 42, 65, 69, 76.

Artwork: Advertising Arts

Acknowledgments

The Publishers would like to thank the following
    people who very kindly supplied bottles of wine
    for photography:
Del Monico, 64 Old Compton Street, London W1;
    28, 29 (Barsac), 59, 62.
Hallgarten Wines Ltd, House of Hallgarten,
    Carkers Lane, London NW5: 48, 49.
J.B. Reynier Ltd, 16 Tachbrook Street, London
    SW1: 39 (Dopff and Irion).